INTERPRETING *the* $\mathcal{P}$salms

INTERPRETING *the*

*P*salms

Issues and approaches

Edited by Philip S. Johnston
and David G. Firth

APOLLOS

APOLLOS (an imprint of Inter-Varsity Press)
38 De Montfort Street, Leicester LE1 7GP, England
Email: ivp@uccf.org.uk
Website: www.ivpbooks.com

First published 2005

British Library Cataloguing in Publication Data
A catalogue record for this book is available from the British Library.

ISBN-13: 978-1-84474-077-3
ISBN-10: 1-84474-077-3

Set in Monotype Garamond 11/13pt
Typeset in Great Britain by Servis Filmsetting Ltd, Manchester
Printed and bound in Great Britain by MPG Books Ltd, Bodmin

*Inter-Varsity Press is the publishing division of the Universities and Colleges Christian
Fellowship (formerly the Inter-Varsity Fellowship), a student movement linking Christian
Unions in universities and colleges throughout Great Britain, and a member movement of the
International Fellowship of Evangelical Students. For more information about local and
national activities write to UCCF, 38 De Montfort Street, Leicester LE1 7GP, email us at
email@uccf.org.uk, or visit the UCCF website at www.uccf.org.uk.*

CONTENTS

CONTRIBUTORS

Craig Broyles is Professor of Religious Studies at Trinity Western University, Canada. He has written *The Conflict of Faith and Experience in the Psalms* (1989) and a commentary on *Psalms* (1999), and edited volumes on *Isaiah* (1997) and *Interpreting the Old Testament* (2001). As a mountain backpacker, Psalm 104 is his favourite.

Dale Brueggemann is Director of Eurasia Education Services and now based in Cambridge, England. He focuses on the development of faculty and curriculum in Bible Schools from North Africa to Eastern Europe, the Middle East and Asia. He has written a survey of Psalms and Wisdom in *They Spoke from God* (2003). Since his army days in Vietnam his favourite has been Psalm 91.

Jerome Creach is the Robert Cleveland Holland Associate Professor of Old Testament at Pittsburgh Theological Seminary, Pennsylvania, USA. He has written *Yahweh as Refuge and the Editing of the Hebrew Psalter* (1996) and the volume on *Joshua* in the Interpretation series. His favourite is Psalm 1.

Timothy Edwards was a teacher in London and Bath for several years before completing an MA in Jewish Civilization at the Hebrew University of Jerusalem. He then moved to Oxford, England, where he has completed a doctorate on the Targum of Psalms. Psalm 63 is his favourite.

David Firth has taught in Zimbabwe and South Africa as well as his native Australia, and is currently Old Testament Tutor and BA Course Leader at Cliff College, Derbyshire, England. He has written *Surrendering Retribution in the Psalms* (2005), and is also interested in the nature of Old Testament narrative texts. Psalm 73 is his favourite.

Jamie Grant is Lecturer in Biblical Studies at the Highland Theological College in Dingwall, Scotland. His research examined kingship themes in the psalms and has been published as *The King as Exemplar* (2004). He loves teaching, preaching and writing on Old Testament poetic texts. He finds it difficult to choose just one favourite psalm but, were you to twist his arm, would probably name Psalm 85.

David Howard grew up in Costa Rica and Colombia, and is now Dean of the Center for Biblical and Theological Foundations and Professor of Old Testament at Bethel Seminary, St Paul, Minnesota, USA. He is the author of *The Structure of Psalms 93–100* (1997), and has also written or edited several books on Old Testament narrative texts. Psalm 113 is a particular favourite.

James Hely Hutchinson is Associate Lecturer in Old Testament at the Faculté Libre de Théologie Évangélique, Vaux-sur-Seine, France. He is engaged in doctoral research on covenant relationships in the Psalter, and has contributed a related article to *The God of Covenant* (2005). He finds Psalm 103 particularly breathtaking.

Philip Johnston is Old Testament Tutor and Director of Studies at Wycliffe Hall, Oxford, England. He has co-authored a book of Hebrew vocabulary analysis (*Les Psaumes*, 1995), and studied the portrayal of death in the psalms and elsewhere (*Shades of Sheol*, 2002). He has also edited journal reviews and a work on biblical and contemporary theology (*The Land of Promise*, 2000). Psalm 90 remains his favourite.

Michael LeFebvre, from Indianapolis, has worked in an international Christian education ministry and in business consulting.

He helped develop curriculum materials on personnel ethics, now translated into several languages. Having trained for Presbyterian ministry, he is currently completing a doctorate at Aberdeen, Scotland. Psalm 131 is his favourite, for its simple expression of total dependence on the Lord.

Tremper Longman is Robert H. Gundry Professor of Biblical Studies at Westmont College in Santa Barbara, California, USA. He has written extensively, including *How to Read the Psalms* (1988), and *Cry of the Soul* (1995) together with psychologist Dan Allender. Psalm 77 is his favourite when life is difficult and Psalm 98 when life is going well.

Dwight Swanson is Senior Lecturer in Biblical Studies at Nazarene Theological College, Manchester, England. With an academic focus on Qumran, he has published *The Temple Scroll and the Bible* (1995), and is now working on the nature of 'Bible' at Qumran. His favourite psalm is currently 57.

Andy Warren-Rothlin is a Translation Consultant for United Bible Societies, based in Jos, Nigeria. He has written mostly on Hebrew grammar, with a thesis on *Modality, Reference and Speech Acts in the Psalms* (1998), but also has interests in Hebrew poetry, medieval European literature, African languages and various aspects of linguistics. Psalm 113 is his favourite.

Gordon Wenham is Professor of Old Testament at the University of Gloucestershire, England. Best known for his commentaries on *Leviticus* (1979), *Numbers* (1981) and *Genesis* (1987, 1994), he has also written *Story as Torah* (2000) and *The Pentateuch* (2003). His favourite psalm is 103.

Gerald Wilson is Professor of Old Testament and Biblical Hebrew at Azusa Pacific University, California, USA. He has published extensively on the Psalms, including a seminal study *The Editing of the Hebrew Psalter* (1985) and a commentary (2002 and forthcoming), and is currently writing one on *Job*. For several years now Psalm 73 has been his favourite.

ABBREVIATIONS

1. General abbreviations

ABD   *Anchor Bible Dictionary*, 6 vols., ed. D. N. Freedman
        (Garden City: Doubleday, 1992)
ANET   *Ancient Near Eastern Texts Relating to the Old Testament*,
        ed. J. B. Pritchard, 3rd ed. (Princeton: Princeton
        University Press, 1969)
ASV   American Standard Version of the Bible
BCE   Before Common Era (=BC)
CANE   *Civilizations of the Ancient Near East*, 4 vols., ed. J. M.
        Sasson (New York: Charles Scribner's Sons, 1995)
CE   Common Era (=AD)
CEV   Contemporary English Version of the Bible
COS   *The Context of Scripture*, 3 vols., ed. W. W. Hallo and
        K. L. Younger, Jr (Leiden: Brill, 1997–2002)
CTA   *Corpus des tablettes en cunéiformes alphabétiques découvertes
        à Ras Sharma-Ugarit de 1929 à 1939*, 2 vols., ed. A.
        Herdner (Paris: Imprimerie nationale, 1963)
DBHE   *Diccionario bíblico hebreo-español*, 12 vols., L. Alonso-
        Schökel (Madrid: Editorial Trotta, 1994)
DCH   *The Dictionary of Classical Hebrew*, 8 vols. projected, ed.
        D. J. A. Clines (Sheffield: Sheffield Academic Press,
        1993–)
DJG   *Dictionary of Jesus and the Gospels*, ed. J. B. Green et al.
        (Leicester: IVP, 1992)
EDDS   *The Encyclopedia of the Dead Sea Scrolls*, ed. L. H.

	Schiffman et al. (Oxford: Oxford University Press, 2000)
ESV	English Standard Version
GNB	Good News Bible
HALOT	*The Hebrew and Aramaic Lexicon of the Old Testament*, 5 vols., L. Köhler, W. Baumgartner and J. J. Stamm, tr. M. E. J. Richardson from 3rd ed. (Leiden: Brill, 1994–2000)
IDBSup	*Interpreter's Dictionary of the Bible: Supplementary Volume*, ed. K. Crim (Nashville: Abingdon, 1976)
ISBE	*International Standard Bible Encyclopedia*, 4 vols., ed. G. W. Bromiley, 2nd ed. (Grand Rapids: Eerdmans, 1979–88)
JPS	Jewish Publication Society Translation of the Tanakh (Old Testament)
LXX	The Septuagint (Old Testament in Greek)
MT	Masoretic Text (Old Testament Hebrew text)
NA²⁷	*Novum Testamentum Graece*, 27th revised ed., ed. B. Aland et al. (Stuttgart, Deutsche Bibelgesellschaft, 1993)
NASB	New American Standard Bible
NIDOTTE	*New International Dictionary of Old Testament Theology and Exegesis*, 5 vols., ed. W. A. VanGemeren (Carlisle: Paternoster, 1997)
NIV	New International Version of the Bible
NJB	New Jerusalem Bible
NJPS	New Jewish Publication Society Translation of the Tanakh (Old Testament)
NLT	New Living Translation of the Bible
NRSV	New Revised Standard Version of the Bible
RANE	*Readings from the Ancient Near East*, ed. B. T. Arnold and B. B. Beyer (Grand Rapids: Baker Academic, 2002)
RSV	Revised Standard Version of the Bible
TDNT	*Theological Dictionary of the New Testament*, 10 vols., ed. G. Kittel and G. Friedrich, tr. G. W. Bromiley (Grand Rapids: Eerdmans, 1964–76)
TDOT	*Theological Dictionary of the Old Testament*, 15 vols. pro-

jected, ed. G. J. Botterweck and H. Ringgren, tr. J. T.
Willis (Grand Rapids: Eerdmans, 1977–)
THAT   *Theologisches Handwörterbuch zum Alten Testament*, 2
vols., ed. E. Jenni and C. Westermann (Zürich:
Theologischer Verlage, 1976)
UBS⁴   *The Greek New Testament*, 4th revised ed., ed. K. Aland
et al. (Stuttgart: Deutsche Bibelgesellschaft and
United Bible Societies, 1994)

Bibliographical abbreviations

AB   Anchor Bible
AGJU   Arbeiten zur Geschichte des antiken Judentums und
des Urchristentums
BASOR   *Bulletin of the American Schools of Oriental Research*
BBB   Bonner biblische Beiträge
BECNT   Baker Exegetical Commentary on the New
Testament
BETL   Bibliotheca ephemeridum theologicarum lovanien-
sium
Bib   *Biblica*
BibInt   *Biblical Interpretation*
BIS   Biblical Interpretation Series
BJSUCSD   Biblical and Judaic Studies from the University of
California, San Diego
BK   *Bibel und Kirche*
BZ   *Biblische Zeitschrift*
BZAW   Beihefte zur Zeitschrift für die alttestamentliche
Wissenschaft
CBQ   *Catholic Biblical Quarterly*
CBQMS   Catholic Biblical Quarterly Monograph Series
ConBOT   Coniectanea biblica: Old Testament Series
CurTM   *Currents in Theology and Mission*
DJD   Discoveries in the Judaean Desert
FCB   Feminist Companion to the Bible
FOTL   Forms of Old Testament Literature
HAR   *Hebrew Annual Review*

HSM	Harvard Semitic Monographs
HTR	Harvard Theological Review
HUCA	Hebrew Union College Annual
JAB	Journal for the Aramaic Bible
JAOS	Journal of the American Oriental Society
JBL	Journal of Biblical Literature
JfS	Journal for Semitics
JJS	Journal of Jewish Studies
JNES	Journal of Near Eastern Studies
JNSL	Journal of Northwest Semitic Languages
JQR	Jewish Quarterly Review
JSJ	Journal for the Study of Judaism in the Persian, Hellenistic and Roman Period
JSOT	Journal for the Study of the Old Testament
JSOTSup	Journal for the Study of the Old Testament: Supplement Series
JSP	Journal for the Study of the Pseudepigrapha
JTS	Journal of Theological Studies
MGWJ	Monatsschrift für Geschichte und Wissenschaft des Judentums
NIBC	New International Biblical Commentary
NIGTC	New International Greek Testament Commentary
NMES	Near and Middle East Series
NSBT	New Studies in Biblical Theology
NTS	New Testament Studies
OTE	Old Testament Essays
OTL	Old Testament Library
OTS	Oudtestamentische Studiën
PBTM	Paternoster Biblical and Theological Monographs
PSB	Princeton Seminary Bulletin
RB	Revue biblique
RevExp	Review and Expositor
RevQ	Revue de Qumran
SABJT	South African Baptist Journal of Theology
SBLDS	Society of Biblical Literature Dissertation Series
SBLMS	Society of Biblical Literature Monograph Series
SBT	Studies in Biblical Theology
SBTS	Sources for Biblical and Theological Study
ScEs	Science et esprit

SJT	*Scottish Journal of Theology*
SK	*Skrif en Kerk*
SOTBT	Studies in Old Testament Biblical Theology
SSEJC	Studies in Early Judaism and Christianity
STDJ	Studies on the Texts of the Desert of Judah
TBC	Torch Bible Commentaries
TBT	*The Bible Today*
ThTo	*Theology Today*
TJ	*Trinity Journal*
TNTC	Tyndale New Testament Commentaries
TOTC	Tyndale Old Testament Commentaries
TPINTC	Trinity Press International New Testament Commentaries
TRu	*Theologische Rundschau*
TynBul	*Tyndale Bulletin*
UF	*Ugarit-Forschungen*
VT	*Vetus Testamentum*
VTSup	Vetus Testamentum Supplements
WBC	Word Biblical Commentary
WTJ	*Westminster Theological Journal*
WMANT	Wissenschaftliche Monographien zum Alten und Neuen Testament
WUNT	Wissenschaftliche Untersuchungen zum Neuen Testament
WW	*Word and World*
ZAW	*Zeitschrift für die alttestamentliche Wissenschaft*
ZTK	*Zeitschrift für Theologie und Kirche*

INTRODUCTION

The book of Psalms is the best loved and most treasured book of the Hebrew Scriptures. It has been precious to countless thousands of faithful Jewish and Christian believers in hundreds of different languages and countries over several millennia, expressing their hopes and fears, inspiring their faith, and renewing their trust in God. Through the psalms, the spiritual insight and religious heritage of a small number of ancient Israelites has had a profound and lasting impact on humanity.

The book of Psalms is also of great importance in biblical scholarship, partly because it is the Old Testament book which portrays most clearly the varied responses of human faith. Thus it counterbalances the more programmatic expositions of legislators, historians, prophets and sages, enabling a richer appreciation of Israelite religion. These responses vary greatly: in time, from (at least) the early monarchy to the late post-exilic era; in social setting, from rulers to temple personnel to ordinary people; and in religious outlook, from exuberant celebration to uncertain trust to hopeless despair. Further, the book of Psalms illustrates well the developing literary deposit of a faith which continuously adapted to new circumstances.

However, Psalms study is in the midst of a sea change. A generation ago the dominant tendency was to study psalms individually, in relation to their literary form and their cultic function. These approaches, pioneered by Gunkel and Mowinckel respectively, remain part of the scholarly agenda, but now jostle for attention alongside many others. As noted in chapter 1, the newer interests include Hebrew poetry, the structure of the Psalter and its various sections, its development from earlier collections to canonical book, and the early interpretative traditions. The large number and diverse contents of the Qumran Psalms fragments have provided new insights, as has renewed interest in the Targum of Psalms.

While much excellent literature on the psalms is already available, it tends to fall into two categories. There are many good introductions for beginning students, with a summary of the psalms themselves and an overview of Psalms scholarship. There are also many important volumes of learned articles, with a focus on the minutiae which contribute to the scholarly enterprise. But there is less literature which bridges the gap between the two, building on introductory work and helping readers to develop their appreciation of Psalms study. This book helps to meet that need, assuming some foundational knowledge gained elsewhere and guiding readers through current issues and approaches.

Part 1 presents contexts ancient and modern, with an overview of current scholarly approaches and a comparison of ancient Near Eastern prayer genres. Part 2 covers central themes of distress (the taproot of lament), praise, king and cult, including an often overlooked feature of the cult. Part 3 gives a sample of approaches concerned in different ways with the content and final form of the Psalter. And Part 4 considers interpretative traditions, both in the shaping of the canonical Psalter and in later Christian and Jewish perspectives. Finally, two appendices collate information helpful for further Psalms study.

This book has been written by members and guests of the Tyndale Fellowship Old Testament Study Group. The draft chapters were circulated electronically and then discussed at the conference in June 2004 (in Nantwich, England), with beneficial interaction amongst contributors and other participants. Through this detailed discussion we all worked together in moulding the book's contents. So while it is not overtly confessional, the volume benefits from a vision of scholarship as complementary and mutually supportive, echoing Paul's vision of the Christian church (1 Cor. 12). The book reflects the diversity of the Tyndale Fellowship itself: some contributors are internationally renowned scholars with a wealth of knowledge, some are competent scholars who are less active due to their teaching commitments, and some are postgraduate students immersed in the detail of current research.

The editors would like to thank all contributors for their happy acceptance of suggested changes, some substantial, in order to keep to strict word limits and to fulfil the book's aims. We particularly thank Dwight Swanson for stepping in at the last minute and working at great speed to contribute the chapter on Qumran. We also thank Philip Duce and his colleagues at Inter-Varsity Press for enabling rapid publication. But more important than the process is the product. So we dedicate this book collectively to all our readers who seek both to interpret the psalms and to appropriate them for their own life and faith.

Philip Johnston and David Firth

NB
  • Quotations are from the NRSV, unless otherwise indicated
  • Verse numbers follow English usage
  • No knowledge of Hebrew is required
  • All biblical references are given in abbreviation
  • All scholarly references are given by abbreviated title

A. PSALMS INTERPRETATION
IN CONTEXT

1. THE PSALMS AND CURRENT STUDY

David M. Howard, Jr

In recent decades, Psalms studies have undergone several important shifts in focus.[1] First, along with the rest of biblical studies, they have focused more attention than previously on texts *as texts*, i.e. as literary entities and canonical wholes. The Psalter is now read more and more as a coherent, unified *book*. Second, studies of Hebrew poetry have broadened to include linguistic analysis alongside literary and structural approaches. Third, the number of methodologies employed for study of the Psalms has greatly expanded. Fourth, issues of text and canon have been reopened, spurred by the discoveries from Qumran. And fifth, classic form-critical categories are undergoing continued refinements and adjustments.

---

1. Here I have reworked and shortened the discussion of my earlier essay, 'Recent', highlighting selected works published since 1999. Fuller bibliography may be accessed via that essay and the works highlighted here. I thank Baker Book House for permission to use some materials from that essay.

Composition and message

Until recently, the Psalter was treated almost universally as a dis-
jointed assortment of diverse compositions, loosely collected
together. The primary connections among the psalms were
judged to have been liturgical, not literary or canonical. The original life setting (*Sitz im Leben*) of most psalms was thought to have
been the rituals of worship and sacrifice at the temple. The
Psalter was understood to have been the hymnbook of Second
Temple Judaism, and it was not read in the same way as most
other canonical books, i.e. with a coherent structure and
message.

Today, however, a shift has taken place, and the prevailing interest in Psalms studies has to do with questions about the
composition, editorial unity and overall message of the Psalter as a
book, a literary and canonical entity that coheres with respect to its
structure and message. Regardless of the authorship and provenance of individual psalms, or the prehistory of various
collections within the Psalter, these were eventually grouped into a
canonical book in the post-exilic period. Studies now abound that
consider the overall structure of the book, the contours of its dis-
parate parts and how they fit together, or the 'story line' that runs
from Ps. 1 to Ps. 150.

These studies can generally be categorized in two major groups:
(1) those dealing with the macrostructure of the Psalter, i.e. overarching patterns and themes, and (2) those dealing with its
microstructure, i.e. connections among smaller groupings of
psalms, especially adjacent psalms.

Macrostructural approaches

A wisdom emphasis?
The publication in 1985 of Gerald H. Wilson's dissertation,
The Editing of the Hebrew Psalter, provided the framework in
which such macrostructural work could unfold in a systematic
fashion. It was a landmark volume, a significant factor in the
recent explosion of interest in the Psalter's final form, building
on the significant pioneering work of Brevard Childs among

others.[2] In his work, Wilson lays a careful methodological foundation for examining the Psalter as a 'book' in that he traces other examples of hymnic collections from the Ancient Near East: the Sumerian Temple Hymn Collection and Catalogues of Hymnic Incipits, and the Qumran Psalms manuscripts. Each of these provides helpful methodological controls for approaching the Psalter. Some have criticized Wilson's work, charging that the Psalter's editorial coherence is merely in the eye of the beholder, with few or no controls. But these criticisms ignore the larger methodological framework that he uses.

Wilson has summarized, refined and advanced his work in numerous essays since 1985, including his essay in this volume. Suffice it to say here that, among other things, he speaks of the 'frames' in the Psalter, including a Royal Covenantal Frame, consisting of Pss. 2, 72, 89 and 144, and a Final Wisdom Frame, consisting of Pss. 1, 73, 90, 107 and 145 (the first psalms of Books I, III, IV and V, along with the final psalm of Book V proper).[3] According to Wilson, the wisdom frame takes precedence over the royal covenantal frame, and thus 'trust in the power of human kings and kingship is ultimately given up, and hopes rest on Yhwh, who rules forever, and who alone is able to save'.[4] The Psalter, then, is ultimately a book of wisdom, containing Yahweh's instruction for the faithful and emphasizing his kingship.[5] Ps. 1, with its instructions about studying the Torah, can be seen as directing readers to study the Psalter in the same way.[6] In this scheme, Book IV (Pss. 90 – 106) immediately follows the Psalter's major break and stands at the editorial centre of the Psalter, with its focus on Yahweh alone as king, in contrast to the apparent failure of the Davidic Covenant which is the focus of Books I–III. In more recent work, Wilson has attempted to account for Walter

---

2. Childs, *Introduction*, pp. 504–525. For previous scholarship in this area, see Howard, *Structure*, pp. 2–9; Mitchell, *Message*, pp. 15–61.

3. Wilson, 'Shaping', pp. 72–82, especially pp. 80–81.

4. Wilson, 'Qumran *Psalms Scroll*', p. 464.

5. Wilson, 'Shape', pp. 137–138.

6. See also, recently, Kuntz, 'Wisdom'.

Brueggemann's suggestion that the major break in the Psalter is after Book II, not Book III,[7] but more work is needed to reconcile the two models.[8] Wilson's sketches of the Psalter's contours are persuasive in the main, and have shaped the scholarly discussion of the Psalter's composition.

Wilson's work has given rise to a spate of books and articles dealing with different aspects of the Psalter's composition and message. Among the most influential is Erich Zenger's work.[9] He argues that the Psalter in its final form was a well-ordered collection intended to function as a literary 'sanctuary' of sorts, i.e. its canonical *Sitz im Leben* was not liturgical or cultic, but rather literary and wisdom-related. The Psalter itself 'is the sanctuary, in which the biblical God wants to reveal himself', at a time of turning away from the temple (the earlier sanctuary) as the primary hope for Israel. For Zenger, 'According to wisdom theology, which shapes the whole Psalter redactionally, *the Psalter itself is the sanctuary* in which God must be sought and praised and from where God's blessing and salvation can proceed.'[10]

A royal/messianic emphasis?
Some scholars, including this writer, have registered objections to some of Wilson's assertions, most notably his almost total subordination of the royal, Davidic theme to that of Yahweh's kingship. Contrary to his analysis that Ps. 2 begins Book I proper (with Ps. 1 serving as the single introduction to the Psalter), a better case can be made that Pss. 1 and 2 together constitute the Psalter's introduction and that Ps. 3 is the beginning of Book I.[11] In this way, the themes of the sovereignty of Yahweh and of his anointed king

---

7. Brueggemann, 'Bounded'.

8. See ch. 12 in this volume, esp. n. 17 and related text.

9. See his programmatic essay, 'The Psalter'.

10. Zenger, idem; emphasis original. He develops this further in 'Der Psalter'.

11. For particulars, see Howard, *Structure*, pp. 200–207, and bibliography. See also Mitchell, *Message*, pp. 73–74; Hosch, 'Psalms 1 and 2', pp. 4–12; Cole, 'Integrated', pp. 75–88; Auwers, 'Voies', pp. 5–26.

that are proclaimed in Ps. 2 also function as keynotes for the entire Psalter. The fact that Ps. 144 is a royal, Davidic psalm, immediately alongside Ps. 145, a kingship of Yahweh psalm, signals that the earthly and the heavenly expressions of Yahweh's kingdom stand together as messages of hope at the end of the Psalter as at the beginning.

One recent, sustained argument in favour of this view is that of David C. Mitchell. He argues that the book is to be interpreted eschatologically and that the Davidic kingship, far from being downplayed and viewed as failed in the Psalter, forms the basis for the eschatological hope in a messianic figure found through-out the collection.[12] He states that 'the messianic theme is central to the purpose of the collection',[13] and he faults Wilson and others for reading the Psalter 'historically', i.e. tying it in specifically with Israel's pre-exilic, exilic and post-exilic situations, rather than eschatologically, whereby the vision looks far beyond these historical periods. Much of Mitchell's argument rests on hypothetical and debatable connections with certain events and with the eschatological programme of Zechariah 9 – 14. However, his work has an overall force and logic that must surely be considered in future discussions of the Psalter's composition and message.[14]

Happily, a rapprochement of sorts is emerging, as Wilson's recent work seems to allow more room for an eschatological (re)reading of the royal psalms, even as he maintains the essential thrust of his original arguments in favour of a dominant wisdom framework.[15]

---

12. Mitchell, *Message*. For specific comments about Wilson's view, see especially pp. 78–82. For further critique and recent bibliography, see Grant's chapter in this volume and his book, *King*.

13. Mitchell, *Message*, p. 87.

14. Recent works on the macrostructural level include Auwers, *Composition*, and Cole, *Shape*.

15. See Wilson, 'King', and his essay in this volume. See also Saur, *Königspsalmen*, who emphasizes the mediating function of the royal psalms in the final form of the Psalter.

Microstructural and other approaches

At the other end of the methodological spectrum from Wilson are works dealing with what might be called the microstructural level, i.e. relationships among individual psalms or small groupings. The earliest book-length treatment of these was my own *The Structure of Psalms 93 – 100*. It assumes that the Psalter should be read as a book with an internal coherence, and tests the hypothesis on the lowest levels by subjecting Pss. 93 – 100 to an exhaustive analysis of every lexeme in every possible relation with every other one. The advantage of this method is that every relation among these psalms should thereby be uncovered, but an obvious danger is that too much will be made of relations that are merely coincidental.[16] A weakness in this particular work is the limited corpus of psalms, in the middle of Book IV; an obvious next step is to consider Book IV in its entirety. Nevertheless, the method forms a necessary counterpart to the macrostructural works, whereby the latter's conclusions can be tested and confirmed.

Jerome F. Creach has forged a third way between macrostructural and microstructural approaches.[17] He takes a semantic field or thematic approach, studying the associated field of one specific lexeme, in this case 'to take refuge' (*ḥsh*). The concept of Yahweh as 'refuge', which occurs first in the programmatic Ps. 2, is found in a majority of psalms and is concentrated in significant sections. Creach uses his findings to comment on the organization of the entire work. This approach should prove to be productive, as other key words that might have been instrumental in shaping the Psalter are studied.

Some sceptical voices have objected that too much is claimed for the Psalter in reading it as a book. Some argue that the proposals advanced disagree too much among themselves for any of them to have validity. However, there is significant agreement among the major proposals; much of the divergence between approaches is

---

16. I attempted to avoid this pitfall by distinguishing between 'key-word links' (the most significant), 'thematic word links' (showing only general connections), and 'incidental repetitions' (not significant at all); see pp. 98–102. My 'Psalm 94' further explains and illustrates the method.

17. Creach, *Choice*.

complementary, not contradictory. The most sustained critique is by Norman Whybray, who sets out to test possible perspectives from which the Psalter might have been edited in the post-exilic period and finds all of them wanting. However, this work has several problems of its own that undermine the argument.[18]

This recent interest in the coherence and overall message of the book of Psalms is in fact a rediscovery of an earlier interest among rabbinic and Christian interpreters. The result is a salutary one, which scholars from all perspectives can embrace.

Hebrew poetry

A second area in which there have been far-reaching changes recently is the study of Hebrew poetry. Significant works have appeared along two major trajectories, indebted respectively to general linguistics and to literary studies, both stylistic and structural.

General linguistic approaches
Several works appeared in the late 1970s and early 1980s attempting to explain Hebrew poetry using linguistic methods, particularly in terms of syntax.[19] For the most part, these works are theoretical, concerned to account for the driving mechanisms of Hebrew poetry and downplaying or ignoring the literary or stylistic dimensions of poetry. Their great advantage is that they reveal things about the workings of Hebrew poetry never seen before with such clarity, and they are rooted in the nature of language itself.

The most ambitious and influential of these works is M. O'Connor's *Hebrew Verse Structure*. He describes Hebrew poetry strictly in terms of syntactical patterns, and argues that syntactical 'constriction' – not metre, rhythm or even parallelism – is the fundamental feature of Hebrew poetry. He asserts, 'Just as most poetic systems are shaped in part by a series of phonological

---

18. Whybray, *Reading*. See Howard, *Structure*, p. 22, n. 31, and 'Review of Whybray'.

19. Collins, *Line-Forms*; Geller, *Parallelism*; O'Connor, *Hebrew*; Berlin, *Dynamics*.

requirements, i.e., by a series of *metrical* constraints, so there are poetic systems shaped in part by a series of *syntactical* requirements, i.e., by a system of syntactic constraints. Among them is Canaanite [i.e. Hebrew and Ugaritic] verse' (p. 65).

O'Connor makes two major contributions: (1) attention to the syntactical patterns underlying Hebrew poetry, and (2) recognition that poetic lines operate under certain constraints. Beyond these, one of his most important specific contributions is his recognition that gapping (i.e. ellipsis) is a major feature of Hebrew poetry and does not generally occur in prose.

One problem with O'Connor's work is its dense and highly technical jargon, and this undoubtedly has inhibited its wider consideration. Another limitation is that, despite its broad-ranging scope – O'Connor studied 1,200 lines of poetry – his explanatory system sometimes fails to do justice to the peculiar poetic features of certain corpora outside his chosen set of lines.

Yet, in the end, O'Connor's system 'works' and deserves wider exposure. The reissue of the work with an 'Afterword' by O'Connor, as well as two articles by William Holladay summarizing and applying the system, should help to remedy this situation.[20] Indeed, at least two major works have now adopted its methodology.[21] Since it operates strictly on the syntactical level, O'Connor's system does not exhaust the *meaning* of a poem and does not deal with the artistry of poetry, but it has opened new doors with its attention to the syntactical fundamentals of language.

Of the remaining works on the syntax of poetry, we should especially highlight Adele Berlin's work, *The Dynamics of Biblical Parallelism*. Like O'Connor, Berlin asserts that parallelism is a linguistic phenomenon, and she states that parallelism and 'terseness' are the two markers of poetic texts (p. 5). She argues persuasively that parallelism has many different aspects and operates on many different levels. It 'may involve semantics, grammar and/or other linguistic features, and it may occur on the level of the word, line,

---

20. Holladay, '*Hebrew* (I)'; '*Hebrew* (II)'.

21. Cloete, *Versification*; Holladay, *Jeremiah 1 and 2*. Cf. further the works cited in O'Connor, *Hebrew* (1997 edition), chapter on 'Contours', pp. 641–642.

couplet, or over a greater textual span' (p. 25). Especially helpful are her observations that parallelism may operate on one level (e.g. phonological) while it does not on another (e.g. lexical or syntactical), and that parallelism on one level raises expectations on another, even when it is not formally present.

Berlin thus goes beyond most syntactically oriented works by insisting that we must devote attention to syntax *and* semantics, as well as to other levels. Referring to Edward Greenstein's argument that syntactical parallelism should define *all* parallelism, she states, 'I cannot agree . . . that syntactic repetition lies at the base of parallelism and that semantic parallelism is a result of this repetition. In many cases, it may be the other way around . . . There is no reason to give syntax priority over semantics (or vice versa); both are important aspects of parallelism.'[22]

By contrast, and in line with the arguments of O'Connor, Charles W. Morris sees syntactics as the foundation upon which other relations build. For him, syntactics deals with the relations of signs to one another, semantics with the relations of signs to the objects denoted, and pragmatics with the relation of signs to their interpreters, i.e. 'all the psychological, biological, and sociological phenomena which occur in the functioning of signs'.[23] Syntactics is the most abstract of these, but it has the greatest explanatory power, since it can explain the workings or the mechanisms of Hebrew poetry in ways that no other approaches can.

Having said this, poetic analysis, which presumably is a tool in the search for *meaning*, must also consider semantics, phonology and morphology. And, as the literary studies below show, there is also an 'art' to understanding poetry. In the search for the meaning of a poem, then, syntax must be foundational, but other approaches must also be enlisted in order to elucidate the meaning of texts more fully.

Stylistic literary approaches

Many studies of Hebrew poetry have recently emphasized literary approaches, whereby individual psalms are treated as coherent

---

22. Berlin, *Dynamics*, p. 23; see her further comments on pp. 21–25.
23. Morris, 'Foundations', p. 108.

wholes and the artistic dimensions of poetry are very much the
focus. Two of the most important are by James Kugel and Robert
Alter.

Kugel's book addresses the nature of parallelism. His fundamental poetic unit is the paired line, or couplet, and he expresses
the relationship between the two as 'A is so, and what's more, B.'
That is, the second line of the pair will advance the thought of
the first line in a 'seconding' manner of some sort. As such, he
overturns the popular notion of parallel lines as essentially syn-
onymous. Kugel resists any system for reading poetry, in contrast
to the works above: 'There is no such thing as an "objective"
approach to biblical texts, no neutral set of literary tools that will
take apart any book or passage and tell us what makes it work.'[24]
Kugel's greatest strength is his explication of the seconding relationship between lines A and B, demolishing the simplistic view
that equates lines A and B. However, his disdain for any foundation in a system or theory of language leaves his approach open to
potentially endless subjectivity.

Alter's is a more literary work.[25] He begins with a discussion of
'The Dynamics of Parallelism' that echoes Kugel's, in that he sees
the second 'verset' of a couplet going beyond the first in any of a
number of ways, only one of which might be synonymity (and that
only very rarely). Others include complementarity, focusing, height-
ening, intensification, specification, consequentiality, contrast and
disjunction. Along with Kugel's observations, this work effectively
demolishes the idea of complete synonymity between lines.[26]

Structural literary approaches
Closely bound up with the turn to stylistic literary studies of
poetry are a myriad of structural studies. The latter differ somewhat from the former in that many end up simply as catalogues of

24. Kugel, *Idea*, p. 302.
25. Alter, *Art*.
26. Essentially the same point is made from a linguistic perspective by
O'Connor, *Hebrew*, pp. 50–52; and Berlin, *Dynamics*, pp. 14–15, 64–65.

large-scale literary devices. The structures of psalms are laid bare (although often without unanimity) with very elaborate diagrams, but too often little is said of a psalm's art or its meaning. This approach is often called *analyse structurelle*, the study of surface structures, as opposed to *analyse structurale*, the deep-structural analysis of French structuralism or semiotics.

Two leading practitioners of this type of analysis are Marc Girard and Pierre Auffret, who have both produced a great number of structural studies. They exhaustively treat repeated patterns within individual psalms, and consider the lowest levels of the word up to the highest levels of the poem.[27] While there are differences between the two,[28] their approach is very similar overall.

Another approach which also includes analysis of poems at all levels is that of J. C. de Moor and his students in the Netherlands.[29] One weakness is that it equates form with meaning in most instances, implying erroneously that the task of interpretation is complete when the structure of a poem is elucidated. Willem S. Prinsloo in South Africa espoused a similar method, calling it a 'text-immanent' approach. This approach is a text-based and text-oriented framework for interpretation, dealing with morphological, syntactical, stylistic and semantic components of poetry. Prinsloo also addressed the needs of those who would preach and teach the texts, certainly a welcome component of his work.[30]

Hermeneutics

In the area of hermeneutics, the Psalms are studied today from a wide

---

27. E.g. Girard, *Psaumes*; Auffret, *Merveilles*; *Là montent*.
28. See Auffret, 'L'étude I'; 'L'étude II'; 'L'étude III', where he responds to Girard's criticisms of his work.
29. This approach is explained in Korpel and de Moor, 'Fundamentals', and exemplified in van der Meer and de Moor, *Structural*.
30. E.g. Prinsloo, 'Psalm 116'; 'Psalm 149'. A representative collection of his essays in Afrikaans is *Psalms*. I thank David Firth for this reference.

range of perspectives, echoing larger trends in biblical studies.[31] Much of this is helpful, in that new ways of understanding texts are brought forward. But there can be problems with some methodologies which seem to have little interest in authorial or textual meaning, e.g. deconstruction and most reader-response approaches.

Several recent works apply a range of different methods to one psalm. For example, Donald K. Berry applies textual, structural, form-critical, rhetorical-critical and reader-oriented methods to Ps. 18, showing the value of each.[32] Jutta Schröten reviews the range of critical approaches to Ps. 118 throughout the history of interpretation, and then offers two parallel readings from synchronic and diachronic perspectives.[33] William H. Bellinger, Jr takes a similar approach to Ps. 61, employing a 'hermeneutic of curiosity' that embraces any and all methods; he uses form, canonical, rhetorical and reader-response criticisms, ending with a theological analysis.[34] A recent multi-author work employs nine different approaches in the study of Ps. 22.[35] Herbert J. Levine takes a more theoretical approach without focusing on any one psalm. He too argues for employing several disciplines, and uses history, anthropology, linguistic philosophy, phenomenology of religion, literary discourse, 'biblical interpretation' and post-Holocaust interpretation.[36]

Some works have focused more on the history of interpretation, including works by John H. Eaton,[37] Lars Olov Eriksson, Uriel Simon and Adele Berlin.[38]

Many critical approaches common today in the academy are also used in Psalms studies. These include sociological and

---

31. McKenzie and Haynes, *To Each*, list no less than fourteen current critical methodologies.
32. Berry, *Psalms*.
33. Schröten, *Entstehung*.
34. Bellinger, *Hermeneutic*. See also his 'Psalm xxvi'.
35. Poorthuis, *Mijn God*.
36. Levine, *Sing*.
37. Eaton, *Psalms of the Way*. Eaton deals with three Torah psalms (1; 19; 119) and three Kingship of Yahweh psalms (93; 97; 99).
38. Eriksson, *Come*; Simon, *Four*; Berlin, *Biblical*.

liberationist approaches,[39] ideological or Two-Thirds World readings,[40] feminist criticism,[41] rhetorical criticism,[42] deconstruction,[43]
speech-act theory,[44] discourse analysis,[45] ecological readings,[46] and
even what might be called physiological readings.[47]

An obvious danger here is that methodologies may themselves
become the *raison d'être* for study, rather than *means* by which to elucidate the meaning of psalms. The pursuit of modern agendas,
however pressing or interesting they might be, should not trump
the pursuit of the ancient authors' meanings.[48]

Text and canon

The discovery in the 1940s and 1950s of at least thirty-nine Psalms
manuscripts in the caves at Qumran and nearby (the Dead Sea
Scrolls) has given rise to new questions about the formation of the
Psalter. The most important of these manuscripts is the so-called
Psalms Scroll (11QPs[a]) discovered in Cave 11 and published by
James Sanders.[49] It contains portions of some thirty-nine psalms
from the biblical Psalter, as well as several others. Its order is radi-

---

39. Pleins, *Psalms*; Reid, *Listening*; Brueggemann, *Israel's Praise*; *Abiding*;
    'Psalms and the Life'; Jesurathnam, 'Towards'.
40. E.g. Croatto, 'Psalm 23:1–6'; Kinoti, 'Psalm 23:1–6'; Moon, 'Psalm
    23:1–6'. These overlap to some extent with those in the previous note.
41. E.g. Tanner, 'Hearing'; Bail, 'Gerechtigkeit'.
42. E.g. Allen, 'Value'; Kuntz, 'King'; Crow, 'Rhetoric'.
43. McCarthy, 'Not-So-Bad' ; Jobling, 'Deconstruction'; Clines, 'World'.
44. Irsigler, 'Psalm-Rede'.
45. Wendland, 'Genre'.
46. Limburg, 'Down-to-Earth'; Urbrock, 'Earth'; Ntreh, 'Survival'.
47. Rendsburg and Rendsburg, 'Physiological'; Levin, 'Right Hand'; Smith,
    'Heart'.
48. I am aware of the hermeneutical and epistemological minefield opened
    by such comments, but cannot engage the issue further here. A recent
    work that deals helpfully with these issues is Vanhoozer, *Is There*.
49. Sanders, *Psalms Scroll*.

cally different from the present canonical order evidenced in all other manuscript traditions. In addition, many other discoveries have fleshed out a picture of a canonical development of the Psalter whereby the first three books (Pss. 1 – 89) appear to have reached a fixed order and arrangement at Qumran much earlier than Books IV and V (Pss. 90 – 150).

Sanders, Wilson and Peter Flint have argued that this scroll represents a valid edition of the Psalms from a variant tradition, i.e. it was considered as the canonical book of Psalms at Qumran, and that Books IV and V were then still fluid in their contents.[50]

However, others have argued that the scroll was not a canonical edition of the Psalter but rather a liturgical book based upon it, an anthology of sorts.[51] As such it was never understood to be canonical, and the radical divergences in order plus the inclusion of non-canonical psalms are due to liturgical reasons and not to a separate canonical tradition.

Even if it were established that the Qumran community regarded the Psalter as canonical, this does not settle the question of what might have been the 'original' version. It is certainly possible that a proto-Masoretic version was considered authoritative by most in Judaism, and that the Qumran 'canon' represented a variant, minority tradition. An analogy here would be the fact that the book of Esther is not found at Qumran, whereas it has been clearly understood as authoritative and canonical in mainstream Jewish (Masoretic) tradition.

Form criticism

Psalms studies for most of the last century have been dominated by form-critical approaches indebted to the work of Hermann

---

50. Sanders, *Psalms Scroll*; Wilson, *Editing*, pp. 63–92; 'Qumran *Psalms Scroll*'; 'Qumran'; Flint, *Dead Sea*, and many publications. See also the essay by Swanson in this volume.

51. See recently Haran, '11QPsa'; Beckwith, 'Early'; Mitchell, *Message*, pp. 21–26, esp. 22–23.

Gunkel. He focused on the literary forms (genres) of individual psalms and paid attention to the life situation (*Sitz im Leben*) that supposedly gave rise to each form.

Sigmund Mowinckel followed Gunkel's classifications, but emphasized especially the cultic background to almost all the psalms. He posited the existence of a so-called 'Enthronement of Yahweh' festival, reconstructed from clues he found in the Psalms. His hypothesis is kept alive by J. H. Eaton,[52] who expands the category of royal psalm to include nearly half the Psalter, by interpreting most individual laments as prayers of the king. This has been disputed by many, but the canonical form of the Psalter partly supports his view, since seventy-three psalms are attributed to David.[53]

Many refinements of Gunkel's work have been made, even though his basic insights still frame the discussion in important ways. For example, Claus Westermann argues that the usual distinction between psalms of praise and thanksgiving is misguided.[54] He labels the first type 'psalms of descriptive praise', where the praises of God *describe* his attributes in general, universal terms, and the second type 'psalms of narrative (or declarative) praise', where God's praises are recited (*declared*) in the specifics of what God has done for the nation or the individual. Westermann overstates the case somewhat, because certainly there are some meaningful distinctions between thanksgiving and praise. Nevertheless, his is a most helpful distinction, revealing that ultimately all the psalms are to be considered as praises.[55]

Erhard Gerstenberger's refinements pay special attention to social settings of the psalms, including a focus on in-group and out-group dynamics.[56] He argues that many psalms arose in the context of 'the small, organic group of family, neighborhood, or community' (the

---

52. Eaton, *Kingship*.

53. See Waltke, 'Canonical', and the discussion above under 'A royal/ messianic emphasis?'

54. Westermann's most important essays are collected in *Praise and Lament*.

55. However, note the qualification in ch. 3 in this volume, under 'Negative conclusions'.

56. Gerstenberger, *Psalms I, II*.

out-groups), not in 'the central temple or famous wisdom acade-
mies' (the in-groups).[57] As such, the origin and the function of many
psalms were not liturgical or connected with the cult at all.

Westermann considered the lament to contain the fullest
rhetorical pattern in expressing Israel's faith, because of the way its
complex structure incorporated the move from despair to praise.
Scholars following him have continued to concentrate significant
energies on the lament.

For example, Anneli Aejmelaeus calls Westermann's complaint
psalms (Gunkel's individual laments) 'prayer psalms of the individual', because of the prominent place of imperative prayer to God.
William H. Bellinger, Jr deals with prophetic elements in the
laments, and (following Begrich) links the 'certainty of a hearing'
with the oracle of salvation, although he downplays the idea of a
cultic prophet who pronounced this oracle. On the other hand,
Raymond Jacques Tournay argues that authentic cultic prophets
did exist, and were the post-exilic levitical singers. Craig C. Broyles
distinguishes between 'psalms of plea', in which God is praised
and asked to intervene on the psalmist's behalf, and 'psalms of
complaint', in which the psalmist challenges God, who is seen
either as an aloof bystander or an active antagonist. The so-called
complaints are not complaints *per se*, but rather intend to summon
God to be faithful to his promises and act on the psalmist's behalf.
Rolf A. Jacobson focuses on the function of direct discourse in
the psalms – quotations from enemies, from the psalmists themselves, from God, and from the community – noting that each has
distinct rhetorical functions.[58]

Turning to the laments in their Ancient Near Eastern context,
Paul W. Ferris, Jr attempts 'to develop a unified comparative
description of the Hebrew communal lament in light of the phenomenon of public lament in neighboring cultures'.[59] He
concludes that there is no connection of dependency between the

57. Gerstenberger, *Psalms I*, p. 33.

58. Aejmelaeus, *Traditional*; Bellinger, *Psalmody*; Tournay, *Seeing*; Broyles,
    Conflict; Jacobson, *Many*.

59. Ferris, *Genre*, p. 13.

Israelite and Mesopotamian laments, but rather that both go back to a common cultural pattern. Walter C. Bouzard, Jr disagrees, arguing that the evidence 'points to the strong possibility of a specifically literary connection' for Hebrew and Mesopotamian collections,[60] although he admits that the evidence for borrowing is only circumstantial. Bouzard questions some of Westermann's structural elements, the 'expression of confidence' and especially the 'certainty of a hearing', since they are not present at all in the Israelite laments he examines (Pss. 44; 60; 74; 79; 80; 83; 89).[61] Walter Brueggemann has advanced an important alternative approach in categorizing psalms by function.[62] He proposes three categories: 'psalms of orientation' are characterized by the absence of tension and portray the world as ordered and good, such as psalms of creation, wisdom, retribution and blessing; 'psalms of disorientation' include essentially the laments; and 'psalms of reorientation' include thanksgivings and hymns of praise. In the last of these, Brueggemann detects a greater sense of excitement than in the 'ordered' psalms of orientation, and he sees evidence that the psalmists have gone through disorientation and progressed to a place of new orientation which is much more secure and mature than the original orientation. Thus thanksgivings and hymns, while they differ in form from each other, are similar in function in that they belong to the new orientation, informed by the psalmists' trouble and by God's gracious intervention.[63]

Conclusion

The potential for Psalms studies in the different areas surveyed above is great, and we can be encouraged by most trends. We

---

60. Bouzard, *We Have*, p. 201.

61. Ibid., pp. 109–113, 204–205.

62. Brueggemann, 'Psalms and the Life', and later writings, especially *Message*.

63. Many other works refine Gunkel's categories or propose new ones. As one example, Johnston's essay in this volume (ch. 3) demonstrates that distress is an important motif often ignored in standard form-critical studies.

should be pleased with the new focus on the unity of the Psalter, in which an eschatological hope can be seen. We can participate enthusiastically in the avenues opened up in studies of Hebrew poetry, where the received text of poems is usually the focus. We can and should discuss which methodological approaches are more valid and helpful and which are less so. We should certainly engage in the ongoing re-evaluations of what is meant by canon in light of the Qumran discoveries. And we have a continuing fruitful avenue of exploration in form-critical approaches.[64] In sum, this ancient hymnbook and prayer book continues to pulsate with its endlessly fascinating qualities and its life-giving power, and we should approach it – and the God whom it reveals – as its humble and grateful beneficiaries.

---

64. I thank Provost Leland V. Eliason and Bethel Seminary for a generous grant that enabled me to participate in the Tyndale Fellowship Old Testament Study Group in Nantwich, at which this paper was first read.

2. THE PSALMS AND ANCIENT NEAR EASTERN PRAYER GENRES

Tremper Longman III

At the heart of many religions is prayer, speech directed toward one's deity. By virtue of being direct address to heaven, prayer is one of the most intimate acts that a devotee can perform. However, though intimate, it is not always warm or celebratory. Prayer can be angry, fearful, or even cold, depending on the nature of the deity and the circumstances of the one who speaks.

The majority of psalms are prayers. As we will describe in more detail below, legitimate prayer in the Bible has one and only one object, Yahweh, though he may be addressed by different names and epithets in the prayers. The prayers of the polytheistic religions of the Ancient Near East address a number of different gods and goddesses, though often prayers dedicated to one deity sound as if that god or goddess is so important that the others do not matter.

The literatures of most Ancient Near Eastern civilizations are rich with prayers of praise and lamentation.[1] The following survey

---

1. The most accessible English translations of selected prayers may be

will only scratch the surface.[2] We should keep one important fact in mind as we explore different prayers in this chapter. We have only a selection of the prayers that were recorded, and certainly these represent an infinitesimal number from the prayers that were uttered. Due to the nature of the case, we have prayers that were preserved either for literary or, probably more importantly, for ritual purposes. In terms of the latter, literary prayers were often combined with sacrifice or some other type of formal worship. In terms of Mesopotamian prayers, the connection is often with incantation ritual.

Mesopotamian prayers

In this section we will treat prayers from the region of Mesopotamia (roughly present-day Iraq) from the first appearance of literary prayers (the second half of the third millennium) down to the end of the neo-Babylonian period (539 BCE). While this includes prayers written in both Sumerian and Akkadian, our focus will be on the former, since the Akkadian-speaking Babylonians and Assyrians basically utilized earlier Sumerian genres, often even writing their prayers in Sumerian.[3]

Hymns

There are a number of hymns from the neo-Sumerian literary corpus.[4] These hymns are of various types, the most popular of which are those dedicated to a number of different gods and goddesses. An example of such a hymn is one dedicated to Enlil

---

found in *ANET*, pp. 365–401, 573–586; *COS*, vol. 1, pp. 37–47 (Egyptian), 156–159 (Hittite), 283–286 (West Semitic), 416–421, 470–476 (Akkadian), 526–534, 552–560 (Sumerian).

2. Furthermore, this survey restricts itself to prayer as genre. For a study of the content and gestures of Israelite prayer in the light of their Ancient Near Eastern counterparts, see Keel, *Symbolism*.

3. Falkenstein and von Soden, *Sumerische*, pp. 57–231.

4. See Hallo, 'Individual', p. 74.

and accessible in a translation by S. N. Kramer.[5] Interestingly, this prayer of praise alternates between third-person description of the majesty of the great god and direct invocation of his name:

> Enlil whose command is far reaching, lofty his word (and) holy,
> Whose pronouncement is unchangeable, who decrees destinies into the
>   distant future . . .
> Enlil, when you marked off holy settlements on earth,
> You built Nippur as your very own city . . . (lines 1–2, 64–65)

But prayers dedicated to gods and goddesses are not the only type of hymns that are extant. Indeed, one of the earliest literary compositions that we have written in Sumerian is an example of a hymn dedicated to a temple, namely the Kesh temple hymn.[6] A later example is the 'Hymn to the Ekur', the magnificent temple dedicated to Enlil at Nippur.[7]

> The great house, it is a mountain great,
> The house of Enlil, it is a mountain great,
> The house of Ninlil, it is a mountain great . . . (lines 1–3)

There are royal hymns as well, but in the case of Sumerian literature, these hymns celebrate the king himself. Among a number of examples, a Shulgi hymn is a particularly interesting example. Here Shulgi, an important neo-Sumerian king (twenty-first century BCE), praises his own great achievements and character. Kramer gave the hymn the title 'King of the Road',[8] because one section extols Shulgi as someone who improved the roads and who could also run the distance between the cities of Nippur and Ur (about a hundred miles) in half the time of a normal runner!

---

5. See *ANET*, pp. 573–576.
6. Described in Jacobsen, *Harps*, pp. 377–385.
7. Translated by Kramer in *ANET*, pp. 582–583.
8. See *ANET*, pp. 584–586. See Klein, *Three*.

I, the king, a hero from the [mother's] womb am I,
I, Shulgi, a mighty man from (the day) I was born am I,
A fierce-eyed lion, born of the *ushumgal*, am I . . .
I, the runner, rose in my strength, all set for the course,
(And) from Nippur to Ur,
I resolved to traverse as if it were (but a distance of) one danna. (lines
   1–3, 39–41)

One group of relatively early Sumerian hymns draws our attention because for the first time we know the name of the one who composed these powerful poems. She was a woman named Enheduanna, the daughter of Sargon, the warrior who managed to push aside the native Sumerian rulers of Mesopotamia and initiate an Akkadian dynasty and empire. For four decades in the twenty-third century BCE she functioned as the high priestess of the moon god Nanna. However, in the cycle of hymns that we have from her, it is not Nanna who is praised but rather Inanna, the goddess of love and war.[9] Among other works attributed to her are forty-two hymns addressed to temples from the southern city of Eridu to the northern city of Sippar and the eastern city of Eshnunna.[10]

We have a fine example of an Akkadian hymn dedicated to the sun god Shamash.[11] The hymn appropriately beings by extolling the god's illuminating radiance:

Illuminator of all, the whole of heaven,
Who makes light the [darkness for mankind] above and below,
Your radiance [spre]ads out like a net [over the world],
You brighten the g[loo]m of the distant mountains.

---

9. See the important work by Hallo and van Dijk, *Exaltation*, as well as the more recent one by de Shong Meador, *Inanna*. The latter mentions that, besides three poems to Inanna, we also have hymns to Nanna and a number of temple hymns that bear her name as composer (p. 37).

10. For an edition of these texts, see Sjoberg and Bergmann, *Collection*.

11. Translations of the Shamash hymn may be found in Lambert, *Babylonian*, pp. 121–138, though the cited translation is from Foster, *Before*, vol. 2, pp. 536–544.

Laments

Sumerian was a language rich in lament literature, both corporate and individual. Many of these lament prayers are embedded in incantation literature. In other words, they are part of a ritual to avoid the danger of malevolent forces. We know a number of different types by their native designations, but in the following we will survey only those most discussed and most relevant for comparison with the biblical book of Psalms.[12]

The balag

We have examples of congregational city laments from the Old Babylonian (1830–1530 BCE), neo-Assyrian (745–626 BCE), neo-Babylonian (626–539 BCE) and Seleucid (post-312 BCE) periods.[13] These have the native designation *balag*, which means harp, and presumably that instrument accompanied these laments. These *balag* laments were written in a dialectical form of Sumerian known as *emesal*, which was the language of the *gala*-priests as they performed their ritual lamentations.[14]

Kutscher has given us a full-length study of one important example of this genre (*a-ab-ba hu-luh-ha*). The primary difference between these and the earlier city laments is in terms of historical specificity. Whereas the neo-Sumerian (2060–1950 BCE) texts are clearly and tightly connected to a particular destruction (namely

---

12. We here omit a study of the famous city laments because they are more relevant as background to the book of Lamentations than to the Psalms. Note the following relevant studies: Dobbs-Allsopp, *Weep*; Ferris, *Genre*; Gwaltney, 'Biblical'.

13. The definitive work on the *balag* is Cohen, *Canonical*. Cohen shows that some of the Old Babylonian *balag* were preserved and redacted into the first millennium. Their continuing use was likely due to their becoming a fixed part of the *gala*-priests' ritual, as witnessed by a catalogue found in Assurbanipal's library. The last *balag* text that we know comes from around 100 BCE.

14. Exactly what *emesal* is has been much debated. The speech elsewhere is often placed in the mouths of women as well as the *gala*-priests, but it is no longer fashionable to refer to *emesal* as a woman's dialect.

that of neo-Sumerian city states), the later congregational laments 'tend to generalize in their description of violence'.[15] In Kutscher's expert opinion, they are not as imaginative in content or as fresh in poetic quality as the earlier texts. He ascribes this difference to their respective places in ritual. As we have seen above, the neo-Sumerian texts were likely composed for the occasion of the rebuilding of temples destroyed during the demise of the Ur III empire. Once they were used in this way, they were then only copied for historical or artistic purposes. The late congregational laments may well have had their origins with a specific historical situation, but they were written for repeated ritual use, for similar though not identical situations. Later, we will note a similarity between the late laments and the psalms of lament.

Ershemma laments

The late congregational laments often had an *ershemma* connected to them.[16] The word means something like the 'lament of the *shem*-drum',[17] and indicates the instrument that accompanied the singing or chanting of the lament by the *gala*-priest. The rituals of the *gala*-priests were usually recited in *emesal*, and so it is not surprising that the *ershemma* are written in that dialect. The most extensive discussion of the *ershemma* is by M. E. Cohen, who notes 194 *ershemma* incipits (first lines) in catalogues, and provides translation and commentary of twenty-six examples.

The *ershemma* is a lamentation connected to the cult. Indeed, from the cultic calendars from the cities of Uruk and Ashur, we see that the *ershemma* concluded the liturgy. It was a song of intercession. In the description of Dalglish, they are 'generally very formal, filled with epithetic and laudatory invocations, often with repetitious formula to induce the deities to repent'.[18]

---

15. Kutscher, *Oh Angry*, p. 4.

16. See the example of *a-ab-ba hu-luh-ha*, edited by Kutscher in *Oh Angry*.

17. However, Hallo ('Lamentations', p. 1872) translates *shem* as 'tambourine' and refers to the laments as 'tambourine laments'.

18. Dalglish, *Psalm Fifty-One*, p. 20.

He divides the extant *ershemmas* into early ones from the First Dynasty of Isin (nineteenth century BCE) and late ones from the first millennium. A number of the former are connected with the actual fall of the Dynasty of Isin wherein the goddess of that city (Nin-Isina) laments the destruction of the city. But others are not connected with an actual destruction and therefore were probably reused in ritual contexts. The late *ershemmas* were the ones, mentioned above, that were connected to the late congregational *balags*.

Shuilla laments

Yet another type of Sumerian lament from the late period are known as *shuilla*, or 'raising of the hand', which may refer to a ritual gesture (perhaps lifting the hand to the mouth as a gesture of prayer) that accompanied the words of the lament. Cooper notes that there are forty-seven *shuilla* texts known through their incipits, though, at the time of his article, only three extant texts could be positively associated with this genre.[19] These Sumerian *shuilla* laments (in *emesal* often with Akkadian interlinear translations) are corporate.

Akkadian literature also attests a vital genre of *shuilla* prayers. However, as opposed to Sumerian examples, the Akkadian prayers are individual laments connected with incantations.[20]

Private prayers

Though many Sumerian compositions are corporate or congregational in character, there are some subgenres that are prayers of individuals. We will illustrate with two types: letter-prayers and the *ershahunga*.

Letter-prayers

Ancient Sumerians understood their gods to be affected by their actions, through which it was possible to displease and even anger their gods. Thus worshippers felt the need to petition their gods so that they would no longer be angry with them. For this purpose, they would go to the temple to be in the presence of their deity,

---

19. Cooper, 'Sumerian'.
20. The definitive study is that of Hunt, *Hymnic*.

represented by a statue or some other material object, and offer
prayers trying to calm the deity down. At some point, it was thought
that if the god could be represented by a statue or an object, then so
could the worshipper. Thus we have examples of votive objects on
which are inscribed prayers. A less expensive alternative developed
as early as the neo-Sumerian period, namely the letter-prayer.[21] A
letter-prayer, as the name suggests, was a prayer inscribed on a clay
tablet and placed in the presence of the god's statue at the temple.
As Hallo describes it, the letter-prayer 'combines the format of a
letter with the function of a prayer'.[22] The prayer was thought to be
continually uttered with the hope of pacifying the god.

Ershahunga prayers

Hallo suggests that the *ershahunga* is the genre that succeeds the
letter-prayer as a private petition to the gods in the midst of some
type of affliction. While attested infrequently in the Middle
Babylonian period (mid-second millennium BCE),[23] the text is well
known in the first millennium with at least 130 *ershahungas* known
from actual examples and citations in catalogues. The native genre
designation *ershahunga* means 'lament that pacifies the heart', and
indicates the petitionary nature of the prayer. Miller well describes
the content of these prayers:

> The petitions of the prayers are both general and specific. They may ask
> the deity to turn to the petitioner to hear or accept the prayer, to be
> gracious, to destroy one's enemies, and to grant protection. Sometimes,
> however, they seek specifically the healing of the sickness that is the
> reason for the lament, release from debt slavery, confirmation of claims
> to one's patrimony, and, of course, release from sin and its
> consequences.[24]

---

21. For a good description of letter-prayers, see Hallo, 'Letters'.
22. In *COS*, vol. 1, p. 532. Examples of letter-prayers are given on pp.
    532–534.
23. Maul, *Herzberuhigungsklagen*, pp. 8–10, gives evidence that these prayers
    existed in the Old Babylonian period.
24. Miller, *They Cried*, p. 17.

Miller later expands upon the latter and notes the growing late concern with moral sin in the prayers of Mesopotamia.

Egyptian prayers

Egyptian prayers are attested from the Old Kingdom period (twenty-ninth to twenty-third centuries BCE) down to the latest periods of time.[25] It is impossible in this brief compass to give a suitable survey of prayer during this time, so we will content ourselves with representative examples.

Redford has indicated that hymns and poetry comprise much of Egyptian literature. He also points out that hymns were sung, and sung in such a fashion that 'the singing of the priests in the temple was likened to the rhythmic clatter of baboons at the rising of the sun'.[26] The reference to the priests is a reminder that many of these hymns were part of the formal worship liturgy of Egypt.[27]

The earliest hymns are found in the Pyramid Texts, which are from the Old Kingdom (particularly Dynasties 5 and 6, 2428–2250 BCE). These are writings from the pyramid walls and include a collection of spells, incantations and hymns. In the words of Foster, the hymns from the Pyramid Texts are 'meant to aid the deceased pharaoh (who was after all a god-king) in returning to his proper sphere with the gods'.[28] The Old Kingdom Pyramid Texts were produced by royalty. These are replaced by the Middle Kingdom Coffin Texts and then the New Kingdom Book of the Dead. These all contain prayers, hymns and spells that enable people to make the journey into the afterlife.[29]

---

25. Assmann, *Agyptische*; Barucq and Daumas, *Hymnes*.

26. Redford, 'Ancient', p. 2237.

27. For which consult te Velde, 'Theology', pp. 1741–1749.

28. Ibid., p. 15.

29. A selection of passages from the Pyramid Texts, the Coffin Texts and the Book of the Dead may be found in *COS*, vol. 1, pp. 3–31.

The hymn to Aten

Certainly the most famous and striking of all Egyptian hymns is the one dedicated to the Aten or sun-disk. Its importance is mainly connected to the theological ideas expressed, being a product of the so-called Amarna heresy. The background of the poem is the Eighteenth Dynasty and in particular Akhenaten, who promoted the worship of the sun-disk in apparent exclusion of all other deities. The Aten is known to have been worshipped at least as early as the Twelfth Dynasty (c. 1900 BCE), but, for reasons that escape us, Akhenaten elevated worship of this deity during his reign.

This hymn expresses the pharaoh's unique religious ideas with a powerful and beautiful style. It begins with a request to Aten that also praises the deity in his function of providing light to the world:

> Let your holy light shine from the height of heaven,
>> O living Aten,
>>> source of all life!
> From eastern horizon risen and streaming,
>> you have flooded the world with your beauty.
> You are majestic, awesome, bedazzling, exalted, overlord of all the earth,
>> yet your rays, they touch lightly, compass the lands
>>> to the limits of all your creation.[30]

What strikes the modern reader is the intimacy that the hymnist (in this case Akhenaten, see below) expresses in his relationship with the god. In the twelfth and final stanza, we read these words:

> And you are in my heart;
>> there is no other who truly knows you
>>> but for your son, Akhenaten.
> May you make him wise with your inmost counsels,

---

30. We take our translation of the hymn from Foster, 'Hymn', pp. 1751–1761.

wise with your power,
that earth may aspire to your godhead,
    its creatures fine as the day you made them.

As implied above, the speaker in the text is the pharaoh himself, which is interesting because we know this hymn from the writing on the tomb wall of one of his high officials (and a later pharaoh himself), Ay.

In any case, this hymn expresses the religious devotion of only a moment in the history of Egyptian theology. Upon the death of this strange pharaoh, the disaffected priesthood apparently had no large problem in reasserting the worship of the multitudinous deities of Egypt, since Akhenaten's monotheism, if that is what it was, never caught on with the people. However, because this is the only extrabiblical attestation of something like monotheism,[31] and due to a similarity between this hymn and Psalm 104 (see below), this is certainly the best-known prayer of ancient Egypt.

Hymns to various deities

More typical are hymns that acknowledge other deities. Even when the focus is on a single god, there is no sense that this is the only god. Among many others, we have hymns to Osiris, Horus, Thoth and the divine pharaohs themselves.[32] As an example of the latter, we cite a hymn from the Papyrus Anastasi II that praises the warrior Ramesses II:

A king from his conception with a majesty like Horus,
    He seized the world by means of his might;
He seized the world by means of his might;
He made the Two Lands bow to his counsel,
    And the Nine Bows are trodden under his feet.

---

31. Though there are some hymns that approach monotheism in their tendency to attribute wide powers to a single god. See *ANET*, pp. 367–368 for examples.
32. For citations and excerpts, see Foster, *Hymns*, pp. 108–115.

All foreign lands are drawn to him bearing their tribute,
  He puts all nations on a single path without descent.[33]

Hittite prayers

Archaeology has recovered a significant number of prayers from
the period of the Hittite empire (mid-second millennium BCE).[34]
These prayers show that the Hittites approached their gods and
goddesses for many of the same reasons as their neighbours.[35] De
Roos, following earlier studies, suggested that Hittite prayers may
be characterized by three elements that may be either independent
of each other or combined into a single prayer. These are *arkuwar*,
mugawar and *walliyatar*.[36]

The first type, *arkuwar*, are prayers in which the supplicants defend
themselves against the gods in the context of suffering of some sort
that is understood as punishment for sin. Perhaps the best-known
prayers from Hatti, the Plague Prayers of Murshili (latter fourteenth
century BCE), should be so characterized. Murshili's prayers are set in
the twentieth year of a plague that has ripped through his country. It
began during the reign of his father Shuppiluliuma I and also
claimed the life of his brother Arnuwanda II. Murshili II confesses
that the plagues were a result of the 'affair of Tudhaliya', whom his
father had killed, though he was in treaty relationship with him.
Murshili, though admitting that the son can inherit the sins of his

---

33. Translation from Foster, *Hymns*, p. 139.
34. The fullest treatment may be found in Lebrun, *Hymnes*. For a selection of
    Hittite hymns in English translation, see those by Goetze, *ANET*, pp.
    393–401; and Beckman, *COS*, vol. 1, pp. 156–160. The citations from the
    Plague Prayers of Murshili II are from *ANET*, p. 400, the Kantuzili
    prayer is from Beckman, *COS*, vol. 1, p. 158 and the quote from the
    Telepinus prayer is from *ANET*, p. 397.
35. Indeed, Guterbock ('Composition'), in a study of a prayer to the
    Hittite god of the sun Ishtanu, argues that many Hittite prayers are
    transformations of Mesopotamian prayers.
36. See de Roos, 'Hittite'.

father, defends himself and pleads with the gods on the basis of the
fact that retribution has been made, in large part by the plague itself:

> What is [this]? Hattusa has made restitution through the plague. It [has
> made restitution] twenty-fold. So it happens. And the souls of the
> Storm-god of Hatti, my lord, [and of] the gods, my lords, are simply not
> appeased. (From the second plague prayer)

The defence is legal, using language from the law court. Indeed, as
de Roos states, 'The Hittites expressed their relations with their
gods not in terms of grateful sentiments, but in terms of justice
and juridical judgment.'[37]

The *mugawar* is an invocation; it is 'the urgent appeal to the god
to come near or to listen'.[38] This is actually an older element of a
Hittite hymn than the *arkuwar*. Kantuzili, a prince from around the
time of Shuppiluliuma I, utters such a prayer to the sun-god,
asking that god to intercede with his personal god, an underworld
deity, when the sun-god descends at night into the underworld:

> O Sun-god, when thou goest down to the nether world [to be] with him,
> forget not to speak with that patron-god of mine and apprise him of
> Kantuzili's plight!

Finally, the *walliyatar* is a song of praise. An example of such a
song may be given from a hymn to Telepinus, the Hattian storm
god. The beginning gives the tenor of the whole:

> Thou, Telepinus, art a noble god; thy name is noble among all gods;
> among the gods art thou noble, O Telepinus. Great art thou, O
> Telepinus; there is no other deity more noble and mighty than thou.

The Hittites thus praised their deities and turned to them when
they were in trouble and suffering. Hymn and lament are the staple
of their conversation with the divine realm.

---

37. Ibid., p. 2000.
38. Ibid.

Syro-Palestinian prayers

While there is a rich tradition of prayers in biblical texts, the same
is not true of other Syro-Palestinian texts. The largest collection of
these extrabiblical texts comes from the digs at Ras Shamra
(ancient Ugarit). The best-known texts from this group are narrative myths, in which the main characters are often appealing to the
gods for help. For instance, at the beginning of the Kirtu text, the
king of that name bemoans the loss of his family in a way that
draws the attention of the gods. Similarly, the opening of the
Aqhat epic features King Danel implicitly requesting that the gods
give him a son. The dominance of narrative myth and lack of
hymnic literature leads van der Toorn to say that 'it should perhaps
be assumed that in places such as Ugarit priests sung the texts of
myths instead of psalms of praise'.[39]
    Nonetheless, as van der Toorn himself recognizes, we do have
an example of a petition to Baal in KTU 1.119:28–34:[40]

> O Baal, drive away the mighty one from our gates,
> the warrior from our walls!
> Bulls, O Baal, we will offer up,
> Vows, Baal, we will pay!
> Male animals, Baal, we will offer up,
> ḫitpu-sacrifices, Baal, we will perform:
> A banquet, Baal, we will serve!
> To the sanctuary, Baal, we will go up,
> the paths to the temple, Baal, we will walk!

Outside the Ugaritic texts, not much can qualify as prayer. In this
context, however, the Aramaic inscription of Zakir, king of
Hamat and Lu'ash, is commonly mentioned. It is not a prayer,
but it alludes to a prayer that the king made in the midst of
battle: 'I lifted up my hand [in a gesture of prayer] to
Be'elshamayn, and Be'elshamayn heard me.' While this attests to

---

39. Van der Toorn, 'Theology', p. 2053.
40. Translation from van der Toorn, 'Theology', p. 2055.

the practice of prayer in this culture, as might be expected, it is not a prayer itself.

Psalms in context

Having completed our survey of Ancient Near Eastern prayers, we are now in a position to offer some contextual comments in regard to similarities and differences with the Israelite book of Psalms.[41] It should be borne in mind that this study is focusing on the genre of prayer, not its style or even its content. In terms of style, it is true that prayers in the various traditions tend to be written in poetry, though prose prayers are known. It is further true that some of the staples of Hebrew poetry (terseness, parallelism, imagery and some secondary poetical devices) are shared with the other languages of the Near East. However, comparative poetics is a major and largely unexplored topic and will remain beyond the purview of this study.[42]

On the other hand, we will make occasional comment about prayers that share content with Ancient Near Eastern prayers and myths. However, this will not be the focus of our attention, partly because to do the topic justice would require a significant discussion of Ancient Near Eastern mythology. Thus, the fact that biblical prayer will sometimes purposively describe Yahweh in the language of a Baal (Ps. 29) or Marduk will largely go unexplored (but see comments on Ps. 104 below). So again, our central concern in this section is with the form or genre of prayer.

Communication with the divine is an integral part of all major Ancient Near Eastern religions. Looking at it from an

---

41. Here I am using 'context' in the technical sense suggested by Hallo, who proposed a comparative study of the Bible in its Ancient Near Eastern environment that takes into consideration similarities and differences, thus avoiding so-called parallelomania. Among many other possible references see Hallo, 'Compare'.

42. Watson, *Classical*, does do some comparative work while he describes the nature of Hebrew poetry.

Israelite perspective, Miller rightly notes that 'when Israel began to pray to the Lord, it did so in the midst of peoples whose arms had long been raised and whose heads had been bowed to the gods that directed their lives and delivered them from disaster'.[43] Indeed, the literatures of Egypt, Sumer, Babylon, Assyria, Egypt and to a lesser extent Canaan give ample evidence of hymns of joy and songs of grief and disappointment.

One must conclude that there is great formal similarity between the prayers of these different cultures. In general, the hymns heap praise on the deities for who they are, what they provide for the world, and what they have done for the community and for the individual. Epithets are used as well as descriptive phrases to extol the deity. Furthermore, the laments of the region share similar concerns. Van der Toorn highlighted four major areas that recur in the laments of the Ancient Near East: physical ailments, social strife, mental problems and disagreement with the divine realm.[44]

In addition to general similarities, there are some more specific ones that have proven illuminating to biblical prayer. We will list a selection of examples here:

1. Sumerian temple hymns may be paralleled to the so-called Zion hymns in the book of Psalms. These are prayers (e.g. Ps. 48) where the place of God's temple is extolled.
2. Hymns concerning kings in the Ancient Near East may find biblical reflex in those psalms that exalt and pray for the king of Israel (Pss. 2; 20; 21).
3. Hallo has drawn attention to the Sumerian background to Isa. 39:9–20.[45] The prayer found in this context is called a *miktam* (see also Pss. 16; 56 – 60), which Hallo suspects is the Hebrew equivalent to a letter-prayer.
4. The Plague Prayers of Murshili in Hittite find a similar motivation to the significantly shorter and – narratively at least –

---

43. Miller, *They Cried*, p. 5.
44. Van der Toorn, *Sin*, pp. 62–67.
45. Most recently in Hallo, 'Lamentations', p. 1879.

more successful plague prayer of David in 2 Sam. 24:17, as well as Psalm 30.

Attempts to find differences are often unpersuasive because they are based on degree rather than kind, and in any case we have only a selection of the prayers.[46] However, it is still instructive to note the differences of degree, while being careful not to read too much into them. I would suggest that Israelite prayers may be differentiated from the prayers of their neighbours by the following emphases:

1. Israelite hymns are more apt to contain praise that extols and thanks God for his actions in history. This statement picks up on the observation that Near Eastern hymns tend to praise their gods by means of attributes and epithets. Again it needs to be emphasized that care should be taken here. After all, ever since the work of Albrektson,[47] it is clear that it is wrong to differentiate the historical religion of Israel from the supposed nature religions of the Ancient Near East. Indeed, in a city lament like the Lamentation over the Destruction of Ur there is no question but that the gods act in the historical realm.

2. The laments of Mesopotamia typically open with praise, whereas the laments of Israel do so only rarely.[48] It is difficult, however, to know what to draw from this. The fact that Israel can adopt an accusatory approach to their God (cf. Ps. 77) may indicate a more intimate relationship or one of less respect. Alternatively, it could also have something to do with the nature of a covenant relationship where the deity makes promises on the basis of which the worshipper may appeal to God. It is certainly inappropriate to suggest as some do that the fact that Mesopotamian prayer opens with praise implies that the

---

46. For an argument that believes the difference of degree implies more substantial differences, see the otherwise excellent survey by Walton, 'Hymns'.

47. Albrektson, *History*.

48. The laments collected by Lambert, '*Dingir.sa.dib.ba*', are exceptional.

worshippers are whining or trying to extort an answer to their prayer.

3. Some of the subgenres of prayer in Mesopotamia (Akkadian *shuillas*, for instance) find their setting in incantation rituals. We have nothing comparable in Israelite prayers.

In terms of genre, the largest and most significant difference is that generated by the deity to whom the prayer is addressed. In the Bible, prayer is legitimately offered only to one God, Yahweh. In the Ancient Near East, there is a plethora of deities to whom the prayer might be addressed. Interestingly, however, prayer is usually addressed to a single deity, even though the other gods' existence is presumed. Sometimes one deity is requested to intercede in relationship with other deities. In any case, however, hymns usually praise a single deity and laments often approach a single deity for help. Presumably, though, the same individual could utter individual prayers to a number of different gods and goddesses.

One reason why the Egyptian prayer to Aten (discussed above) is so often brought into comparison with biblical prayers is that Akhenaten's worship of the deified sun-disk is fundamentally closest to the biblical religion, since Aten is glorified as the One God. This may explain the other reason why this hymn is frequently discussed, and that is that there is a special relationship between it and Ps. 104. Foster posits a definite connection between the Israelite psalm and the Egyptian one, which he suggests is at least half a century older, due to 'overall tone, parallelism of certain more general ideas, and [similarity] in at least one specific passage'. He suggests the Israelite poem is dependent on the Egyptian. This may well be the case, the Israelite poet being attracted to the monotheistic tendencies expressed by the foreign poem, but the text also demonstrates non-Egyptian ideas, most concretely illustrated by a reference to the sea monster Leviathan.[49]

However, even if Foster is correct that Ps. 104 is directly influenced by the Egyptian prayer to Aten, this is an exception

---

49. For the quote and the argument in this paragraph, see Foster, 'Hymn', p. 1759.

rather than a rule.[50] The similarities that we have seen above, in large measure, are born not from influence and borrowing but from common concerns and similar experiences.[51]

Conclusion

Our survey reveals that the Psalms are far from unique in their literary environment. Hymns and laments are found in all the religions of the region, indicating the personal nature of the relationship between humans and their gods. The uniqueness of Israelite prayer is found not in form but in the nature of the deity addressed. Yahweh is the only true God, the only one that counts. This is why the Psalms remain an inspiration for twenty-first-century prayers.

---

50. Many draw a parallel between Ps. 29 and Ugaritic ideas. While this is likely appropriate, the comparisons are with mythological ideas rather than poetic form and so this particular connection is not discussed here.

51. In any case, we must be careful about extending similarities into large-scale hypotheses about the origins or use of the Psalms. The banner example of taking this wrong road is the reconstruction of a *Sitz im Leben* for the Psalms in an annual re-enthronement festival à la Mowinckel.

B. THE PSALMS AND KEY THEMES

3. THE PSALMS AND DISTRESS

Philip S. Johnston

Introduction

The snares of death encompassed me;
the pangs of Sheol laid hold on me;
I suffered distress and anguish. (116:3)

Distress is one of the most common themes of the Psalter. Particularly in the first half of the book, psalm after psalm portrays distress and anguish in eloquent description and graphic metaphor. The writers feel besieged, constricted, burdened, bogged down, submerged and drowning. They are frequently helpless and occasionally hopeless. Surrounded by enemies, suffering physically, punished by God, they cry out to him for relief and deliverance. This is certainly a dominant motif in this precious book.

Distress in the psalms elicits mixed responses today. For many who use them devotionally, this is one of their most appealing features. The psalms portray situations of outward difficulty and inner turmoil with which readers easily identify. The distress of these ancient Israelites mirrors the distress of their own world and individual lives. The situations may be very different, but human reactions and emotions are often very similar. So the struggle to maintain faith in trying circumstances today is given powerful expression by the similar struggles of psalmists many centuries ago. However, for many other current readers the frequent portrayal of distress does not match their own experience. Baying enemies and threatening waters do not convey their own life of faith. So the daily discipline of reading, reciting or chanting a psalm becomes more a duty than a joy.

Distress is not a heading found in most scholarly treatments of the Psalms, despite its thematic prevalence. This doesn't mean it isn't pondered and discussed. But it does mean that it has been subsumed under other headings. Since Gunkel's pioneering form-critical study in the early twentieth century, most study of the Psalms has been dominated by his approach. Obviously distress occurs most frequently in the lament psalms, both individual and communal, so it is usually discussed in relation to them. But it also occurs in many other categories regardless of their exact delineation, notably in thanksgivings, but also in royal psalms (which follow other form-critical categories anyway), wisdom psalms, and so on, e.g.:

> you brought up my soul from Sheol . . .
> Weeping may linger for the night. (30:3, 5 – individual thanksgiving)

> cords of death . . . torrents of perdition . . .
> strong enemy . . . (18:4, 17 – royal; individual thanksgiving in form)

> How long will you assail a person,
> will you batter your victim . . . (62:3 – individual confidence)

> But as for me, my feet had almost stumbled;
> my steps had nearly slipped. (73:2 – wisdom)

> Those who plough ploughed on my back;
> they made their furrows long. (129:3 – communal
>   thanksgiving/confidence)

Indeed, the only main form-critical category where distress is not portrayed is the hymn. Thus this theme cuts across form-critical analysis, and study of it draws eclectically from across the Psalter.

Description of distress

Distress, then, is almost ubiquitous in the Psalter. How is it portrayed? We will first note several recurrent themes, and then comment more generally on its portrayal.

Personal suffering

First, there are frequent descriptions of personal suffering. Several of these are vivid, extended treatments, indicating a combination of physical, mental and emotional anguish, e.g.:

> . . . I am languishing . . . my bones are shaking with terror.
> My soul also is struck with terror . . .
> I am weary with my moaning;
> every night I flood my bed with tears;
> I drench my couch with my weeping.
> My eyes waste away because of grief;
> they grow weak . . . (6:2–7)

> I am poured out like water,
> and all my bones are out of joint;
> my heart is like wax;
> it is melted within my breast;
> my mouth is dried up like a potsherd,
> and my tongue sticks to my jaws;
> you lay me in the dust of death . . .
> My hands and feet have shrivelled;
> I can count all my bones . . . (22:14–17)

> There is no soundness in my flesh . . .
> there is no health in my bones . . .
> My wounds grow foul and fester . . .

I am utterly bowed down and prostrate;
all day long I go around mourning.
For my loins are filled with burning,
and there is no soundness in my flesh.
I am utterly spent and crushed;
I groan because of the tumult of my heart . . .
My heart throbs, my strength fails me;
as for the light of my eyes – it also has gone from me. (38:3–10)

To these can be added many briefer but similarly vivid descriptions of turmoil.[1] The psalmists are often poor and needy,[2] and sense with foreboding the immanence of death.[3] They are frequently unhappy, dispirited, ill at ease, restless. This can easily lead to personal despondency and a lack of self-worth, e.g. 'I am a worm, and not human' (22:6).

Some psalms indicate the cause of distress as unwarranted enmity or personal failure (see below), but many more leave the cause unexpressed. Yahweh's anger, the enemies' scheming and the psalmists' suffering are intertwined in a savage pastiche of jarring colours, but causal connections are often omitted. However, for all their vividness, the biblical psalms do not portray personal suffering in as detailed or as diagnostic a fashion as many Akkadian psalms, e.g. the well-known Prayer to Ishtar.[4]

Personal distress is also often tied up with a sense of isolation. The distressed psalmist feels beleaguered, cut off from family and friends, distant from temple and community, and often far removed from God himself. Pss. 42 – 43 give an extended portrait of physical, social and spiritual isolation; many other psalms give briefer but equally poignant snapshots in a variety of imagery, e.g.:

---

1. E.g. 31:9–10; 32:3–4; 39:3; 102:4; 119:143. Westermann labels 119:143 'spiritual suffering' (*Praise and Lament*, p. 36), presumably from the context.

2. E.g. 86:1; 109:22.

3. E.g. 102:11; 109:23.

4. Especially lines 46–90; *ANET*, pp. 383–385; reprinted in *RANE*, pp. 199–201. Westermann provides a succinct comparison, *Praise and Lament*, pp. 36–42. See also Walton, *Ancient*, ch. 6.

> I am like an owl of the wilderness,
> like a little owl of the waste places.
> . . . like a lonely bird on the housetop. (102:6–7)

The isolation is felt keenly and hurts deeply.

Communal suffering

There are fewer portrayals of communal distress, mainly because there are fewer communal laments, and these are generally less specific. But they can be equally harrowing, e.g.:

> You have made us like sheep for slaughter,
> and have scattered us among the nations.
> You have sold your people for a trifle,
> demanding no high price for them.
> You have made us the taunt of our neighbours,
> the derision and scorn of those around us . . .
> you have broken us in the haunt of jackals,
> and covered us with deep darkness . . .
> Because of you we are being killed all day long,
> and accounted as sheep for the slaughter . . .
> For we sink down to the dust;
> our bodies cling to the ground. (44:11–25)

> Why should the nations say, 'Where is their God?'
> Let the avenging of the outpoured blood of your servants
> be known among the nations before our eyes.
> Let the groans of the prisoners come before you;
> according to your great power preserve those doomed to die. (79:10–11)

Communal distress is much more pointedly attributed to enemies, who are identified as its main cause. But the blame is often also directed to God for allowing it to occur, whether or not it is accepted by the community as deserved.[5]

---

5. Accepted: 79:8; 80:18 (implicitly); 85:2; 90:8; not accepted: 44:17–21; no comment: Pss. 60; 74; 83; 126; 137.

Oppressive enemies

Enemies abound in the psalms, and are explicitly mentioned in over a quarter of them.[6] Several features mark their portrayal, including their actions, their words and their nature. They are over-whelmingly numerous and fiercely aggressive. They conspire, threaten, arm themselves, set traps, ambush, pursue, and do every-thing possible to destroy the vulnerable psalmists. For instance:

> Consider how many are my foes,
> and with what violent hatred they hate me. (25:19)

> Guard me, O LORD, from the hands of the wicked;
> protect me from the violent
> who have planned my downfall.
> The arrogant have hidden a trap for me,
> and with cords they have spread a net;
> along the road they have set snares for me. (140:4–5)

> He has prepared his deadly weapons,
> making his arrows fiery shafts. (7:13)

> They track me down; now they surround me;
> they set their eyes to cast me to the ground.
> They are like a lion eager to tear,
> like a young lion lurking in ambush. (17:11–12)

> They sit in ambush in the villages;
> in hiding-places they murder the innocent.
> Their eyes stealthily watch for the helpless;
> they lurk in secret like a lion in its covert;
> they lurk that they may seize the poor;
> they seize the poor and drag them off in their net.
> They stoop, they crouch,
> and the helpless fall by their might. (10:8–10)

---

6. In 36 psalms; so Westermann, *Praise and Lament*, p. 189. This section draws on his summary.

The enemies are often portrayed as animals, particularly lions.[7] Ps. 22 even juxtaposes three animal images in chiastic pattern: oxen (vv. 12, 21), lions (vv. 13, 20) and dogs (vv. 16, 20).

The enemies blithely bear false witness against the psalmists.[8] And their words addressed directly to the psalmists are equally wounding. Sometimes they are confrontational, with open mockery and delight at the psalmists' misfortune.

> But at my stumbling they gathered in glee,
> they gathered together against me;
> ruffians whom I did not know
> tore at me without ceasing;
> they impiously mocked more and more,
> gnashing at me with their teeth. (35:15–16)[9]

At other times they dissimulate this under a cloak of apparent friendship, whereas all along they are scheming treacherously.

> My enemies wonder in malice
> when I will die, and my name perish.
> And when they come to see me, they utter empty words,
> while their hearts gather mischief;
> when they go out, they tell it abroad. (41:5–6)[10]

No wonder one exasperated psalmist feels 'beset as a city under siege' (31:21), while another concludes:

> Their mouths are filled with cursing and deceit and oppression;
> under their tongues are mischief and iniquity. (10:7)

---

7. Animals: 10:9; 59:6; 74:19; lions: 7:2; 10:9; 57:41; 58:6.

8. E.g. 27:12; 35:11.

9. Similarly 13:4; 22:17; 38:16; 39:8; 42:10; 69:9; 89:51; 102:8; 119:42, 51.

10. Similarly 28:3; 41:6; 52:2–4; 55:21; 62:4; 119:69; 144:11.

The enemies are described as generally perverse and specifically godless, in that they do not acknowledge Yahweh and his laws.[11]

Nature and death

Often a focus of delight and joy in the psalms, the natural world can also be a realm of danger and threat. The land may be stricken by drought and famine, without immediate attribution to enemy activity or divine punishment. Individuals may be overcome by the ordinary hazards of wild animals and unforeseen danger. One source of danger which features frequently is water. While essential to life and a source of blessing, water is also frequently a threat, both in the sudden torrents and flash floods of the rainy season and in the unknown and unmastered high seas.[12]

Water and the resultant mud and mire are frequent images of distress, with the psalmist variously stuck, sucked down, trapped, helpless against rising water, swept away and drowning. This is one of the most pervasive sets of images in the entire Psalter, reflected in a wide variety of detail and length, and always evoking danger and eliciting fear. It is developed in two noteworthy directions. First, pounding water can convey a sense of unrelenting, successive difficulties sent by God, e.g.:

> Deep calls to deep at the thunder of your cataracts;
> all your waves and your billows have gone over me. (42:7)

Second, waters often lead to or represent Sheol.[13] Thus there is a strong association between 'the torrents of perdition' and 'the

---

11. E.g. 5:10; 10:3; 14:1–4; 26:10; 28:4f.; 36:1–4; 52:1–7; 54:3; 55:10–15; 73:6, 27; 86:14; 109:17; 119:85, 139.

12. 107:26f. The Israelites were inexperienced sailors, since the shoreline lacked natural harbours and was mostly controlled by non-Israelites (despite Gen. 49:13; Deut. 33:19). Thus Israelite sea travel is seldom mentioned (e.g. 1 Kgs 22:48), and they borrowed foreign expertise (1 Kgs 9:26–28; Jon. 1:5).

13. For fuller discussion and references, see Johnston, *Shades*, particularly chs. 3 and 5.b.

cords/snares of death/Sheol' (18:4f. // 2 Sam. 22:5f.).[14] Ps. 88 notes the overwhelming waters in its fullest and bleakest portrayal of the underworld:

> For my soul is full of troubles,
> and my life draws near to Sheol.
> I am counted among those who go down to the Pit;
> I am like those who have no help,
> like those forsaken among the dead,
> like the slain that lie in the grave,
> like those whom you remember no more,
> for they are cut off from your hand.
> You have put me in the depths of the Pit,
> in the regions dark and deep.
> Your wrath lies heavy upon me,
> and you overwhelm me with all your waves. (88:3–7)

The underworld has many other grim associations, as Ps. 88 shows. There are quasi-physical features like bars and gates, and it is a land of no return.[15] But just as important in the psalms are the non-physical aspects: the silence, the sleep of death, the non-remembrance, the pointlessness.[16] And above all, there is the godforsakenness, the separation from Yahweh and the inability to offer him prayer or praise.[17]

Some psalmists talk directly of experiencing Sheol. This occurs occasionally in laments,[18] and more frequently in thanksgivings.[19] Gunkel suggested plausibly that the writers could speak more

---

14. The latter collocation also occurs in 116:3.

15. Cf. 9:13; 107:18; also Isa. 38:10; Jon. 2:6; Job 16:22.

16. E.g. 9:18; 13:4; 30:9; 94:17.

17. E.g. 6:5; 88:5; 115:17.

18. Sheol: 6:5; 88:3; pit: 28:1; 69:15; 143:7; depths: 130:1. Possibly also: ground, dust: 7:5; sleep of death: 13:3; dust of death: 22:15; terrors of death: 55:4.

19. Half of Gunkel's individual thanksgivings have underworld terms, e.g.: Sheol: 18:5; 30:3; 116:3; pit: 40:2. Possibly also: mighty waters: 32:6; deadly thing: 41:8; destruction: 92:7; gates of death: 107:18; death: 118:18.

confidently once the danger had passed.[20] This is partly true, though his analysis is complicated by thanksgiving sections within lament psalms. Pedersen and Barth argued that these psalmists really had an actual experience of Sheol. This takes their vivid language seriously, but builds on flawed anthropology, psychology and exegesis.[21] Nevertheless, the force of language used by these psalmists shows that their experiences were extremely harrowing and their feelings desperate.[22]

General features

Perhaps the most striking general feature, at least to modern readers, is the vividness of language and directness of approach. The terms and metaphors are strong, stark, evocative, even haunting.[23] Unlike most modern prayers, attempts to qualify or justify the current situation are rare, while pleas of desperation and outbursts of indignation are frequent. Brueggemann summarizes well:

> The speakers of these psalms are in a vulnerable, regressed situation in which the voice of desperate, fear-filled, hate-filled reality is unleashed and no longer covered by the niceties of conventional sapiential teaching.[24]

> The surprise of Israel's prayer is that the *extravagance of praise* does not silence or censor Israel's need but seems to legitimate and authorise a second extravagance, the *extravagance of complaint*, lament, accusation, petition, indignation, assault, and insistence.[25]

---

20. Gunkel, *Introduction*, p. 131. He wrote that '"sheol" is almost always avoided' (*Einleitung*, p. 185, my translation), but unfortunately his qualification was lost in the published English translation, '"sheol" is avoided'. See further Johnston, *Shades*, pp. 88f.

21. Pedersen, *Israel I–II*, pp. 466–469; Barth, *Errettung*, pp. 111–112 et passim; see further Johnston, *Shades*, pp. 89–93.

22. Brueggemann notes Freud's perspective that 'the utter abandonment of pretense is a prerequisite to new joy', 'Psalms and the Life', reprint p. 21.

23. See Brown, *Seeing*.

24. Brueggemann, 'Psalms and the Life', reprint pp. 19f.

25. Brueggemann, 'Psalms as Prayer', reprint p. 54, emphasis original.

Equally striking is the lack of precision. Enemies abound, but individual enemies are never identified and national ones only seldom. Personal adversity is frequent, but the circumstances are always vague. This aspect is particularly problematic for the identification of specific historical or socio-ritual occasions for the psalms (see below), but particularly helpful for later appropriation of the psalms, whether within ancient Israel or by later believers.[26]

Similarly, there is often an imprecision of time frame, conveyed by the frequent switch of verbal tenses (or aspects) and compounded by the uncertainty of interpreting these in poetry. This can be illustrated repeatedly by comparing various English translations, e.g. for Ps. 116:1–2:

NRSV: I love the LORD, because he has heard my voice and my
       supplications.
       Because he inclined his ear to me, therefore I will call on him as
       long as I live.

NJPS: I love the LORD for he hears my voice, my pleas;
      For he turns his ear to me, whenever I call.

The vivid language and captivating imagery remain forcefully stereotypical. Traps and nets, dogs and lions, water and pits, death and Sheol, etc., are often juxtaposed kaleidoscopically to become alternative and interchangeable images, a common stock of expressions for distress. The distinctiveness of each poem lies not so much in its unique images (though these do occur occasionally) as in its unique blend of the common ones.

The psalms which portray distress mostly move on from it. As form-critical analysis has clearly demonstrated, laments nearly always progress in some way, notably with an assertion of being heard, a vow of future praise or even a defiant outburst of present praise. And thanksgivings by definition have moved on. Distress is very real, but it is not final.

---

26. Cf. (among many) Miller, *Interpreting*, p. 51: 'the language of the psalms is *open* and *metaphorical*'.

Causes of distress

As regularly noted, there are three main agents of distress identified in the psalms: God, enemies and self.[27] This covers a wide range of interpersonal relationships. It also covers the grammatical spectrum of first person (I/we), second person (you, Yahweh) and third person (he/they, the enemies). All three are regularly cited in individual laments as causing distress, whereas in communal laments the enemies are more frequently the cause.

God

God is frequently portrayed as the cause of current distress. This is often conveyed in the searching questions 'Why?'[28] or 'How long?'[29] The communal laments also express this in statements of 'startling bitterness',[30] e.g.:

> you have rejected us and abased us . . . (44:9)

> You have made your people suffer hard things;
> you have given us wine to drink that made us reel. (60:3)

> you have afflicted us . . . (90:15)

However, these stop short of outright condemnation of Yahweh and rejection of him. For all their incomprehension, bewilderment and anger, the psalmists do not abandon God. The individual laments tend to adopt a less confrontational approach, expressing

---

27. E.g. Broyles, *Conflict*, p. 21; Miller, *Interpreting*, p. 48. Westermann calls these the basic dimensions of the laments, *Praise and Lament*, p. 169.

28. E.g. individual: 10:1; 22:1; 42:9; 43:2; 88:14; communal: 44:23f.; 74:1.

29. E.g. individual: 6:3; 13:1f. (x 4); 35:17; communal: 79:5; 80:4; (85:5); 89:46; 90:13.

30. So Westermann, *Praise and Lament*, p. 177, who calls this 'the heart of the lament of the people'.

perplexity by negative petitions for God *not* to hide, be silent, be distant, forsake, rebuke or cast off the psalmist.[31] But they still see God as a primary cause of their distress, e.g.:

> Remove your stroke from me;
> I am worn down by the blows of your hand. (39:10)

Enemies

As noted above, enemies proliferate in both individual and communal psalms. However, their portrayal differs. The enemies in communal psalms are sometimes named, e.g. Edom (60:9; 137:7), local nations plus Assyria (83:5–8), Babylon (137:9), and otherwise they are clearly external enemies.[32] Thus the communal laments portray times of military threat or defeat.

By contrast, the enemies in the individual psalms, whether laments or thanksgivings, are much harder to identify. Various specific proposals have been made, notably false accusers (Schmidt), national enemies (Birkeland) and sorcerers (Mowinckel). These have already been well surveyed and critiqued elsewhere,[33] and none has been widely accepted.

More helpfully, Miller suggests we should look beyond the psalms to Old Testament narrative for 'a wealth of illustrative possibilities':

> These stories thus offer us clues for understanding the laments by
> suggesting the kinds of opposition to which the laments allude and
> giving us some indication of the sorts of contexts that would have been
> in mind or appropriate for those psalms that cry out against the taunters
> of the Lord and the people.[34]

---

31. E.g. 6:1; 27:9; 28:1. Westermann, *Praise and Lament*, p. 185, sees this as a 'retreat from the complaint against God'.
32. E.g. 74:4–8; 79:1–4; 89:40–43.
33. E.g. Miller, *Interpreting*, p. 50; Day, *Psalms*, pp. 21–29.
34. Miller, *Interpreting*, p. 55, and more generally pp. 52–63, on the contexts of taunt (*ḥrp*): Judg. 8:15; 1 Sam. 17; 25; 2 Kgs 18 – 19; Neh. 4:2–4; 6:13. Similarly Brueggemann, 'From Hurt', reprint pp. 77–82.

Similarly, the lives of Hannah and particularly Jeremiah give us plausible contexts for individual laments.[35] These contexts are merely suggestive, but powerfully so.

Westermann notes other interesting features of hostility in individual psalms: it is directed towards a single person, who becomes completely isolated from friends; it is overwhelming and seemingly irresistible; and it occurs within the community, yet threatens its fabric of common faith. He also suggests that a focus on the enemy's apparent success led to the development of a new psalm form, which discusses the wicked and the righteous in wisdom style.[36]

Self

A few psalms contain a direct confession of sin and/or plea for absolution:

> I confess my iniquity;
> I am sorry for my sin. (38:18)

> Wash me thoroughly from my iniquity,
> and cleanse me from my sin. (51:2)

> If you, O Lord, should mark iniquities . . .
> But there is forgiveness with you . . . (130:3)

This is so rare that Westermann concludes, 'whenever we meet a confession of sin, consciousness of a specific offence is presupposed.'[37] However, there is insufficient evidence to substantiate this. While the heading of Ps. 51 proposes one such occasion,

---

35. For Hannah see also van Zyl, '1 Sam. 1:2 – 2:11'.

36. Seen in Pss. 14; 36; 37; 52; 53; 58; Westermann, *Praise and Lament*, pp. 191–193.

37. Westermann, *Praise and Lament*, p. 274. Regarding the traditional Christian use of the so-called penitential psalms, he comments that 'the confession of sin has become the Christianized form of the lament' (p. 274).

neither the body of that psalm nor texts elsewhere are as specific.

Even fewer psalms contain references to sin in general as marking humanity, meriting divine judgment and requiring attention. One such is:

> You chastise man [*'îš*] in punishment for sin . . . every man [*'ādām*] is a
> mere breath. (39:11, lit.)

While 'man' here could be the psalmist, the collocation of *'îš* and *'ādām* suggests a more generalized statement.[38] However, these references are rare.[39]

A few psalms link sin and suffering, notably:[40]

> While I kept silence, my body wasted away . . .
> Then I acknowledged my sin to you . . . (32:3–5)

> . . . there is no health in my bones because of my sin. (38:3)

> Deliver me from all my transgressions . . .
> I am worn down by the blows of your hand. (39:8–10)

> . . . heal me, for I have sinned against you. (41:4)

This association mostly occurs in reference to the psalmists themselves, implying that their own sins have led to their suffering, rather than that sin is the general cause of suffering, as Mays rightly notes.[41] Others argue against even this personalized association.[42]

---

38. Similarly Craigie, *Psalms 1 – 50*, p. 310: 'general principle'.

39. Perhaps implicitly 90:7f. Johnston also posits a link in 89:47f. between divine judgment and human mortality, *Shades*, pp. 82f.

40. Mays, *Psalms*, p. 163, adds 6:1; 88:7, which give no reason for divine anger; and 107:17–22, a historical reminiscence.

41. Mays, *Psalms*, p. 164.

42. E.g. Lindström, *Suffering*, argues this strongly though sometimes awkwardly; see Johnston, Review of Lindström.

By contrast, a larger number of psalms contain protestations of innocence.[43] This is such a marked feature that some see these as a subcategory of laments, or as part of a larger group of 'Prayers of the Accused'.[44] Retrospective claims of innocence also occur in thanksgivings, e.g. 18:20–24. Thus, though both are represented, protest of innocence features more in the Psalter than acceptance of guilt. It is generally the poor and needy who cry to Yahweh for deliverance from distress which is not of their own making.[45]

Responses to distress

Petition
The first and most obvious response to distress is to appeal to God. Indeed, this is the very essence of the Psalter. As Broyles notes pithily, 'A lament psalm is not lamentation. It does more than simply bemoan current hardship. It seeks change . . . A lament psalm is primarily an *appeal*.'[46] Noting this primacy of the appeal, several scholars suggest that 'petition' would be a better term for many psalms than 'lament',[47] but retain the latter given its widespread adoption.

The basis of appeal varies. Communal laments often cite God's past deeds and promises to the nation, e.g.:

We have heard with our ears, O God,
our ancestors have told us,

---

43. For a recent thorough treatment of Pss. 7, 17, 18, 26 and 44, see Kwakkel, *According*.

44. So Schmidt, listing over 30 psalms which indicated a temple trial, followed with modifications by Beyerlin and Delekat; see further ch. 6 in this volume.

45. See e.g. Kraus, *Theology*, pp. 150–154.

46. Broyles, *Conflict*, p. 14, emphasis original. Broyles then focuses his attention on the appeal 'because, quite simply, we have more to work with', p. 22.

47. E.g. Westermann, *Praise and Lament*, p. 34.

what deeds you performed in their days,
in the days of old ... (44:1)

By contrast, individual laments focus more on God's nature and personal commitment to the believer and almost never cite his past activity on behalf of the nation.[48] While the community appeals in a variety of ways to the national or royal covenants bestowed by God, individuals focus on their personal relationship with God, though this difference is blurred in a few irregular psalms.[49] But whatever the basis, the appeal remains trenchant.

Negative conclusions

A few psalms record very little or even no amelioration.[50] Ps. 39 contains patient waiting and moral resolve, and acknowledges divine punishment for sin, at least in principle (though not for any specific sin noted). But the hope for a response remains unfulfilled. The psalmist can only conclude sadly:

Hear my prayer ...
before I depart and am no more. (39:12–13)

Even more poignant is Ps. 88, the bleakest of all the psalms. Here there are lengthy and emotive descriptions of divine displeasure, social isolation and imminent death,[51] and the psalm ends in darkness, literally as well as metaphorically. The only glimmer of light is that the psalmist can still pray. He is still able to appeal to Yahweh. But there is no hint of response or hope of improvement.

---

48. Partial exceptions: 22:4f. notes unspecified historical events; 51:18 implies the exile (but in a communal coda to an individual lament).

49. E.g. Ps. 66, which has individual and communal elements, refers to the exodus.

50. Besides those noted here, a few have only minimal hope, e.g. Ps. 38 and possibly Ps. 143.

51. On this last aspect see Johnston, *Shades*, pp. 95f.

These psalms must temper the assertion by Westermann that all psalms move beyond lament.[52] Most do, in one form or another. But Ps. 88 clearly does not, as other scholars have pointedly commented.[53] The inclusion of these few unrelieved psalms in the Psalter is vivid testimony to ancient Israel's willingness to retain a record of unresolved anguish. And it has enabled many a believer in subsequent eras to express similar anguish, using them as both a model and a resource.

Positive conclusions

Nevertheless, as noted, most psalmic clouds of distress have silver linings. The vast majority of laments contain some expression of confidence, however embryonic, and many contain either a vow or an expression of praise. For Bellinger, 'this positive word is so pervasive it must be an established part of the psalm type'.[54] And the thanksgivings by definition have already moved beyond distress. Sometimes the change of mood encapsulated within a psalm is dramatic, none more so than in Ps. 6:

> Depart from me, all you workers of evil,
> for the LORD has heard the sound of my weeping. (6:8)

This has given rise to many posited explanations, which generally fall into one of three groups.[55]

---

52. Westermann repeatedly asserts this, e.g. 'there are no Psalms which do not progress beyond petition and lament' (*Praise and Lament*, p. 74); 'There is not a single Psalm of lament that stops with lamentation' (p. 266). He interprets the motif 'the dead do not praise Yahweh' as an implicit petition (pp. 157–159, cf. p. 75 n. 24), but does not discuss Pss. 39 and 88 in detail, either here or in *Living*.

53. E.g. Brueggemann, commenting that this psalm 'is a resource as precious as it is peculiar', 'Psalms and the Life', reprint p. 13. Also Nowell, 'Psalm 88', p. 105.

54. Bellinger, *Reading*, p. 55.

55. For recent summaries, see e.g. Day, *Psalms*, pp. 30–32; Brueggemann, 'From Hurt', pp. 72–74.

First, there are cultic explanations. Begrich developed the concept of an oracle, similar to the 'salvation oracles' in Isaiah 40 – 55, pronounced by a priest or cultic prophet to the lamenter in the middle of his prayer.[56] However, while such oracles are occasionally incorporated in psalms, including some laments,[57] it is surprising that none is recorded at the point of shift from lament to praise. Also, while a salvation oracle may have effected a change of perspective and a positive conclusion for an original author, it is hard to see how such an interpretation fits with ongoing cultic use.[58] Podechard made a different cultic proposal: these are really thanksgivings, with the original lament prefixed to them in dramatized form. But if the lament is dramatized, there is all the more reason for the oracle to be included as the high point of the re-enactment.[59]

Secondly, there are psychological and/or spiritual explanations. A long-standing view still proposed by some is that the very act of petition and the mention of Yahweh's name give the psalmists new hope and inner resolve, enabling them to conclude with a more positive perspective.[60] Cartledge suggests that making a vow brings about the psalmists' change of attitude, given the importance of the vow in ancient Israel.[61] These could certainly be contributing factors. Kim finds the reason in the ideology of holy war, with renewed trust in Yahweh as divine warrior causing the sudden change of mood.[62] This is possible, though it fails to

---

56. Begrich, 'priesterliche', following Küchler; accepted by many, including Mowinckel, *Psalms*, vol. 1, p. 219; Westermann, 'in some instances', *Praise and Lament*, p. 65; Bellinger, 'best available explanation', *Reading*, p. 56.

57. E.g. Pss. 12:5; 21:8–12; 35:3; 60:6–8; 108:7–9; 62:11–12; 80:8; 91:14–16.

58. See further Day, *Psalms*, pp. 31f.; Williamson, 'Reading', pp. 5–7. The latter also notes the lack of oracle in the communal laments, where a cultic setting is inherently likely.

59. So Cartledge, 'Conditional', p. 80.

60. E.g. S. B. Frost, J. W. Wevers; so Brueggemann, 'From Hurt', reprint p. 73.

61. Cartledge, 'Conditional', pp. 81–91.

62. Kim, 'Holy War', illustrates this for Ps. 3.

explain why the change occurs where it does, and the link with holy warfare is tenuous.[63]

Thirdly, there are literary explanations. Weiser suggested that these are really thanksgivings, to which a powerful lament has been added at some point.[64] However, while a few psalms do appear composite (e.g. 19; 40), this hypothesis seems artificial for the great variety of relevant laments. More helpfully, Williamson suggests that laments should be seen as composed in the perspective of their hopeful conclusion, not their sorrowful beginning.[65] Though this questions a basic feature of form criticism, it fits our intuitive approach to literature. Whereas Gunkel proposed distinctly different contexts for laments and thanksgivings, this proposal implies a spectrum of contexts for the composition of a spectrum of psalms, from outright despair to complete confidence.

Thanks and praise

Fuller and more joyful responses to distress are expressed in thanksgiving, both within laments and in the thanksgiving psalms themselves. Many of the latter are exuberant in their joy. But some have a subdued mood more typical of laments (e.g. 30), and a few psalms have features of both forms making classification difficult (e.g. 9; 10; 40; 41). This again implies that distress and well-being are two ends of a spectrum rather than two completely distinct situations, and that lament and thanksgiving are likewise two poles on a continuum of psalmic forms. There is much overlap in the progression from one to the other.

It is also worth noting the canonical shape of the Psalter itself. The book begins predominantly with lament, and moves increasingly to praise. Of course, as with most observations on the Psalter, this is a generalization. The early psalms contain many declarations of trust and praise, while the later 'psalms of ascent'

---

63. Miller, Review of Kim, p. 89, notes that this motif would fit the
    communal laments better, yet these lack sudden mood changes.
64. Weiser, *Psalms*, pp. 70, 80.
65. Williamson, 'Reading', pp. 7–15, citing Hezekiah's prayer in Isa. 38 as
    illustration.

(120 – 134) reflect times of distress, and four laments (140 – 143) precede the final praise psalms. Nevertheless, in general the Psalter follows the same pattern as many individual psalms, moving beyond an experience of distress to a declaration of praise.

Conclusion

As noted at the outset, distress is a pervasive theme which defies the scholarly boundaries of form criticism. This is not to deny the value of form-critical study which, as Broyles notes, 'directs the interpreter toward the principal aim or use of a type of psalm'.[66] However, it does underline the point frequently made, that form-critical categories represent not so much moulds into which religious poetry had to be squeezed, but rather basic formats which could be used and developed with great ingenuity and variety.[67]

The theme of distress is also somewhat tangential to that other great preoccupation of twentieth-century psalms study, the quest for socio-religious settings.[68] It is possible to envisage the recital of distress at great festivals, whether of enthronement (Mowinckel), covenant renewal (Weiser) or Zion (Kraus), but the relevant psalms give little if any suggestion of this. Aspects of them might reflect various juridical ordeals, but the evidence is too sparse for the various reconstructions proposed.[69] Distress in lament and thanksgiving would fit a domestic cult setting,[70] but again this is

66. Broyles, *Conflict*, p. 26. For a recent overview of form-critical study, see Nasuti, *Defining*.
67. E.g. Gillingham, *Poems*, p. 207.
68. See further ch. 6.
69. Johnston, 'Ordeals', critiques proposed river ordeal echoes (McCarter) and temple drinking ordeals (van der Toorn).
70. Gerstenberger, *Der bittende Mensch*; also *Theologies*, pp. 57f., 79–82. Similarly Albertz, *History 1*, p. 100: 'to a large degree [the individual psalms of lament and oracles of salvation] still breathe the spirit characteristic of personal piety as this was practised in the families'.

hard to substantiate. These psalms as much as others are clearly linked to the cult, whether by explicit mention of vow, great congregation, etc., or implicitly, as in change of voice.[71]

The portrayal of distress in the psalms is partly illuminated by form-critical study, but at its heart lies the relationship of the psalmists to Yahweh. It is to him that they appeal in their distress, to him that they look for relief, and to him that they offer praise. As Mays comments:

> The theological setting-in-life in which all the prayers for help can be read is the relation of an *'ebed* [servant] to an *'adon* [lord]. It is more important in accounting for their formation and use than particular personal situations and cultic institutions . . . It furnishes the common identity that goes with the use of the prayers.[72]

In summary, distress is ubiquitous in the psalms, affecting individuals and communities. It is portrayed in a profusion of human and natural images, in vivid, evocative, stereotypical language, and is attributed as much to God as to human enemies or the psalmists themselves. But distress is always recounted in an appeal to Yahweh, and the sufferer nearly always moves on to some expression of hope. Both the occasional acceptance of unmitigated lament and the frequent progression beyond it are defining characteristics of psalmic prayer, and potent aspects for those who wish to appropriate them today.[73]

---

71. See Mandolfo, *God*, for whom voice change in laments reflects an earlier function as ritual dialogue.
72. Mays, *Lord Reigns*, pp. 29f.
73. Brueggemann, 'Costly Loss', notes the psychological, sociological and theological importance of lament. For further application today, see Sheppard, 'Theology', pp. 149–152; Boulton, 'Forsaking'.

4. THE PSALMS AND PRAISE

James Hely Hutchinson

Introduction

Like so many human activities, praise comes to us both naturally and unnaturally. C. S. Lewis once observed that 'the humblest, and at the same time most balanced and capacious minds, praised most, while the cranks, misfits and malcontents praised least'. Praise, he concluded, 'almost seems to be inner health made audible', the natural overflow of a heart that delights in a certain object.[1] Conversely, as Paul Beauchamp writes, 'praise is not natural to our selfishness'.[2] If the book of Psalms is, as the traditional Hebrew title has it, the 'book of praises'[3] *par excellence*, this is only because the psalmists turn their thoughts away from themselves and on to the

---

1. Lewis, *Reflections*, pp. 80–81.

2. Beauchamp, 'prière', p. 35.

3. The earliest extant attestation of the phrase *sēper tĕhillîm* as a probable designation of the Psalter is in 4Q 491, dated to the later first century BC (Auwers, *Composition*, p. 109 n. 339).

object of supreme delight – the Creator God, Israel's Redeemer, Yahweh himself. This close correlation between theology and doxology emerges at every turn in the Psalter. My task will be to demonstrate, and enlarge upon, this truth; in particular, I shall offer ten propositions regarding the Psalter's praise that arise from lexical, grammatical, poetic, form-critical and canonical considerations.

Vocabulary of praise

According to my first proposition, *use of the key verb* hll *highlights the fact that praise in the Psalter is ascribed supremely to Yahweh and that he is worthy to receive it.* No reader of the Psalms can fail to be struck by the recurrence of the summons to 'praise the LORD' (traditionally 'Hallelujah'). The active form of the Hebrew root *hll* (*piel*) features seventy-five times in the book, with the object of the praise always God (almost exclusively as Yahweh/Yah),[4] his name or his word. The passive participle (*měhullāl, pual*), meaning 'worthy of praise', is similarly reserved exclusively for Yahweh (18:3; 48:1; 96:4; 113:3; 145:3). The reflexive form (*hithpael*) 'exult' is less relevant to our purposes, but does appear with Yahweh as its object on three occasions (63:11; 64:10; 105:3). As for what this key verb can tell us about the nature of praise, Helmer Ringgren cites three verbs which are used in parallel with *hll* (*piel*) and which suggest that the mode of praising is 'singing' and 'telling',[5] and seven parallel verbs which indicate that the activity consists in, or is closely tied to, 'thanking', 'glorifying', 'magnifying', 'extolling', 'blessing', 'invoking' and 'rejoicing'.[6] I may already assert my second proposition: *the*

---

4. Also as Elohim in 44:8.

5. Ringgren, '*hll*', p. 406: *šyr, zmr* (*piel*), *spr* (*piel*).

6. Hebrew verbs *ydh* (*hiphil*), *kbd* (*piel*), *rwm* (*polel*), *šbḥ* (*piel*), *brk* (*piel*), *zkr* (*hiphil*), *rnn* (*piel*). Ringgren also cites *ṣhl*, although this is less relevant since it is not found in the Psalter. Strictly speaking, *rnn* (*piel*) does not occur in parallel to *hll* (*piel*) in the Psalter, although it is closely identified with the noun *těhillâ* (33:1; 145:1, 7), and the noun *rinnâ* is employed in conjunction with *hll* (*piel*, 63:5).

activity of praising in the Psalter is essentially vocal. Verbs like these suggest that it would not be the norm for Yahweh to be praised silently, in a corner!

We may be tempted to think that, by examining each occurrence of these verbs in turn, we could give an exhaustive account of the nature of praise in the Psalms; but we need to dismiss any such optimism. Consider the beginning of Ps. 8: 'O LORD, our Sovereign, how majestic is your name in all the earth!' The psalmist is here engaged in the activity of praise, yet its vocabulary is absent. But even if we were to limit our aim to lexical analysis alone, the investigation would prove to be more complex than Ringgren's list of verbs might suggest. Take the case of Ps. 145, which stands out as the only psalm specifically designated in its superscription as a *těhillâ* ('praise', a cognate noun of *hll*). Of all the terms that connote the act of praise in this psalm, only seven overlap with Ringgren's list. Again, in the short Ps. 117, which is typically viewed as setting forth the Psalter's praise in its most basic and regular form,[7] it is striking that the verb used in parallel with *hll* (namely *šbḥ, piel*) is found only seven times in the book of Psalms, whereas the important parallel verb *ydh* (*hiphil*), occurring sixty-four times in the Psalter, is not found in this paradigmatic praise psalm. Further, van Gemeren identifies as many as seventeen Hebrew roots in his attempt to capture the idea of the praise of Yahweh in the Psalms, suggesting that they can function as synonyms of one another;[8] yet *šbḥ* is not one of them! The fluidity of the Psalter's use of vocabulary to convey the concept of praise, and the dangers of reductionism inherent in lexical analysis alone, are evident from even these few remarks.

Grammar of praise

My second proposition (above) does not entail that the person praising God be in the company of others. Praise is frequently

---

7. E.g. Allen, *Psalms 101 – 150*, p. 158.

8. VanGemeren, 'Psalms', p. 777.

offered to Yahweh by individuals: for example, the headings of
Pss. 7 and 18 specify that the praise offered in these psalms is
found on the lips of David. That said, we need to bear in mind
that the call to praise in the Psalter usually takes a plural form
(*hallělû*, e.g. 135:1; *hôdû*, e.g. 136:1). Since English is not a highly
inflected language, we are liable to overlook this point, although
the Authorized Version's translation of 'hallelujah' as 'praise *ye* the
LORD'[9] reminds us that there was a time when the singular and
plural of the second person were distinguished. It does seem –
and this is my third proposition – that from the Psalter's perspective *the most appropriate locus of praise is a congregational setting, praise
being typically conducted simultaneously on both the horizontal and vertical
axes*. That there is a peculiar privilege attached to praising God in
the presence of other worshippers may be seen from the outlook
of individuals in distress: they sometimes spell out the fact that
they look forward to the glorious prospect of praising God in a
corporate context. Take the case of Ps. 109. The bulk of the psalm
is taken up with a prayer that arises from the circumstances
described in vv. 2–5: 'wicked and deceitful mouths are opened'
against the psalmist; he is being attacked gratuitously; his love is
being met with hatred. Anticipating answered prayer and deliverance from these circumstances, the psalmist speaks of a time
when he will praise Yahweh abundantly 'in the midst of the
throng' (v. 30). Ps. 26 presents a similar scenario.

Why might the psalmist be conscious of the privilege of praising God in the company of others? Part of the answer seems to lie
with the fact that in some psalms, although Yahweh remains the
object of praise, he is spoken *about* rather than spoken *to*. In
Ps. 136, for example, the psalmist calls upon the assembly to praise
Yahweh, and gives ample justification for this summons; yet we are
not told that he or the others in the assembly turn to God at any
point. There is, then, truth in the thesis that praise is advertising[10]
– indeed, this is a helpful corrective to the idea that praise, even in
a corporate context, takes place only in what is considered to be

---

9. My emphasis.

10. As developed by Payne, 'Confessions', pp. 2–5.

the private world of the believer's relationship with God on the vertical axis. But we must be careful to avoid reductionism. The advertising analogy would have greater applicability if the psalmists spoke *exclusively* about God and called upon others to do the same. Yet cases of direct praise of Yahweh are numerous, as already stated in relation to Pss. 7 and 18. Even where psalmists urge others to praise Yahweh, their concern is not simply that the addressees should publicize God's greatness (e.g. 96:3, 10; 145:4) but also that they should express this greatness directly to God (e.g. 66:3; 92:4). Further, it is unthinkable that the psalmists would have divorced the Godward movement from the humanward summons. Indeed, to return to the case of Ps. 136, it is telling that much of the psalm's content is anticipated in the preceding psalm (with which it is apparently paired), where we find the Godward movement enacted briefly along the way (135:13). Nor is this atypical: it is striking how readily (unselfconsciously, it would seem) the psalmists switch between the second and third persons in their praise of Yahweh. Thus in 99:3–4 we observe a shift from statements made *about* Yahweh, including an emphatic third-person pronoun, to statements being made *to* Yahweh, with emphatic second-person pronouns occurring twice at this point. Again, in Ps. 118, the psalmist moves several times between speaking about Yahweh and addressing him directly (the latter in vv. 21, 25, 28). Or in the short Ps. 93, the name Yahweh features five times in five verses; the first, second and fourth of these occurrences are in third-person contexts, while the third and fifth are vocatives.[11]

We must note the reasons given for praising Yahweh. To employ Claus Westermann's terminology,[12] *praise in the Psalter is both descriptive of Yahweh's character and deeds, and declarative of his particular acts of deliverance* – my fourth proposition. In both cases, the grounds for praise are frequently signalled by the causal use of the

---

11. Interestingly, we even find the psalmist shifting between self-exhortation and direct address of Yahweh, as in the case of the transition between 104:1a ('Bless the LORD, O my soul') and its immediate outworking in v. 1b ('O LORD my God, you are very great').

12. Westermann, *Praise and Lament*, p. 31.

conjunction *kî* (usually translated 'for', 'because'),[13] although this understanding is not universally accepted. Frank Crüsemann's contention that *kî* introduces direct speech[14] should not be dismissed too quickly, for the closely related nominalizing use of *kî* ('that . . .') can certainly introduce the content of praise (100:3 provides a clear example: 'Know *that* the LORD is God').[15] In any case, causal and nominalizing uses of *kî* can be hard to distinguish.[16] Consider the praise formula that receives particular prominence in Book V (107:1; 118:1; 136:1, etc.), translated as follows by the NRSV: 'O give thanks to the LORD, for he is good; for his steadfast love endures for ever.' There seems to be scant difference between praising Yahweh '*because* his steadfast love endures for ever' and praising Yahweh '*that* his steadfast love endures for ever', or indeed praising Yahweh with the words 'his steadfast love endures for ever'.[17] That said, 95:6–7 secures the idea that, at least on occasion, the psalmists present grounds or motivations for praising Yahweh, since here a nominalizing use is ruled out: the obeisance required by verse 6 ('let us bow down . . . let us kneel') is anchored in the truths of verse 7 ('*for* he is our God . . .').[18] Further, 100:5, which constitutes the first instance in the Psalter of the prominent praise formula just noted, seems to require a causal understanding of *kî* for similar reasons: the act of entering Yahweh's gates and courts (v. 4), parallel to praising him, is driven by a recognition of the fact that '[he] is good; his steadfast love (*ḥesed*) endures for ever'. We assume, then, that the double *kî* in the praise formula furnishes a double reason for praising Yahweh: he is good, and his *ḥesed* is everlasting.[19] But a more extensive treatment of the motive

---

13. In the same category is the causal use of *'ăšer/šĕ*, as exemplified by 124:6 ('Blessed be the LORD, for he has not given us as prey to their teeth'; a.t.).

14. Crüsemann, *Studien*, pp. 32–35.

15. My emphasis.

16. For further discussion regarding Crüsemann's position, see Kuntz, 'Grounds', pp. 165–169.

17. My emphasis.

18. My emphasis.

19. The meaning of *ḥesed* is discussed below.

clauses, such as is provided by Kenneth Kuntz,[20] would highlight
as grounds of praise not only Yahweh's attributes (in particular his
incomparability, sovereignty, majesty and righteousness, as well as
his goodness and *ḥesed*), but also his many marvellous deeds (in
creation and salvation). Indeed, James Mays and others have
insightfully commented that in psalm praise we find the ancient
equivalent of the 'statement of faith' or creed used in many
Christian churches today: here is what Yahweh's true worshippers
believe about him.[21] With regard to Westermann's second category, praise which follows specific acts of divine intervention in
the psalmists' lives, a good example is in 116:1: 'I love the LORD,
because [*kî*] he has heard my voice and my supplications.'

Poetry of praise

Those who know this God express their beliefs about him with
enthusiasm. According to my fifth proposition, *praise has an emotional dimension*. This emerges from the poetic character of the
psalms and especially from particular devices used to heighten the
praise mood. In Ps. 103, Yahweh is praised for his benefits considered from the successive standpoints of one individual (vv. 1–5),
the whole covenant community (vv. 6–18), and the entire created
order (vv. 19–22). Alongside this widening of the horizon, there is
a crescendo in the intensity with which the truths are expressed,
culminating in the urgent threefold plural imperative of the last
three verses. It is difficult to imagine this psalm being read in a
neutral tone! Likewise, it is hard to escape the intensity of feeling
conveyed by the tenfold exhortation 'praise' (imperative or jussive)
featuring in vv. 1–7 of Ps. 148, or the parataxis (i.e. piling up of
one entity after another) of vv. 7–12 of the same psalm as appeal
to praise Yahweh is made in rapid succession to denizens of the

---

20. Kuntz, 'Grounds', pp. 169–183. However, we should note that his study is
    confined to the form-critical category of the hymn (see discussion
    below).
21. Mays, *Lord Reigns*, p. 65.

sea, weather phenomena, mountains, trees, animals and various categories of people. Again, consider the effects of refrains in Pss. 107 and 136, *inclusio* in Ps. 118, and staircase parallelism in 29:1–2, 7–8 (coupled with ellipsis in these last two verses).[22] It is harder to be sure of the function of alphabetic acrostics, within which the praise of Pss. 111, 112 and 145 is set, but one possibility is that this form gives the impression of comprehensiveness in terms of covering the subject matter from every angle.[23]

There are pitfalls to avoid here. There is a false antithesis in the assertion that Ps. 148 is not to be 'analysed word for word . . . [but] to be enjoyed, to be revelled in'.[24] The affective component in praise is no licence for jettisoning our critical faculties. Similarly, praise is not, *pace* Walter Brueggemann,[25] a medium through which ambiguity is promoted: such a suggestion runs counter to the creed-like character of the psalmists' affirmations mentioned above. In addition, it should not be said of the purer praise psalms that they sanction 'doxology without reason'.[26] Brueggemann disparages some psalms for what he perceives to be their excessive emphasis on the summons to praise at the expense of articulating reasons for that summons. In particular, he speaks of Ps. 150 as 'all summons and no reason',[27] 'a communal act of utter release and ecstasy' in praise of 'a god [who] does nothing and has done nothing and will do nothing'.[28] But the reasons for praising Yahweh are given in v. 2: 'his mighty deeds . . . his surpassing greatness.' Our fourth and fifth propositions must be held together.

---

22. Watson, *Classical*, pp. 150–155.

23. Ibid., p. 198. Watson also suggests that acrostics were designed to display the author's skill.

24. Sedgwick, 'Message', p. 209.

25. Brueggemann, 'Praise', reprint pp. 113–114.

26. Brueggemann, *Israel's Praise*, pp. 89–121.

27. Ibid., p. 92.

28. Ibid., p. 108. Addressing American Christian culture, Brueggemann is concerned that praise without reason can serve to legitimate 'a social order that cannot be criticized or changed, even if it is unjust'.

Categories of praise?

My observations thus far have afforded some useful insights, but they have left us bereft of a cohesive, overarching framework for understanding the nature and the theological import of the Psalter's praise. The limitation I noted with respect to lexical investigation has not been rectified by grammatical considerations, and we cannot assume that the poetic devices I have listed are *automatic* indicators of a praise context. For example, although we know intuitively that 8:1 expresses praise of Yahweh, the approaches adopted thus far do not reliably cater for it. How, then, does one capture more adequately the concept of praise in the Psalter?

The answer which dominated Psalms scholarship for much of the twentieth century lies in the form-critical *Gattung* (or genre), with certain psalms categorized as hymns of praise. This indeed is the case for Ps. 8. But there are several problems here. First, there have been significant inconsistencies in the methods employed to determine such classifications. Even Hermann Gunkel's five major categories are not all of comparable status: his royal psalms represent a class governed by content rather than form.[29] Again, Hans-Joachim Kraus's proposed overhaul of Gunkel's classification, while supposedly based on terms used in the Psalter, includes one category, 'festival psalms and liturgies', which is not so based.[30] Secondly, the classifications are not free from the perils of isolated lexical analysis noted above. In particular, Gunkel's thanksgiving category is closely tied to the verb *ydh* (*hiphil*), usually translated 'thank'. Westermann, however, maintains that there is a mismatch between the meaning of this Hebrew verb and the English 'thank' or the German 'danken'. He observes that the verb is never used in the Old Testament to convey an expression of thanks between humans – *brk*, often translated 'bless', does duty for this idea – and argues that its usage in relation to God cannot be understood independently of the broader concept of praise.[31]

---

29. Day, *Psalms*, p. 12.
30. Ibid., p. 14.
31. Westermann, *Praise and Lament*, pp. 25–27.

In line with my fourth proposition above, I am following Westermann in preferring to speak of 'declarative praise' where Gunkel and others speak of 'thanksgiving'. I am also assuming that Ps. 100 (entitled *mizmôr lĕtôdâ*, 'a psalm of thanksgiving')[32] is no less a paradigm of psalm praise than Ps. 145 (*tĕhillâ*, 'praise'). There is a third difficulty with seeking to pin down the Psalter's praise by genre. Even if scholars could agree on an appropriate taxonomy, the practical problem would still have to be faced that many psalms seem to defy classification: for instance, praise can be mingled with features of wisdom,[33] and is often found in the same context as complaint.

Does *Sitz im Leben* (the social context) fare any better as a basis for identifying the praise which the Psalter sets forth? This criterion has obvious attractions: if it can be demonstrated that a psalm belongs to, say, the feast of Booths (as seems likely with Ps. 81), then it will be appropriate to assume it forms part of the corpus of praise (in keeping with the data of Lev. 23:33–43). However, suggestions as to a psalm's *Sitz im Leben* are tentative at best, speculative at worst; and, as is the case with the *Gattungen*, scholars have embraced widely differing views. For Gunkel, it is axiomatic that his category of hymn to Yahweh has a parallel in 'the king at a festive meal [who] would not dispense with songs sung in his praise . . .';[34] yet this is unproven. Again, Mowinckel's proposed enthronement festival not only lacks any Old Testament attestation but is inherently improbable given the differences between Israelite kingship and that of Canaan and Mesopotamia. Nor are there solid grounds for accepting Weiser's proposed alternative, a covenant festival in which the hymn of praise to Yahweh serves as 'that cultic rite by means of which the congregation "co-operates" in the divine dispensation of salvation . . .'[35]

I do not wish to dismiss form criticism outright. Sensitivity to

---

32. The second term is a noun cognate of *ydh* (*hiphil*). As in the case of Ps.
    145, this is a unique designation within the Psalter.

33. See Allen's treatment of the form of Ps. 107 (*Psalms 101 – 150*, p. 84).

34. Gunkel, *Psalms*, p. 13.

35. Weiser, *Psalms*, p. 55.

genre and to the background of a psalm's composition are important elements of responsible exegesis; and the form critic is able to
emancipate us from slavery to tying the Psalter's praise to certain
words or constructions. But my sixth proposition is built on an
observation that emerges from the difficulty of classification
inherent in form criticism, namely that lament and praise are often
found in the one psalm: *praise is frequently the fruit of a transformation
in outlook which the psalmist embraces in the midst of crisis or difficulty.* This
is classically the case in the well-known Ps. 22, or in Ps. 73 where
the psalmist shifts from a position of all but abandoning his trust
in God to one in which he revels in the fact that 'God is the
strength of [his] heart and [his] portion for ever' (v. 26) and desires
to 'tell of all [the Lord GOD's] works' (v. 28). But this sixth proposition applies again and again to psalms which are traditionally
categorized as laments: witness, for example, the movement from
lament to praise evidenced in each of the Davidic psalms from
54 to 64, or in Ps. 109, discussed briefly above. Indeed, the form-
critical conclusion that individual laments are 'by far the most
common type of psalm'[36] proves to be misleading, for 'the cry to
God . . . by nature . . . is always underway from supplication to
praise'.[37] Even the gloomiest psalm touches on the importance of
seeing Yahweh praised (88:10–11), even if it cannot be said that
the psalmist himself emerges from the gloom. Indeed, here, as
elsewhere (6:5; 9:13–14; 30:9), *praise is considered to be a corollary of the
believer's very existence* – my seventh proposition. It is, to quote from
the title of Ronald Allen's work, 'a matter of life and breath',[38] for
the psalmists see fit to plead with Yahweh for deliverance from
death precisely so that they can continue to praise him.

Canon of praise

If we step back and reflect on the fact that each of the five books

---

36. So Day, *Psalms*, p. 12, following Gunkel. Cf. Appendix 1.

37. Westermann, *Praise and Lament*, p. 75.

38. Allen, *Praise!*

of the Psalter concludes with a doxology,[39] we find an additional
reason to question the idea that lament is the dominant note in the
collection. For the message of the Psalter is greater than the sum
of its parts. Over the last twenty years, form criticism has gradually
given way to canonical criticism as the chief paradigm of psalm
study, or rather of Psalter study, since the new paradigm pioneered
by Childs and Wilson sets much store by the overall shape of the
book of Psalms.[40] One feature of this shape is a shift from lament
to praise that takes place not merely within individual psalms but
also across the Psalter as a whole. Running alongside this progression is a gradual shift of focus from the individual to the
community (in line with my third proposition regarding the corporate context of praise).[41] Although 'the book of Psalms is not
arranged to trace [the route to praise] in a clear, direct and simple
way',[42] yet the concentration of clusters of purer praise psalms in
the fourth and fifth books (Pss. 93 – 100; 111 – 118; 145 – 150)
forms part of the overall message of the Psalter. Far from being
'all summons and no reason', Ps. 150 presupposes the context of
the whole collection.[43]

In order to appreciate the significance of this concentration of
praise at the end of the Psalter, we must reflect on a related result
of canonical criticism. Following the work of Wilson,[44] it is recognized that several psalms taken up with covenantal concerns are
strategically positioned at the 'seams' between books, and that Ps.
89 in particular plays a pivotal role: the crisis of Yahweh's apparent unfaithfulness to the Davidic covenant, triggered by the
events of the Babylonian exile, is answered in the subsequent

---

39. 41:13; 72:18–19; 89:52; 106:48; 146 – 150. Ps. 145:21 signals the beginning
    of Book Five's (and the Psalter's) lengthy closing doxology. Cf. Wilson,
    Editing, pp. 193–194; Miller, 'End', reprint pp. 313–314.

40. See ch. 12 in this volume.

41. Cf. Wilson, 'Shape', p. 139.

42. Brueggemann, 'Bounded', p. 79 n. 2; reprint p. 203 n. 2.

43. Brueggemann comes close to conceding this latter point in 'Bounded',
    p. 67; reprint pp. 192–193.

44. Wilson, 'Use', pp. 85–94.

unfolding of the Psalter. The answer given at the end of Book IV, in Pss. 105 – 106, is that the covenant made with Abraham proved to be inviolable in Moses' day, even in the face of such displays of Israelite rebellion as the golden calf incident of Exod. 32 or the Baal-Peor incident of Num. 25: the implication is that Yahweh's commitment to the Abrahamic covenant remains unshakeable despite the exile. Ps. 106 closes with a petition made by the exiles that amounts to prayer for Yahweh to act once again in line with his promises to Abraham by restoring them to their land (v. 47), and we see this prayer answered at the beginning of the following psalm, which also marks the start of Book V (107:1–3). These observations require that we interpret *ḥesed* in the praise formula of 107:1 as Yahweh's covenant faithfulness. Viewed through the crisis of the exile, this praise formula takes on fresh significance and leads to an eighth proposition: *praise in the Psalter arises particularly from a circumstance-defying belief that Yahweh's covenant promises will come to realization – through the arrival of the Davidic king.*

Formulating the proposition in this way, I am presupposing that the glorious answers to prayer set forth in Ps. 107 and developed throughout Book V were never realized in the post-exilic period, to which the final form of the Psalter dates.[45] In other words, there is an eschatological or teleological thrust to the book of Psalms, as signalled right from the start by the introductory and programmatic Ps. 2.[46] The community of Israelites into whose hands the Psalter first came may have been back in the land, but they were still liable to be bewildered by Yahweh's apparent cancellation of his promises to David. The Psalter insists that the king of Ps. 2 will appear – an absolutely supreme and righteous ruler who will be greater than Solomon (Pss. 45; 72), in whom the Abrahamic promises will find fulfilment (72:17b), a 'horn . . . for David'

---

45. Wilson dates the final form to the late first century AD (*Psalms 1*, p. 30). But see McFall, 'Evidence', p. 225, and especially the discussion in Auwers, *Composition*, pp. 161–170.

46. For the eschatological role of Ps. 2, see Childs, *Introduction*, p. 516. For the scholarly consensus on its introductory role, see e.g. Zenger, 'Der Psalter', p. 116.

(132:17) whose coming will prove that Yahweh has not renounced his commitment to the Davidic covenant. Book V couches this glorious prospect in the imagery of a return from exile (Ps. 107), a new exodus (Pss. 114; 135 – 136) and a journey to Zion (Pss. 120 – 134); yet post-exilic worshippers, despite being physically present in Jerusalem, must await the fulfilment of these realities. They correspond to the righteous individual of Ps. 119 whose delight is in Yahweh's word, but who faces persecution. They do of course join in the praise in line with the exhortations of, for example, Pss. 146 – 150, but in an anticipatory sense: the time when 'everything that breathes [praises] the LORD' (150:5; cf. Ps. 148) is a long way from their experience. Against the background of the teleological structure of the Psalter, the summons made to 'all the earth' (100:1) and all nations (117:1) to praise Yahweh makes good sense: not only is the final destination of Ps. 150 in view, but also the answer to the crisis of Ps. 89 lies, as we have seen, with the fulfilment of the Abrahamic covenant whose salvific scope encompasses all peoples (Gen. 12:3).

At the same time, the Psalter looks forward to the destruction of those who oppose Yahweh, his messiah and the covenant people (Pss. 2; 149). This leads to a ninth proposition: *the polemic of praise consists in the overthrow of Yahweh's rivals.* Put simply, Yahweh is praised as God (100:3). In the words of Brueggemann: 'Doxology to Yahweh attacks the claim of every other god and every other loyalty.'[47] The wordplay at 96:5 is striking: 'all the gods of the peoples are no gods at all' (a.t.), the people's *'ĕlōhîm* being branded *'ĕlîlîm*, idols. In Pss. 93 – 100 Yahweh is praised for his transcendent majesty, and this is seen to include his future role as judge of all the earth (96:13; 98:9). Given the covenantal framework within which the Psalter's unfolding message is set, the psalmists' demands in the imprecatory psalms (e.g. Pss. 109; 137) that their enemies be cursed may be regarded as the obverse of his *ḥesed*: in the end, those who curse God's people will themselves be cursed (Gen. 12:3).

Attention to the shape of the book of Psalms has also highlighted the strategic placement of wisdom psalms (notably Pss. 1;

---

47. Brueggemann, 'Praise', reprint p. 118.

73; 90), which in turn underline the necessity of fearing Yahweh and obeying his revealed instruction (cf. also Pss. 19; 119). This obedience is presented as entirely compatible with praise (note the blending of these themes in Pss. 81; 95; 101; 103), for praise is the fitting activity of the righteous (33:1; 140:13) and a product of wisdom (2:10–11; 111:10). Indeed, *the Psalter insists on marrying exuberant praise not only with obedience but also with fearful trembling* – my tenth proposition. The alternation between rejoicing and trembling in Pss. 95 – 100 brings this out in a particularly striking manner. If Ps. 95 begins with the twofold injunction to 'make a joyful noise' (vv. 1–2), it ends with a warning not to harden one's heart to the voice of him who 'swore in [his] wrath, "They will certainly not enter my rest"' (vv. 7–11, a.t.). Worshippers who major on exuberant rejoicing (Pss. 96; 98) at the expense of bowing before Yahweh's holiness (Pss. 97; 99), or vice versa, will have lost their balance in their praise life.

Model of praise

Lewis's phrase 'inner health made audible' has proven to be peculiarly appropriate as an encapsulation of the Psalter's idea of praise. Yahweh is praised by those who recognize he is 'God of gods' and 'Lord of lords' (136:2–3) and who 'do not forget all his benefits' (103:2) – in times of trial as well as in favourable circumstances, individually and (especially) corporately, for as long as they have breath and in view of the day when everything that has breath joins them in this activity. And what was true when the Psalter was being compiled is also true in our era of redemptive history. To be sure, we enjoy the privilege of a clearer and sharper revelation of the 'horn for David'. We are conscious that, as Ps. 2 suggests and as Heb. 1, quoting numerous psalms, makes clear, the king stands on a par with Yahweh, and we are mindful that his coming marked the real end of the exile (cf. Mark 1:2–3). By faith in the Lord Jesus Christ, we have already, in one sense, come to the heavenly Jerusalem (Heb. 12:18–24). On the other hand, we must await the day when his enemies are made his footstool (Ps. 110:1), and keep pressing on in the journey towards 'the city that is to come' (Heb. 13:14). We must trust that the promises made to Abraham and David, encompassed by the new covenant and guaranteed by Christ's blood, will one day be fully and finally accomplished. As we wait, perhaps facing persecution, we turn to Yahweh, as our God and Father, and to his king – and we praise them for the wonder of the gospel. Again and again, we too shall need to make the shift from lament to praise that is possible thanks to God's covenant faithfulness.

5. THE PSALMS AND THE KING

Jamie A. Grant

Introduction

The casual reader of the Psalter may well ask, 'Why does the king deserve special consideration? Why does he merit a chapter all to himself?' There are some psalms which are clearly 'royal', but not so many. Many psalms bear 'Davidic' superscriptions, but does that make any difference to our reading of these poems? Does a 'David' superscription alone make a psalm royal? Equally, the student may conclude that 'kingship' was once an important issue when scholarly discussion focused on 'sacral' and 'sacerdotal kingship' and 'the Great Autumn Festival' – but these are discussions of a bygone era, and the foci of debate have changed a great deal since then.[1] So why devote a whole chapter to consideration of the psalms and kingship?

It can reasonably be argued that whilst the royal themes of the

---

1. See Clines, 'Psalms', for helpful discussion of these questions. Starbuck also discusses some of these questions with regard to royal psalms in the context of the Ancient Near East in *Court Oracles*.

Psalter are not always obvious, they are significant. Whilst the king-ship background to the psalms is not as visible as praise or lament or cult, it is just as important to a right understanding of the theology of the Psalter. The Davidic king is not conspicuous, but there is a sense in which he subtly dominates the book of Psalms. The genre category of Royal Psalms may reflect relatively few psalms, yet the concept of kingship is significant if we are to understand the Psalter properly, which is why this topic deserves our particular attention.

There are certain questions that must be addressed if we are to grasp the significance of 'kingship' for proper interpretation of the Psalms. (1) Genre: are royal psalms properly described as a form-critical category and are there really so few truly 'royal' psalms in the Psalter? (2) The anonymous 'I': is this the king speaking? Some-times? Always? Never? (3) Canonical reading: is there significance in the placement of royal psalms at the 'seams' of the Psalter? (4) Reinterpretation: why are the royal psalms still in the Psalter at all? After all, the book reached its final form long after the demise of the Davidic monarchy. (5) Psalmic kingship: why is the Psalter so positive about kingship when the rest of the Old Testament (espe-cially the Deuteronomistic History) is decidedly ambivalent about whether kingship is a good thing or not? (6) Current relevance: does a royal milieu in the Psalms make any difference to our reading of the individual poems as Christians living in the twenty-first century? These questions we seek to address.

Genre and kingship

Up until the 1990s psalm studies were largely dominated by discus-sion of genre questions. As discussed elsewhere in this book, the individual poems of the Psalter were grouped into categories according to their type, and one of Gunkel's types was Royal Psalms. Gunkel comments, 'The internal unity of [these] psalms[2] stems from the fact that they are *concerned entirely with kings*.'[3] This

---

2. Pss. 2; 28; 20; 21; 45; 72; 101; 110; 132; 144:1–11.

3. Gunkel, *Introduction*, p. 99.

summary definition of royal psalms immediately raises some concern. First, as Gunkel readily admits,[4] this is not a genre classification at all – it is an association based on similarity of content rather than form. According to Gunkel's definition, the royal psalms could vary in form between individual complaints and individual thanksgiving songs as long as they focus entirely on kingship. This leads to a second word of caution. Why must a psalm be concerned 'entirely' with kings for it to qualify as a royal psalm? It is now widely acknowledged that relatively few individual psalms fit neatly within their genre categories without any influence from other psalm types,[5] yet mixed psalms which are dominated by lament, for example, are still categorized as 'lament psalms'. Should the same approach not be applied to the royal psalms?[6] Therefore, it seems a worthwhile task to revisit the question: what makes a royal psalm *royal*?

Second, in terms of establishing a royal milieu for an individual composition, Gunkel focuses on royal nomenclature. He suggests that use of such terms as 'king', 'anointed', 'David' and 'Yahweh's servant' indicate a background in the kingship of Israel and Judah.[7] Whilst this is clearly a logical starting point for any discussion of psalms grounded in kingship, the question arises as to whether such terms are the *only* reliable indication of a royal setting. This uncertainty is accentuated by the fact that two of the ten psalms which Gunkel highlights as royal lack any of these

---

4. Ibid., p. 325.

5. See, helpfully, Grogan, *Prayer*, pp. 51–54.

6. The most glaring exclusion from Gunkel's list of royal psalms is Ps. 89, which focuses almost entirely on Yahweh's covenant with the Davidic king – its gracious magnitude and crashing failure. Yet Gunkel (somewhat grudgingly, it appears) only allows the possibility that vv. 47–52 of this psalm have a royal focus (*Introduction*, pp. 99–100). As we will see below, a good argument can be made for a royal backdrop to some of the anonymous songs of the individual, but these are all excluded from Gunkel's category by dint of his insistence that royal psalms must be 'entirely' focused on kings.

7. Gunkel, *Introduction*, p. 99.

naming characteristics in the psalms themselves (101 and 110).[8]
This creates a tension for Gunkel's definition of poems that are
'royal'. Based on their content, he intuitively sees that Pss. 101 and
110 have a setting in kingship, yet neither of them meet his form-
critical criteria for the royal psalms. The implications of this
expansion in the royal category are significant. Gunkel's reasoning
is based on content – the duties which the individual fulfils in
Ps. 101 are the duties of the king,[9] and the priestly rule imagery of
Ps. 110 is also reminiscent of kingship.[10] This expansion of the
royal category based on the content of individual compositions
allows for the argument that there are many more psalms scattered
throughout the Psalter which draw upon kingship themes and
ideals.[11] Gunkel 'allows' two anonymous 'Davidic' psalms to be
seen as royal psalms because of their kingly content. This being
the case, could there not be more such psalms – perhaps even
many more?

Anonymous kingship

John Eaton picks up on this ambiguity in Gunkel's definition of
royal psalms and suggests that there are indeed many more psalms
in the Psalter which are based in kingship.[12] He argues that

---

8. The superscriptions of Pss. 101 and 110 include the name of David, but
   Gunkel and other form critics tend to deny any significance to the
   superscriptions and hence these are largely ignored in their discussion
   (Bullock, *Encountering*, p. 24).
9. Gunkel, *Introduction*, pp. 99, 109.
10. Ibid., pp. 102, 109.
11. Even within the form-critical school there were those who argued for a
    much broader number of royal psalms in the Psalter. Sigmund
    Mowinckel, for example, ultimately concluded that there are 'many
    I-laments . . . in which the "I" is not just an "Everyman", but the king of
    the people . . .' (from the Foreword to the 1961 reprint of *Psalmenstudien*,
    cited in Eaton, *Kingship*, pp. 12–13).
12. Eaton, *Kingship*, pp. 1–26.

Gunkel's treatment of Pss. 101 and 110 should be applied to all the anonymous 'I' psalms, especially those that bear a Davidic super-scription. Eaton highlights several criteria which suggest that there may be a royal background to a good number of the anonymous psalms. First, there is the testimony of the chronicler who associ-ates David with psalmody and the preparations for temple worship. Eaton suggests that we should understand the psalms' Davidic superscriptions in light of this association.[13] Second, we must remember that the king had responsibilities with regard to public (temple) worship, where many of the psalms would have been used.[14] Third, Eaton goes on to highlight twenty-four charac-teristics found in the anonymous psalms which can reasonably be taken to indicate a royal background: the enemies of the anony-mous speaker are often foreign armies,[15] or the anonymous 'I' is presented as victorious over these armies,[16] or it is clear that his deliverance has national repercussions,[17] or Yahweh's honour is bound up with the fate of the psalmist[18] and so on.[19] All of these characteristics combine to indicate that the king is, perhaps, the most likely candidate to be the speaker in many of the anonymous psalms. Furthermore, Eaton argues that the anonymous 'I' psalms (particularly the individual laments) are clearly homogenous, and therefore many of them seem to reflect a royal background. Hence, our 'default position' in interpreting the psalms of the indi-vidual should be to see them as royal, such a conclusion only to be rejected if there is no compelling indication of kingship in the content of the psalm.[20] When Eaton's theory is adopted, a further

---

13. 'In spite of problems of detail, [the Davidic superscriptions] can reasonably be taken as an indication of the large place which royal psalmody has in the collection' (ibid., p. 20). See also Wallace, 'Chronicles', pp. 267–291.

14. Eaton, *Kingship*, p. 22; Waltke, 'Theology', p. 1102.

15. Pss. 3:6; 27:3; 55:21, etc.

16. For example, Ps. 118:10–12.

17. For example, Ps. 22:29–31.

18. Pss. 23:3; 25:11; 31:3, etc.

19. Eaton, *Kingship*, pp. 23–24.

20. Ibid., pp. 22–23.

fifty-four psalms are added to Gunkel's original eleven, thus giving the Psalter a decidedly more 'royal' flavour.

What of Eaton's argument? Is the book of Psalms more royal than a prima-facie reading would suggest? Stephen Croft assesses the issue of the identity of the unnamed individual in the psalms and comes to a more nuanced but broadly similar conclusion. He suggests that a number of possible individuals could fit the specific setting implied by an individual psalm, such as cultic ministers, wisdom teachers or private individuals. However, even taking these other possibilities into account, Croft still concludes that the Psalter is much more royal than Gunkel's genre classification suggests.[21] Furthermore, it would be fair to say that most commentators find Eaton's thesis at least broadly convincing.[22] The strengths of Eaton's argument are (1) the refusal simply to ignore the Davidic superscriptions, since they do seem to suggest some sort of royal background, and (2) the desire to let the *content* of the individual compositions speak, and many poems make most sense when heard as the words of the Davidic king.[23]

Canonical kingship

The profile of psalm studies has changed dramatically over the last twenty years. The genre categories of Gunkel and Mowinckel dominated academic study of the Psalter from the 1930s until 1985, when Gerald Wilson's ground-breaking work *The Editing of*

---

21. Croft, *Identity*, p. 80. One difficulty with Croft's suggestions is that, whilst we do have indication of the Davidic king's involvement in psalmody and public worship, we have no unambiguous indication of the participation of any of the other hypothetical individuals in a psalmic context.

22. See, for example, Miller, *Interpreting*, pp. 135–136; Creach, *Yahweh*, pp. 65–66, or Waltke, 'Theology', pp. 1101–1102.

23. Eaton does go too far in places when he suggests that some psalms should be understood as royal because the turn of phrase found within them effectively 'sounds regal' – see, for example, the discussion of Ps. 73 (*Kingship*, p. 76).

the Hebrew Psalter was published.[24] Wilson argues that the order of the psalms in the Psalter is not entirely random, as was simply presupposed by the form-critical school,[25] but that there are signs of deliberate ordering of the psalms to reflect the theological concerns of the book's editors. He suggests that psalms were purposefully placed alongside one another to highlight themes which may run through a number of psalms in a group. The great significance of Wilson's work is that psalms are given a literary context for interpretation. Previously, it was always assumed that psalms were contextless compositions – hermetically sealed literary units that did not communicate with the surrounding material. Context, however, changes the way in which we read everything.[26]

Looking for interaction between psalms within a context means that the contemporary reader can seek out themes and emphases or look for threads running through pairs or groups of psalms which point to topics that the editors of the final form of the Psalter wished to emphasize. Details of the canonical method are addressed elsewhere in this book,[27] but one key aspect of this method is that psalms placed in certain positions within the Psalter take on a special significance.[28] In particular, the psalms which are placed at the beginning and end of the five 'books' of the Psalter take on special importance.[29] Wilson's argument that the seam psalms of Books I–III take on added editorial significance further accentuates the weight of the royal psalms within the book as a whole.

---

24. See chs. 1 and 12 of this volume.

25. Claus Westermann suggests that the reason for the lack of discussion of the shape of the Psalter in form-critical circles 'lies simply in the fact that in laying the foundation for his interpretation of the Psalms, Gunkel above all had no interest in how the collection was handed down to us' (*Praise and Lament*, p. 251).

26. See Mays's helpful discussion for a fuller understanding of the significance of context ('Question', pp. 14–20).

27. See further chs. 8 and 12 of this volume.

28. Grant, *King*, pp. 16–17.

29. Wilson, 'Use', pp. 85–94; deClaissé-Walford, *Reading*.

Wilson contends that through reading the royal psalms which are placed at the seams of Books I–III we can plot a 'narrative' which traces the rise and fall of the Davidic monarchy. Ps. 2 describes the inauguration of the Davidic covenant, Ps. 72 reflects the transition of Davidic covenant to successive generations of Israelite kings, and Ps. 89 laments Yahweh's apparent rejection of the Davidic covenant.[30] Questions have been raised about how well this narrative theory works in its detail, especially with regard to the canonical function of Ps. 2 and the suggestion that royal psalms play a less significant role in Books IV–V.

Wilson argues that Ps. 2 lies at the seam of Book I, providing an opening Davidic bracket which is closed by Ps. 72 at the end of Book II.[31] However, it seems much more likely that Pss. 1 and 2 combine to provide a joint introduction to the *whole* Psalter. This is evidenced in their common lack of superscription and various linguistic links between the two psalms, including a bracketing *inclusio* based in the word 'blessed' (*'ašrê*, Pss. 1:1; 2:12). Therefore it is probably better to see Ps. 2, not so much as part of a narrative of the rise and fall of the Davidic covenant, but as part of the introductory hermeneutical paradigm for the interpretation of the whole book of Psalms.[32]

Equally, Wilson contends that Ps. 89 presents the failure of the Davidic monarchy, and that the narrative continues into Book IV with an emphasis on the fact that David no longer reigns – Yahweh does! Readers of the psalms were not to worry about the demise of the Davidic king, but to trust explicitly in Yahweh instead. Therefore Wilson comments that the emphasis on royal psalms is less significant in Books IV and V than it is in Books I–III.[33] For various reasons, this idea does not seem to give full voice to the royal emphases which are found in Books IV and V.

---

30. Wilson, *Psalms 1*, pp. 123–124.

31. Thus Ps. 2 serves as 'the introduction to the first book or the combined first and second books' (Wilson, 'Use', p. 88).

32. Sheppard, *Wisdom*, pp. 136–143; Miller, 'Kingship', p. 128; Mays, 'Place', p. 10; Grant, *King*, pp. 227–229.

33. Wilson, 'Shaping', pp. 76, 81; *Editing*, p. 227.

For example, we see the return of the Davidic king in Pss. 101 –
103, the strongly eschatological presentation of the Davidic
monarch in Ps. 110 (very reminiscent of Ps. 2), and the fact that
the last voice heard in the Psalter prior to the concluding doxology
(Pss. 146 – 150) belongs to the Davidic king (Pss. 138 – 145). All of
these features seem to indicate a very active royal thread in Books
IV and V.[34] So, whether there is a narrative based around the
Davidic covenant in the Psalter or not, it is clear on a broader level
that the royal psalms are used at key junctures throughout the
book of Psalms, further emphasizing the importance of the kingship theme within the book.[35]

Continuing kingship

Three final questions need to be addressed: Why are the royal psalms
retained in the Psalter? Why is the psalmic view of kingship so
different from the rest of the Old Testament? And what is the
significance of the royal psalms for contemporary Christian readers?

    The first of these is a fascinating question. Just why are there
any kingship poems in the book of Psalms at all? Most scholars
would acknowledge that the origins of the royal psalms are
grounded in the realities of the Davidic monarchy first in Israel
and then in Judah.[36] This being the case, why do any royal psalms

---

34. See Howard, *Structure*, pp. 201–202; Mitchell, *Message*, pp. 87, 224;
    Shepherd, *Book*, pp. 443–444; Grant, *King*, pp. 33–39; Vincent, 'Shape'.
35. Even if Ps. 2 is not part of a broader kingship narrative, its position in the
    Psalter, as part of the introduction to the whole book which provides a
    paradigm for interpretation, is still highly significant.
36. Gunkel suggests that the royal psalms reflect the real-life settings and
    circumstances of the Davidic kings – 'the particular occasions of the
    individual royal poems are often clear' (*Introduction*, pp. 102–103). Most
    commentators agree that the royal psalms are founded in the historical
    realities of the Israelite monarchy, except Erhard Gerstenberger who sees
    them as originating in post-exilic, eschatological, messianic thought
    (*Psalms I*, pp. 48–49).

remain in the Psalter? Why did the editors retain poems which celebrate enthronement ceremonies and royal weddings long after
the monarchy ceased to exist?

Democratization and *reinterpretation* are the keys to continuing
kingship in the Psalter. Psalms are purposefully unspecific about
their historical details and setting. The psalmist may well plead his
cause before God because of his enemies, but we are not told who
these enemies are. The poets often lament because of the opposition of the wicked, but these foes are not identified for us and the
circumstances that inspired the lament are not made clear. The
writers celebrate great heights of joy and deliverance in the psalms,
but again the historical details of these testimonies are never laid
out before the reader. Why is it so?

Psalms were, in the main, deliberately written to be as broadly
applicable as possible. The psalms are originally poetic accounts of
humankind speaking to God, yet through canonization these have
become the Word of God spoken to his people. Based firmly in
this idea of humanity in relationship with God, the psalms express
every emotion conceivable (confidence, despair, joy, trust, etc.) and
the whole point is that this expression of human emotion directed
towards God is available to be adapted to a wide variety of circumstances. The psalmist's enemies may be the armies of Assyria or
Babylon, yet the poet's expression of trust in Yahweh's vindication
could equally well be applied to the lowly Israelite who is unjustly
opposed by a neighbour or colleague. The point is that prince and
pauper have equal access to the God of creation and covenant.
The words may have originated on the lips of the king, but the
principles are just as valid for the ordinary labourer. The circumstances differ, but the spiritual truths do not. This is called
democratization – the words written by a *specific* individual
grounded in *specific* circumstances can be appropriated by *all*
people in a *wide variety* of circumstances as they adopt the expression of the psalmist's thoughts and emotions to reflect their own.[37]

---

37. Hence, as noted above, there is much debate regarding Eaton's argument
    concerning the number of royal psalms in the Psalter. Were we not
    looking for these indicators we would never have guessed that there are as

Alongside the generalizing effects of democratization, another factor has led to the retention of the royal psalms in the Psalter: reinterpretation. Democratization has shrouded the 'royalty' of some of the anonymous psalms; reinterpretation, on the other hand, maintains the currency of the more obviously royal psalms.

Why keep a psalm which celebrates the enthronement of the king when there is no king? It is kept because it has come to mean something different. Ps. 2, for example, was probably recited at the coronation of each new Davidic king,[38] but retains its prominent place in the Psalter because its meaning for the covenant community has changed with their change of circumstances. This process of reinterpretation of the psalms seems to have occurred quite naturally.[39] Imagine four hypothetical readers of Ps. 2: a Davidic/Solomonic era reader, a later pre-exilic reader, a post-exilic reader, and an early Christian reader. Each of these readers would approach and appropriate Ps. 2 in a slightly different way.[40]

Ps. 2's focus on Yahweh's universal rule through his king based in Zion would perhaps have resonated most with the

---

many kingship psalms. The experiences of the 'psalmist-king' can be applied in general terms to a multitude of circumstances, so the 'anonymous I' in the psalms effectively becomes an 'everyman' for believers everywhere and in every generation. That is why the psalms have retained such strong appeal to believers of both Jewish and Christian communities throughout the ages – quite simply, people can relate to what they read. See Miller, *Interpreting*, pp. 23–27; Durham, 'King', p. 428; Allen, 'David', pp. 544–546 for further discussion.

38. Mays, *Psalms*, p. 45; deClaissé-Walford, *Reading*, pp. 101–102.

39. VanGemeren, 'Psalms', p. 14.

40. Mays comments, 'As the career of Israel passed through dramatic changes, the givens of the settings of earlier psalms changed. Traditional patterns and vocabularies took on modified significance and roles. Older psalms were reinterpreted to fit new conditions, and new psalms were written in continuity with classic conventions but expressing the needs and thoughts of later times' ('Question', pp. 14–15).

Davidic/Solomonic reader when Israel was a relatively major player on the Ancient Near Eastern stage and their experience of human kingship was fairly positive.[41] By contrast, the later pre-exilic reader, who lived when Judah was politically insignificant and whose experience of kingship was much more mixed (if not negative), would experience a strong degree of cognitive dissonance in reading this psalm.[42] The theology of Ps. 2 would be far removed from the reality of their situation. This leads to a process of reinterpretation. If Ps. 2 is not fulfilled in the present kingship, its fulfilment must lie elsewhere, perhaps in a future king of Israel. So a degree of eschatological expectation is added to the reading: 'Yahweh reigns, by all means, but surely the king spoken of is not our king. This must be a king who is still to come.'[43] This is true all the more so for the post-exilic reader, for whom the king has become a very distant historical reality.[44] So, is it at all surprising that the early Christian community read and understood Ps. 2 in the light of Jesus the Messiah (Acts 4:24–28; 13:32–33)?[45]

Is this process of reinterpretation legitimate? There is a sense in which it is inevitable, such is the effect of the ahistoricity of the psalms. They are *designed* to be appropriated in the way that is most relevant to the community of believers in their setting. This is not wrong, since such reinterpretation is inherent to psalmody.[46] So the royal psalms are retained in the Psalter due to processes of democratization and reinterpretation. They point us to the ultimate Davidic king who is also the ultimate 'everyman', setting an example of piety for all readers of the psalms to follow.

---

41. deClaissé-Walford, *Reading*, p. 99; Grant, *King*, pp. 33–39.

42. Craigie, *Psalms 1 – 50*, pp. 65–68.

43. Jacobson writes, 'The messianic reinterpretation of the royal psalms developed as a response to the failure of the Davidic monarchy' ('Royal', p. 198).

44. Vincent, 'Shape', pp. 61–82.

45. Ormseth, 'Psalms', p. 119.

46. Waltke, 'Canonical', pp. 3–18.

Psalmic kingship

A theological problem remains, however. Why are the Psalms so positive about kingship when the rest of the Old Testament (especially Deuteronomy and its associated historical books) is not?[47] The question carries two presuppositions which must be assessed if we are to address the issue properly: first, that the Psalter is overwhelmingly positive about kingship and, second, that the rest of the Old Testament is not.

Taking the latter point first, it is often said that the perception of human kingship in the Old Testament is mixed and, with the exception of the Psalter, never unambiguously positive. However, the Old Testament's view of kingship is not quite as bleak as is sometimes suggested. Gerald Gerbrandt argues convincingly that it is not kingship *per se* that is viewed negatively in the Old Testament. Rather it was the people's desire to have a king 'like the other nations' that provokes the condemnation of Yahweh and Samuel in 1 Samuel 8 – 12.[48] The problem is not the request for a king in and of itself, but that the people should have known that their king was to be markedly different from their Ancient Near Eastern counterparts.[49] David Howard develops this argument in a couple of articles demonstrating that in fact the various parts of the Old Testament are not ideologically opposed to kingship.[50] Rather, the Old Testament is positive about kingship which is practised in accordance with the law of the King, and negative about kingship that rejects Yahweh and his ways.[51]

---

47. See, for example, McConville, *Deuteronomy*, p. 306; 'King', pp. 277–278.

48. Gerbrandt, *Kingship*.

49. In particular, condemnation stems from the fact that the people desired a king as military leader rather than trusting in Yahweh for deliverance as they ought. Ancient Near Eastern kings were primarily seen as military leaders, but the Israelite king was to trust in Yahweh rather than military strength (Deut. 17:16; Gerbrandt, *Kingship*, pp. 101, 170–171, 190).

50. Howard, 'Case Deuteronomy', pp. 19–35; 'Case Narrative', pp. 101–115.

51. See also Gerbrandt, *Kingship*, pp. 40–41, 189–194.

However, it could still be argued that the royal psalms, especially the explicitly royal psalms, seem to be uncritically positive about kingship, as opposed to a more cautious attitude in the rest of the Old Testament. In response, first, it must be remembered that psalms are occasional literature – they are meant to teach us *something*, but their intent is not to provide us with a complete picture. This is true of the royal psalms which celebrate all that is (or can be) good about human kingship set alongside the rule of the Great King. They are positive because kingship can be a good thing, but they are not written as a thesis on the relative merits and demerits of kingship. Second, the Psalter is not unaware of the downsides of human kingship. Ps. 89:38–52, for example, discusses Yahweh's apparent rejection of the Davidic line and the prophetic background to these events would be quite clear to readers of this psalm – the House of David fell because the kings of this noble line rejected Yahweh and his ways.

A third element should be borne in mind, however, and that is the whole dynamic of contextual interpretation in the Psalter. The explicit royal psalms seem to have a very positive view of kingship, but how does their canonical context influence their interpretation? We do not have the scope in this article to give a contextual reading of all the royal psalms, but it does appear that the editors of the Psalter sought to direct their readers to a particular understanding of the future Davidic king by placing some of the royal psalms in a very specific context. As we have seen above, the retention of the royal psalms in significant places throughout the Psalter is ultimately reinterpreted eschatologically, creating the expectation of a future king who will live up to the content of these royal psalms (universal rule with complete societal justice, etc.). What is more, it seems that these same editors direct the reader's attention to a future king who goes beyond even the best examples of kingship found in Israel's history – the future king will be the one who actually fulfils the ideal of kingship, Deuteronomy's kingship law (Deut. 17:14–20).[52]

---

52. Grant, *King*.

We noted above the significant placement of Ps. 2 as part of the introduction to the Psalter. It is interesting that this first and most prominent of the royal psalms is paired with a psalm which celebrates the torah ('instruction') of Yahweh (Ps. 1).[53] The themes of torah and kingship are linked in the introduction to the Psalter, which seeks to provide a paradigm for the interpretation of all that follows in the book. Kingship is linked with torah from the outset of the Psalter and, interestingly, the next explicitly royal psalms in the Psalter are Pss. 18, 20 and 21 which also revolve around a torah psalm (Ps. 19).[54] Surely this primes the reader's curiosity: 'Are torah and kingship poems linked elsewhere in the Psalms?' There is one more explicitly torah-focused psalm in the book (Ps. 119) and, perhaps not surprisingly, we discover that it follows Ps. 118 where, it can be argued, the king leads the people in an act of antiphonal worship.[55] Why link these royal psalms with the theme of torah?

The most obvious canonical association of torah and kingship themes is found in Deuteronomy 17:14–20, where the only positive responsibility placed on the Israelite king is that: 'When he takes the throne of his kingdom, he is to write out a copy of this instruction [torah] for himself – taken from the priests who are Levites – into a book. And he is to keep it with him and read it all the days of his life, so that he will learn to fear Yahweh his God, to keep all the words of this instruction [torah] and to follow all these statutes.'[56] Basically, the kingship law indicates that, above all else, the king is meant to be the paradigmatic Israelite believer. How does he become such? By internalizing Yahweh's torah and allowing it to influence every aspect of his life and rule.[57] This is what all kings in Israel were meant to be like – archetypal believers, examples for all other Israelites to follow. But, of course, each of the actual kings of Israel failed in this task to a greater or lesser degree.

---

53. Miller, 'Beginning', pp. 83–92; Auffret, *Literary*; Sheppard, *Wisdom*, pp. 136–143.

54. Allen, 'David', p. 546; Miller, 'Kingship'.

55. See further, Grant, *King*, pp. 127–128.

56. Deut. 17:18–19 (a.t.).

57. Miller, *Deuteronomy*, p. 148; Sonnet, *Book*, p. 76; Sarna, *Book*, p. 38.

The association of these same themes of torah and kingship in juxtaposed psalms is designed to direct our attention back to the kingship law. A context is provided for these explicitly royal psalms, and that context (as always) influences their interpretation. Yes, kingship is celebrated in Pss. 2, 18, 20, 21 and 118, but their contextual reading points to the *ideal* of kingship rather than the *reality* of kingship experienced throughout Israel's history. The thoughts of the reader are not directed towards the best examples of kingship (David or Josiah), they are directed rather to the ideal of kingship. The coming king will be the one who keeps the kingship law, the ultimate exemplar of torah-piety lived out in reality.[58]

So both presuppositions mentioned above are called into question. Perhaps the Old Testament is not so markedly negative about kingship and perhaps the Psalter is not so uncritically positive about royalty. The Psalter does have its own view on kingship: it celebrates the institution at its very best, but it is also aware of the failures of the kings. The retention of the royal psalms in the final canonical book is a sign that the Old Testament covenant community always suspected that there must be more to Yahwistic kingship than the Davidic kings themselves could ever offer.[59]

Kingship – so what?

Do these observations about the Psalms and the king make any difference at all for a Christian reading the Psalter in the twenty-first century? How do they affect our understanding of the Psalms?

---

58. 'The ideal of human kingship, introduced by the story of human failure and the gracious accommodation of God to it (in 1 Sam. 8–12; 2 Sam. 7), remains, however, for messianic appropriation' (McConville, *Deuteronomy*, p. 306). See also Miller, *Deuteronomy*, p. 149; Grant, *King*, pp. 273–280, 291–295.

59. Eaton suggests that the royal psalms 'originally had reference to the monarchy of early Israel and functioned in that setting. But from the outset they had a prophetic character . . . they served to nourish the messianic hope . . .' (*Psalms*, p. 33).

There are two main implications to be drawn. First, on a theological level, we are pointed towards a more subtle and developed messianism in the Psalter than is often portrayed. Over many centuries, Pss. 2, 72 and 110 have been hailed as messianic, pointing towards a triumphant ruler who would fulfil the psalmic standards of universal rule, societal justice and lordship with Yahweh. However, these images are very different from the earthly, visible ministry of the 'Greater David'. On the other hand, the expansion of the definition of royal psalms by Eaton, Croft and others leads us to a very different messianic image from the Psalms. It points towards a king who is very deeply human, who experiences the same heights of joy and depths of despair as all humanity. This image of the king in the Psalter brings to life the assurance that 'we do not have a high priest unable to sympathize with our weaknesses, rather one tested in every way we are, yet without sin'.[60] The king in these psalms is often presented as petitioner, praying to Yahweh for help, and today Jesus continues to pray for Yahweh's deliverance, but now he prays on *our* behalf as one who is intimately aware of the daily realities of being human (Heb. 7:25).

Second, on a practical level, we are presented with the image of the king as exemplar for the people, grounded in the torah of Yahweh and entirely dependent on him. One of the reasons why the king of Israel has such a prominent role in the Psalter is that he fulfilled a representative function within the Old Testament theocracy, simultaneously representing Yahweh to the people and the people to Yahweh.[61] This is borne out in the co-regency imagery of the explicitly royal psalms and in the lament prayers of the 'I' psalms with a royal background. The juxtaposition of royal and torah psalms that we have looked at above points the reader to a particular picture of the king as an exemplar of piety and lifestyle. Pss. 1 and 2 present us with a picture of the individual rooted in the torah (Ps. 1:2–3) and of the king rooted in dependence upon Yahweh (Ps. 2:12). These images jointly provide an introduction to the book as a whole and the linguistic overlap

60. Heb. 10:15 (a.t.).
61. De Pinto, 'Torah', pp. 160–161; Miller, 'Current', pp. 135–136.

between the two psalms indicates that the two figures actually merge as one: the individual in Ps. 1 is to be read as the king and the king in Ps. 2 is to be understood as the unnamed individual.[62] Ps. 1 'democratizes' the royalty of Ps. 2, but at the same time Ps. 2 adds a royal flavour to the 'everyman' inclusiveness of Ps. 1. The figures of king and anonymous believer merge.[63] This ambiguity presents us, as believing readers, with an example to follow – the king is presented as one grounded in the word of Yahweh and consciously taking refuge in him, and we believers are to do no less. The true king has set an example for all who would follow him, basing his life in the torah (Luke 4:16–21) and living his life in dependence upon his Father (John 5:30).

Conclusion

Rereading the royal psalms Christologically, we see a picture of Jesus the King as our *representative* and our *example*. Seeing the significance of kingship in the Psalter gives us a fuller understanding of the humanity of our Messiah and a fuller awareness of the piety that should typify our lives day by day. The royal nature of the Psalms is both obvious and subtle, but the implications of this kingship theme are significant.

> The stone the builders rejected has become the capstone.
> Yahweh has done this thing and it is wonderful in our eyes.
> This is the day that Yahweh has made; let us rejoice and be glad in it.[64]

---

62. Miller, 'Beginning', pp. 90–91.
63. Grant, *King*, pp. 280–289.
64. Ps. 118:22–23 (a.t.).

© Jamie A. Grant, 2005.

6. THE PSALMS AND THE CULT

Jerome F. D. Creach

The question of the psalms' relationship to the cult dominated psalms research in the first three quarters of the twentieth century. That topic has receded into the background, however, as scholars now focus on questions of how the canonical book is arranged, how it grew to its present form, and what theological impact the book is intended to make.[1] Current interest in the shape of the final collection is so pronounced that some students may be tempted to bypass the question of the psalms and the cult altogether. The data concerning the order of the Psalter is more certain than the hypothetical settings proposed for many psalms, and the shape of the book may seem more pertinent to faith than the supposed use of psalms in ancient Israelite worship. Indeed, the study of the psalms and the cult may seem like a stale academic exercise better left in the dustbin of scholarly history.

Despite this present devaluation, the subject holds important theological treasures for those who are patient enough to explore

---

1. See Howard, ch. 1 in this volume.

it. After all, the scholars who first sought to know the psalms' relationship to the cult developed their approach as a reaction to the prevailing methods of their day (mainly historical and literary criticisms) that then made the psalms seem like lifeless artefacts. They believed their new approach, known as form criticism, could bring the psalms to life for a contemporary audience by showing that these poems emerged from real-life situations. If those situations could be recovered, they averred, we could hear in the psalms the voices of Israelites crying out to and praising God in everyday circumstances.[2]

This approach to the psalms is important theologically because it reminds us that the psalms were originally wed to rituals that gave concrete expression to the psalms' claims of faith, statements of thanksgiving, words of praise, and pleas for deliverance. Just as ritual without ethics and commitment makes for an empty faith, so too spiritual expression without sacrifice makes for faith with no tangible imprint. The word of God is powerful because it is incarnational. By maintaining the link between the psalms and the cult we can, in some limited way, experience more fully the Word that both became flesh and demands fleshly expressions of devotion.

Origins of the question: Hermann Gunkel

The study of the psalms and the cult may be traced to the work of German scholar Hermann Gunkel whose publications appeared between 1904 and 1933.[3] When Gunkel began his research most scholars considered psalms artistic pieces that they could interpret in light of the life circumstances of their authors.[4] Although Gunkel thought the Psalter contained the spiritual songs of pious Israelites who lived during the Maccabean period (167–164 BCE),

---

2. Campbell, 'Form Criticism', pp. 15–31.

3. See the summary of this period of research in Stamm, 'Vierteljahrhundert', pp. 34–41; a briefer but helpful treatment is available in English in Gerstenberger, 'Psalms', pp. 179–188.

4. Haller, 'Jahrzehnt', pp. 378–383.

he did not believe it was possible to recover anything about the composers. The language of these poems was too general and stereotyped to do so. To illustrate the point Gunkel noted a primary difference between David's lament over Saul and Jonathan in 2 Sam. 1:19–27 and the psalms in the Psalter: 'In his dirge, David mentions Saul and Jonathan by name, so why do the Psalms not mention the name of one person who lived at the time of the poet?'[5] Gunkel concluded that this absence of historical and personal notation was due to the psalms' origin in the public and official events of Israelite community life. Therefore he believed the main tasks of interpretation were to categorize the psalms according to genre and to identify the setting in life (*Sitz im Leben*) that gave rise to a particular type of psalm. Gunkel assumed Israel's cult was the setting for practically all genres of psalms.[6] The only exception was the so-called wisdom psalms, which he believed arose in situations of instruction, among 'the old men in the gate or in the market'.[7]

Some of Gunkel's conclusions have been rejected, and rightly so. For example, he thought the genres of the psalms developed from originally pure types that could be easily identified with particular cultic settings, to later mixed genres and liturgies. It is clear now that genres are adapted to their settings and therefore are never really pure. Similarly, his view of the development of Israel's religion can no longer be held. He thought Israel's faith began in primitive expressions, matured and reached its zenith in the great prophets, and then deteriorated into legalistic expressions. Despite these now passé ideas, Gunkel raised two primary questions that continue to set the agenda for the study of the relationship between the psalms and the cult: first, are the psalms in the Psalter cultic in origin or do they merely bear the stamp of a cultural milieu in which the cult was a pervasive influence? Second, what specific cultic events and practices lie behind the psalms and gave rise to them? Both of these questions will be considered in the following

---

5. Gunkel, *Introduction*, p. 7; *Einleitung*, p. 10.

6. Ibid.

7. Gunkel, *Introduction*, p. 21; *Einleitung*, p. 30.

discussion. Before engaging these subjects, however, it is necessary to establish a working definition of 'cult' and to consider the general evidence that the psalms are cultic literature.

The nature of the cult and the use of cultic lyrics

What is the cult?

A primary challenge in exploring the relationship between the psalms and the cult is to establish a definition of 'cult' that allows some determination of what psalms are or are not cultic. Generally stated, the cult is 'the socially established and regulated holy acts and words in which the encounter and communion of the Deity with the congregation is established, developed, and brought to its ultimate goal'.[8] Put another way, cult is 'the material expression and social organization of pious living'.[9] These definitions distinguish cultic activity from private prayer and personal piety, a distinction that may be helpful conceptually for modern readers of the psalms. For ancient people, however, the line between public and personal was never so exact. Indeed, in ancient society the cult facilitated contact with a reality to which the cult participant ascribed 'life-creating, order-establishing, and meaning-giving power'.[10] Therefore all of life was punctuated by sacral activity of a communal and ritualistic character.[11] E. Gerstenberger illustrates well the pervasiveness of the cult (in a scholar's reconstruction at least) when he proposes that some psalms arise from familial healing ceremonies mediated by ritual experts from the extended family.[12] Hence cultic activity was part of even the most personal and intimate affairs, if cult is defined broadly as a social phenomenon. Moreover, as official public worship changed in the post-exilic period (after 539 BCE), it likely

---

8. Mowinckel, *Psalms*, vol. 1, p. 15.

9. Ridderbos, 'Psalmen', p. 235.

10. Stolz, *Psalmen*, p. 7.

11. Buss, 'Meaning'.

12. Gerstenberger, *Der bittende Mensch*, pp. 167–169.

included a broader range of expressions than ever before, making the identification of non-cultic psalms even more difficult. Therefore the problem for a study of the psalms and the cult is this: if the cult permeated ancient life and reflected the ever-present organized expression of piety, how can the psalms *not* be cultic? In one sense, of course, all the psalms *are* cultic. To distinguish the nature of the psalms more exactly, however, it may be helpful to think of the cult in historical, not just sociological terms. A guiding question then might be, what is the relationship of the psalms to the official worship system of the first temple (before 587 BCE)? This line of enquiry allows for negative verification and provides a kind of anchor for the study of the psalms' relationship to the cult. Those psalms that do not reflect the worship of the Jerusalem temple before the exile, though perhaps cultic in some sense, may be sorted by using such a historical criterion. This delineation between first and second temple cults is important at some point in the exploration of the psalms' relationship to the cult. It is helpful first, however, to retrace the general idea that the psalms are by and large cultic material, a realization that came to the fore in the work of Gunkel.

Role of lyrics in the cult

Gunkel was concerned to show that the psalms represented the lyrical component of the cult.[13] There is ample evidence in Old Testament narratives to prove the general point that rituals and lyrics were inextricably bound in cultic practice.[14] For example, Lev. 9:22–24 states that Aaron and Moses blessed the Israelites, noting specifically that Aaron 'lifted his hands towards the people' (v. 22). Although the contents of the blessing are not given, this type of setting and action are surely assumed when Num. 6:22–26 gives the words of the Aaronic blessing. Later in the book of Numbers, when the Israelites came to Beer (meaning 'well') to seek water, they sang, 'Spring up, O well! – Sing to it! – the well

---

13. Gunkel, *Introduction*, p. 11; *Einleitung*, p. 16.
14. Note the fuller list of examples in Gunkel, *Introduction*, pp. 7–13; *Einleitung*, pp. 10–19.

that the leaders sank, that the nobles of the people dug, with the sceptre, with the staff' (Num. 21:17–18). Here the search for water was ritualized and was accompanied by an appropriate song. Perhaps the best general example, however, is the account of Israel's celebration after the defeat of Pharaoh and his army at the Red Sea in Exod. 15:1–21. The text reports that Miriam and the women of the camp danced, played tambourines (v. 20) and praised God, saying, 'Sing to the LORD, for he has triumphed gloriously; horse and rider he has thrown into the sea' (v. 21b). The fact that other texts portray victory celebrations similarly – women dancing, playing instruments, and singing – shows this type of event had accepted rituals and included music (Judg. 11:34; 1 Sam. 18:6–9).

Cultic use of the psalms: external evidence

In addition to these general illustrations of lyrics bound to cultic acts, there are texts outside the psalms that provide direct evidence that some psalms were used in the cult. Num. 10:35–36 reports that when the ark moved from its place Moses would say, 'Arise, O LORD, let your enemies be scattered, and your foes flee before you' (v. 35), and likewise when the ark came back to its place he would say, 'Return, O LORD of the ten thousand thousands of Israel' (v. 36). This narrative helps make sense of numerous passages in the psalms that ask God to 'arise' (68:1) or 'return' (132:8). Such language should be heard as part of a ceremony that had as its centrepiece a procession of the ark in celebration of the victory of God over his enemies (see particularly 24:7–10).[15]

At least two texts outside the Psalter attest directly to the cultic use of particular psalms. According to 1 Chr. 15:1 – 16:36, David led a procession of the ark to Jerusalem, accompanied by Levites appointed to play and sing. They brought up the ark 'with shouting, to the sound of the horn, trumpets, and cymbals, and made loud music on harps and lyres' (1 Chr. 15:28). When the ark was in place David 'appointed the singing of praises to the LORD by Asaph and his kindred' (16:7). The content of their praise is

---

15. Cross, *Canaanite*, pp. 91–111.

reported to be segments of Pss. 105, 95 and 106 (1 Chr. 16:8–34). To be sure, the original version of this event in 2 Sam. 6 is less elaborate and does not include these details related to the psalms, but it is significant that the chronicler, who is supremely interested in worship, connects the psalms and this cultic act.

Jer. 33:10–11 likewise associates a particular psalm with a cultic act. The passage reports Jeremiah's prophecy that when the Lord restores good fortune to Judah there will once again be occasion to bring thank offerings to the temple (see Lev. 7:11–18). Such offerings, Jeremiah declares, will be accompanied by the words of Ps. 136:1: 'Give thanks to the LORD of hosts, for the LORD is good, for his steadfast love endures for ever!' (Jer. 33:11) The implications of this passage, however, are not limited to the use of this particular verse or psalm. The common expression 'give thanks' comes from the same root word (yadâ) as the name of the thanksgiving offering in Hebrew (tôdâ; Lev. 7:12). Hence it is reasonable to assume that there is a connection between the thanksgiving offering and the words 'give thanks', 'I give thanks' and the like, wherever they appear. The Jeremian text indicates that the act of making a thanksgiving offering (116:12–19; cf. Job 33:19–28) appeared in tandem with a thanksgiving song (116:1–11).

These final two examples give direct evidence that the psalms were used in the cult, but do they suggest that the lyrics as we have them in the Psalter originated in a setting of worship? Even Jer. 33:10–11 is not proof of such an origin, though it does indicate that the first line of Ps. 136 was closely associated with cultic rituals. Moreover, 1 Chr. 15:1 – 16:36 is interesting, but it would seem to illustrate a rather obvious fact, namely, that in the time of the chronicler psalms were used in various worship settings. To clarify further the questions of how the psalms are related to the cult and whether or not the psalms originated in the cult, we must turn to the psalms themselves.

Cultic use of the psalms: internal evidence

Psalm headings

Perhaps the clearest indicator of the cultic *use* of psalms is psalm superscriptions. This information in the headings falls into two main categories. Some psalm titles include notes about an occasion on which a psalm was used. For example, the heading of Ps. 30 identifies the psalm as 'a song at the dedication of the temple', presumably a reference to the dedication of the second temple in 515 BCE; the title of Ps. 38 identifies the work it introduces as 'for the memorial offering', though this cannot be identified further; Ps. 92 designates the psalm as 'a song for the Sabbath'. The headings of Pss. 120 – 134 may also indicate cultic use. They all contain the note 'a song of ascents' (with a slight variant in Ps. 121). It is often assumed that this element of the title designates these psalms for use in pilgrimages to Jerusalem.[16]

Psalm titles contain a variety of comments that appear to be musical directives: 'with stringed instruments' (Pss. 4; 6; 54; 55; 61; 67; 76); 'for the flutes' (Ps. 5); 'according to . . .' ('*al*) plus any of a variety of terms: 'the deer of the dawn' (Ps. 22); 'the lilies' (Pss. 45; 69); 'the dove on far-off terebinths' (Ps. 56). Note the use of this type of direction in relation to musical performance in 1 Chr. 15:20–21. The elusive *selâ* may also be classified with information in psalm titles even though it appears at breaks in the bodies of the psalms.[17]

These various notes on the performance of psalms were almost certainly added in a later stage of development when the psalms became written documents. They point to one important dimension of the psalms' relationship to the cult, namely, as the liturgy of the second temple. In the case of Pss. 120 – 134 the grouping as a whole shows signs of being edited for pilgrimage in the post-exilic period, even though some members of the collection were originally northern compositions.[18] Hence there is evidence at different levels that some psalms were adapted for a particular cultic use. Evidence of a cultic origin is found mainly in the

---

16. See the history of interpretation summarized in Crow, *Songs*, pp. 1–27.

17. See the brief but excellent survey of opinions in Tate, *Psalms 51 – 100*, p. 33 n. 5a.

18. Crow, *Songs*, pp. 159–187.

bodies of psalms, i.e. in the poetic lines themselves. To this data we now turn.

The bodies of psalms

As noted earlier, Gunkel thought the formulaic character of most psalmic language indicated that the psalms had their origin in the cult. There are other signs of cultic origins in the bodies of psalms as well. For example, the psalms' frequent references to ritual acts suggest the psalms were to be performed. The psalms mention performance of songs by singing (81:1–2; 144:9; 147:7) and playing instruments (81:2–3; 144:9; 147:7; 149:3; 150:3–5). There are also references to ritual clapping and shouting (47:1), dancing (149:3), processing to the holy place (132:7), and making sacrifices (118:27).[19] Most importantly, the examples cited here are almost all directive statements. They invite or call worshippers to sing, dance, or otherwise perform ritual acts (the only exception may be 132:7). This list of references to ritual acts can be expanded greatly if we include the imperative calls to worship that begin so many psalms of praise (47:1; 95:1–2; 96:1–3; 98:1; 100:1; 105:1–2; 113:1; 134:1–2).

In addition to these direct statements about cultic performance, the antiphonal quality of many psalms suggests a relationship to the cult. Ps. 118 opens with an invitation to praise, 'O give thanks to the LORD, for he is good' (v. 1a), followed by a statement of God's worthiness to be praised, presumably spoken by the congregation, 'his steadfast love endures for ever' (v. 1b; see v. 29). The response in v. 1b then recurs throughout the next three verses, showing that the psalm is to be spoken publicly, as various groups (Israel, v. 2; house of Aaron, v. 3; those who fear the Lord, v. 4) are called to utter the words, 'His steadfast love endures for ever' (see also 115:9–11; 135:19–20; 136). The refrain is introduced by the Hebrew particle *kî*, which is often taken as a causative, and thus rendered 'for' or 'because'.[20] It gives the reason why God should be praised. As 118:1–4 makes clear, however, the clause which *kî*

---

19. *ḥag* is more 'festal sacrifice' than 'festal procession' (NRSV); cf. translation as 'offering' in Mal. 2:3.

20. E.g. Williams, *Hebrew*, pp. 72–73.

introduces does more than express motivation for praise and thanksgiving. The refrain participates in the thanksgiving called for as the congregation's response.[21]

In some psalms a shift in voices seems to indicate a performance that involved more than one person. For example, Ps. 75 begins with a declaration of praise spoken by a worshipper (v. 1). Then Yahweh himself speaks for the rest of the psalm (vv. 2–10). Similarly, Ps. 81:1–5a expresses a call to worship and a congregation's response, but v. 5b introduces 'a voice I had not known', the voice of God who speaks to the end of the psalm (vv. 6–16). Such features give these psalms a dramatic character. They perhaps indicate the participation of a cultic prophetic in worship.[22] Regardless of who speaks, however, the multiple voices point to community use.

These examples give credence to the notion that the language of many psalms was shaped by the cult, if not originating in it. The identification of specific cult rituals and practices that lie behind the psalms is much more difficult. Equally problematic is the question of whether particular psalms arose in the cult of the first temple or in later expressions of worship. To advance the discussion of how and when psalms were specifically used in the cult (and to argue that they were indeed cultic) requires a comparison of Israel's cult to the worship systems of other Ancient Near Eastern peoples. Their cults and their use of lyric material serve, in effect, as models for scholars' attempts to reconstruct Israel's use of the psalms. As with all such reconstructions, this work also requires scholars to use their imagination. Given available knowledge about cult practices in neighbouring societies and the contents and tenor of the psalms, what practices likely stand behind the biblical psalms?

Theories of cultic settings

Space does not allow a comprehensive survey of theories on the cultic use of psalms. The discussion that follows includes repre-

---

21. Miller, *They Cried*, pp. 206–207.
22. So Johnson, *Cultic*.

sentative work that has either attracted much attention or is typical of the kind of hypotheses put forward.

Community psalms and Israel's festivals

S. Mowinckel made creative use of the extrabiblical evidence, particularly the Babylonian Akitu or New Year festival. The Babylonian festival featured a declaration of the kingship of Marduk, the chief deity of the Babylonian pantheon. For Mowinckel this information was essential for understanding the use of psalms in Israel's worship. He proposed a New Year festival in the autumn in Israel, at the time identified in later texts with the harvest festival (Exod. 23:16; 34:24; Lev. 23:23ff.). He thought that the centre of this celebration was a claim of Yahweh's kingship. The key psalms in his schema were the so-called enthronement psalms which have at their centre the theme of Yahweh as king (Pss. 47; 93; 95 – 99). Mowinckel believed the final day of the festival was a grand enactment of Yahweh's enthronement, marked by a procession of the ark to the temple. Hence the words 'The LORD is king' (93:1; 97:1; 99:1) should be rendered 'The LORD *has become* king', for this line constituted a cultic shout at the culmination of the parade to the holy place.[23]

Mowinckel thought further that this celebration of Yahweh's kingship was led in large part by the Israelite king, whose rule was also reaffirmed and celebrated in various rituals during the New Year festival, as was the case in Babylon. Hence he thought the enthronement psalms came from the cult of the first temple. Mowinckel rightly saw that the so-called royal psalms presented the human king's earthly rule as parallel to the heavenly rule of God, and that these psalms presented the king as God's appointed representative (Pss. 2; 89:2–39; 110). Read in light of Babylonian records of the Akitu festival, this delineation of Israel's king indicated to Mowinckel that the king, as God's representative, stood at the centre of the New Year celebration and of the cult in general. For Mowinckel, the 'I' of the psalms was read in most cases as the voice of the king. The king was not expressing

---

23. Mowinckel, *Psalms*, vol. 1, pp. 106–192.

personal complaints for the most part; rather, he was representing Israel's 'corporate personality'. So the king's reign, his struggles with enemies, his victories and defeats, were ritually enacted in the festival.[24]

Reactions to Mowinckel's work reflect the difficulty of the question, the scarcity of evidence, and the polyvalence of the language of the psalms. Three prominent opinions on Mowinckel's theory provide illustration. (a) Some scholars reject Mowinckel's notion of a central festival. They note that the Old Testament contains no direct evidence of such a celebration. Moreover, some critics have pointed out that Mowinckel relies too heavily on rabbinical material which cannot be used to reconstruct a festival in the monarchical period.[25]

(b) Other scholars not only accept Mowinckel's view that a Babylonian-like event occurred in Israel, but they also postulate that Israel's cult fitted a general pattern in Ancient Near Eastern religious expression. Among the more radical proposals was that put forward by scholars in the so-called Myth and Ritual school. They held that the Israelite king stood in the place of God in the cult and was himself understood as a semi-divine character. The Myth and Ritual adherents hence pressed Mowinckel's ideas in ways he did not intend.[26]

(c) Perhaps the most common reaction to Mowinckel's work, however, was general agreement, but with suggested modifications. For example, Gunkel agreed with Mowinckel that a New Year festival was celebrated in ancient Israel and that the ceremony centred on Yahweh's kingship. He disagreed with him, however, on the cultic nature of the enthronement psalms, as they now appear in the Psalter. Gunkel's objection was based on

---

24. Eaton (*Kingship*) states the case for the royal identity of the individual quite strongly; Croft (*Identity*) argues similarly, but nuances the argument in a propitious way.

25. Mowinckel, *Psalms*, vol. 1, pp. 121–125. See the summary of critiques in Stamm, 'Vierteljahrhundert', pp. 48–49; for an excellent evaluation in English, see Eaton, 'Psalms and Worship', pp. 241–272.

26. Gerstenberger, 'Psalms', p. 216.

the fact that the enthronement poems occur in bits and pieces also in Isa. 40 – 66, a portion of the book of Isaiah that dates to the Babylonian exile (587–539 BCE) or afterward.[27] For the great prophet of the exile, these poetic lines are eschatological in that they look forward to God's reign, which would be displayed in the return of Judah to its homeland. Gunkel thought it logical that the prophet had reinterpreted the enthronement material for his own historical situation. Since the enthronement psalms in the Psalter are identical in form and content to what we have in the latter part of Isaiah, it also seemed to follow that these psalms are not the cultic originals, but later eschatological poems influenced by Isa. 40 – 66.[28] Therefore for Gunkel the psalms in question, in present form at least, were not from the first temple period, but later.

Weiser shared Mowinckel's assumption of a central festival of the first temple and of the psalms as the liturgy of that festival. But he argued that the festival setting for the majority of the psalms was a 'covenant festival of Yahweh' in which the Sinai covenant was remembered and renewed. His reconstruction is based on two primary pieces of data: first, the covenant and its renewal predominates in the Hexateuch (Genesis – Joshua) and should therefore be taken as the primary cultic emphasis of early Israel (see Josh. 24). Second, Weiser notes that very few psalms (Pss. 65; 67; 85; 126) contain emphases that would be at home in the agricultural festivals, which he believes were later developments away from Israel's original emphasis on covenant.[29] His theory made sense of the so-called anti-cultic psalms (40:6; 50:14; 51:15–17; 69:31), which stand theologically close to the prophets who criticized the practice of ritual without ethics (Amos 5:21–26).[30] It also accounted for the fact that sacrifice and the agricultural festivals are hardly mentioned in the psalms, a point

27. Isa. 40:10; 44:23; 49:13; 55:12; 59:19; 60:1; 62:11.

28. Gunkel, *Introduction*, pp. 80–81; *Einleitung*, p. 116.

29. Weiser, *Psalms*, p. 27.

30. See Szörenyi, *Psalmen*, pp. 320–333; and the summary of his work in Clines, 'Psalm Research I', p. 107.

Eerdmans used earlier to deny the psalms' origin in the cult.[31] It is interesting to note, however, how Weiser begins his discussion of the covenant festival liturgy:

> No proper ritual of the Covenant Festival of Yahweh has been handed down to us from Old Testament times, such as has been preserved, for instance, from the Babylonian New Year Festival and the Akitu Festival at Uruk, giving instructions for the execution of the cultic acts and for the recitals of the priests.[32]

And yet Weiser proceeds to say with confidence, 'The liturgy which we find in Ps. 50 is part of the order of the feast of the renewal of the Covenant which was celebrated at the Temple of Jerusalem.'[33] Weiser's criticism of Mowinckel's theory, that the Old Testament never mentions an enthronement festival, turns back upon his own thesis, for the covenant festival too is a reconstruction that remains hypothetical, however attractive it may be.[34] Moreover, the weaknesses of Weiser's thesis, as of Mowinckel's, are magnified when the proposed festival is allowed to act as a magnet that attracts virtually every psalm into its orbit.

Cultic rituals and psalms of the individual

Just as there are competing theories regarding how the psalms were used in national cultic events, there are also many and various views of how the poems functioned in ceremonies centring on individuals. As we have already seen, some scholars understand the 'I' of these psalms to be the king. There are several interrelated theories, however, that attempt to explain how some psalms functioned in the lives of ordinary Israelites. Mowinckel located numerous individual complaint psalms in occasions of sickness and requests for healing (applied to ordinary Israelites, but perhaps composed originally for the king). He believed these psalms

---

31. Ridderbos, 'Psalmen', p. 241.

32. Weiser, *Psalms*, p. 35.

33. Ibid.

34. Szörenyi, *Psalmen*, pp. 213–214.

should be read against the particular backdrop of sickness caused by curses or spells cast by the psalmists' enemies, enemies labelled 'evildoers' (Ps. 10:15). Mowinckel imagined healing from such maladies took place in the temple, in rituals designed for such circumstances and carried out by priests (so again for Mowinckel these psalms were part of the worship of the first temple).[35]

Schmidt proposed that some of these psalms actually grew out of a judicial process in which an accused person sought vindication through a trial in the temple. The notion that such a procedure was available is supported by numerous texts (1 Kgs 8:31–32; Deut. 17:8–13; 21:1–8). Deut. 17:8–13 most clearly identifies the temple and the Levites on duty as the locus of judgment. Ps. 17 is a parade example of a psalm that might be read against this backdrop. It begins with a call for hearing in vv. 1–2 ('Hear a just cause, O LORD'), and the rest of the psalm is filled with images of adversaries who falsely accuse the psalmist. The fact that the psalmist asks for God's favourable judgment and for the Lord to confront the accusers (v. 13) lends credence to Schmidt's proposal. His thesis has continued to maintain adherents. W. Beyerlin supported and expanded the theory, proposing that Pss. 3, 4, 5, 7, 11, 17, 23, 26, 27, 57 and 63 arose from an institutional setting in which such a judicial process was carried out.[36] L. Delekat proposed a setting similar to that of Schmidt and Beyerlin, but he emphasized the overnight stay in the temple, which many of these psalms imply. Delekat describes in amazing detail what took place during the night, how the accused received oracles, had dreams, and underwent ordeals. He proposed that the psalms expressing this experience were inscribed on temple or sanctuary walls by the accused.[37] Recently, K. van der Toorn has revised these theories that focus on a judicial process by focusing on the ordeal that the accused underwent during the night in the temple. He proposes that the psalmist submitted to a drinking

35. Mowinckel, *Psalms*, vol. 2, pp. 1–8.

36. Schmidt, *Gebet*; Beyerlin, *Rettung*, p. 141; see the summary in Gerstenberger, 'Psalms', pp. 203–205.

37. Delekat, *Asylie*.

ordeal, like that described in Num. 5:11–31, hence the frequent references to a cup in these psalms (11:6; 16:5; 23:6).[38] This final expression of the thesis in a general way illustrates both the strengths and weaknesses of them all. Van der Toorn is right to emphasize the temple setting of the psalms in question, for there are frequent references to seeing God's face (11:7) or dwelling in the holy place (23:6). To make the psalms fit the details of his thesis, however, he must apply some of the data in ways that seem contrary to their intention. For example, it is unlikely that the references to a cup in these psalms refer to ordeals, since they connote celebration (23:5), symbolize God's protection (16:5), or indicate judgment upon the psalmist's enemies (11:6).[39]

In the case of the cultic settings of many psalms, the only new data available to support fresh proposals is that which comes from the scholar's imagination. The primary exception is the discovery and appropriation of new texts. Particularly important for understanding the cultic background of the psalms is the body of material uncovered from 1929 at Ras Shamra (ancient Ugarit) near the coast of Syria. These works continue to be translated and evaluated for their comparative value. Drawing largely from this material, for example, P. K. McCarter has proposed that psalms using water as a symbol of distress originated in river ordeals meant to determine guilt or innocence (18:18; 32:6; 66:10–12).[40] In the end, however, such theories suffer from the same weaknesses as those mentioned above. The proposed ritual (or ordeal in this case) is not mentioned elsewhere in the Old Testament, and the evidence of the psalms must be manipulated too much to fit the pattern of the comparative material.

This does not mean, however, that gains in knowledge are no longer possible in this area. Gerstenberger offers a promising explanation for some psalms that seem to arise from situations of illness. Using sociological models, Old Testament narratives that depict the nature and setting of prayer, and Mesopotamian ritual

---

38. Van der Toorn, 'Ordeal', pp. 40–42.

39. See the evaluation of these theories in Johnston, 'Ordeals'.

40. McCarter, 'River Ordeal', pp. 403–412.

texts, Gerstenberger proposes that many of these psalms grew out of family ceremonies of healing in which a local cult figure officiated. To support the notion of such a ceremony in the home, he notes that Hezekiah seeks a 'ritual expert' (Isaiah) when he is sick (Isa. 38). Likewise, 2 Sam. 12 depicts David practising penitence at home. According to Gerstenberger, these examples raise the possibility, indeed the likelihood, that many psalms had their setting in the second temple period and apart from the official worship of the temple itself.[41] He proposes that many psalms of sickness reflect a kind of 'group therapy' process, in which a ritual expert from the clan or tribe restores the infirmed to full communion with the family group.[42]

The current state of the question

What the foregoing survey reveals perhaps most clearly is that the relationship between the psalms and the cult is very difficult to determine because it is multifaceted. The psalms were used as primary liturgical material in the second temple period (and beyond) as psalm superscriptions and some Old Testament narratives (1 Chr. 15 – 16) clearly indicate. The liturgical features of some psalms suggest further that they actually originated in the cult of the first or second temple. Nevertheless, the number of psalms that are cultic and the exact manner in which they were performed eludes us, with the possible exception of the song of thanksgiving, which almost certainly was used in the first temple (see Jer. 33:10–11). Features of even some of these psalms, however, show the issue to be complex. Ps. 30 bears classic signs of the song of thanksgiving: description of being rescued (vv. 1–3, 11), inclusion of terminology for giving thanks (v. 12); but it was apparently used differently in the second temple period, according to its superscription: 'a song at the dedication of the temple'. Similarly, the language of individual thanksgiving dominates

---

41. Gerstenberger, *Der bittende Mensch*, pp. 167–169.
42. Ibid., p. 165.

Ps. 129 (vv. 1a, 2–4), but the work was adapted for community use, as the phrase 'let Israel say' (v. 1b) attests.

Psalms scholars in the early twenty-first century must deal with the question of the psalms and the cult in light of at least two important trends. The first regards a shift in the perceived date of psalms. While Gunkel thought the psalms were late compositions, based on cultic originals, and Mowinckel believed most of the psalms in the Psalter are the cultic originals from the first temple, there is now some movement towards the idea that many psalms grew out of the cult of the second temple. With this proposal, Gerstenberger also suggests a different social setting for many psalms. He imagines a cult that is much less centralized, with worship taking place in many local communities of Jews scattered around the ancient world. Many scholars now find a place in the cult of the post-exilic diaspora for psalms that seem designed to instruct, psalms which Gunkel thought were set among the elders in the gate. Gerstenberger states the matter this way:

> These early Jewish communities fought against religious extermination, insisting on the one, exclusive, and invisible God, on his *tôrâ*, on his Sabbath, and on his stipulations concerning food, marriage, and all the other matters of daily life. They hoped for the restitution of the Davidic empire and God's revenge upon all oppressors. To maintain such a dynamic tradition the Jews studied the written heritage of their ancestors. Teaching this revealed will of God became the very backbone of communal and individual existence. At this point wisdom influence entered Jewish life and, most of all, Jewish cult.[43]

By treating the psalms in such a context Gerstenberger has been able to advance the discussion of specific cultic settings for other psalms as well. His proposal on the *Sitz im Leben* of the individual complaint psalms is particularly important. Given the dearth of direct evidence of cultic practice in ancient Israel, his use of sociological models, supported by Mesopotamian ritual texts and Old

---

43. Gerstenberger, *Psalms I*, p. 20.

Testament narratives, is one of the most promising models for future research.[44]

The current interest in the Psalter as a literary product has also impacted the discussion of the psalms' relationship to the cult. There is now an increased awareness that some psalms in present form bear signs of editorial manipulation, which raise anew questions about what elements in the psalms are cultic. Ps. 2:10–12 is a good example. J. J. M. Roberts proposes the address to the 'kings of the earth' had in mind rulers of Israel's subservient territories who were present for an Israelite king's coronation. He finds support for this view in records of similar Egyptian ceremonies in which vassals were instructed to pay homage to Pharaoh.[45] Roberts's discussion is quite helpful for understanding the possible origins of these poetic lines. Nevertheless, the fact that Ps. 2:12a warns the foreign kings with language so similar to Ps. 1:6b raises the possibility that the end of Ps. 2 was given its present form in the Psalter to enhance its connection to Ps. 1 as a dual introduction to the book. Regardless of which perspective is right, it is interesting that this dynamic in current scholarship brings us back, albeit by a different path, to the question of Gunkel: are the psalms in present form cultic, or do they merely draw from cultic forms and language?

---

44. Note Long's favourable analysis of such use of sociology in 'Recent',
   p. 44.
45. Roberts, 'Religio-Political', p. 132.

7. THE PSALMS AND CULT SYMBOLISM: THE CASE OF THE CHERUBIM-ARK

Craig C. Broyles

Whether we read the Psalms as prayers of David or as poems for private meditation, and whether we read them according to the canons of form criticism or recent literary approaches, or we scan their themes to construct our theology, we read them primarily as literature. An investigation of the symbolism associated with the cherubim-ark in the Psalms, however, reveals that they were shaped by liturgy and ritual, and not merely by literary, thematic or theological concerns. The value of this investigation is not merely historical because it also aids in the solution of several interpretive cruxes in the Psalms. Psalms were not simply to be read; they were to be performed. Belief was expressed verbally and visually.

It is commonly assumed that once the ark of the covenant was installed in Solomon's temple, it was never seen publicly again.[1]

---

1. For example, some scholars deny that key psalms discussed below give any evidence of ark processions in the Psalms: Hillers, 'Ritual', pp. 48–55; Cooper, 'Ps. 24:7–10', pp. 37–60.

This article will argue, however, that the cherubim-ark was used regularly in festival processions at the temple in the pre-exilic period. By this sacred symbol Yahweh's kingship was presented to the worshipping congregation not only as an imaginative metaphor but as a visual symbol. And this King was portrayed not by a static image, as one sitting enthroned, but by a dynamic ritual, as a victorious warrior-king ascending to his palace in triumphal procession. This study will thus help us to recover from the Scriptures the significance of these old symbols that served to link the various roles that God assumes: he is God of the skies, King, Warrior and Judge.

The cherubim-ark elsewhere in the Old Testament

Because the cherubim are mentioned only twice in the Psalms and the ark only once, we must first explore texts outside the Psalter to identify what these sacred objects symbolized and what divine attributes and terminology were associated with them.[2] (The key terms and associations that recur in the Psalms have been *italicized*.)

The ark's construction

In the so-called priestly strand of the Pentateuch, the ark is designated as 'the ark of the testimony' (*'ărōn-hā'ēdut*, Exod. 25:22). Unlike the description of when Solomon brought the ark into the temple (1 Kgs 6 – 8), here the two cherubim are 'of one piece with the mercy-seat', which rests on top of the ark (vv. 17, 20). Further, according to Lev. 16:2, Yahweh's theophanic '*cloud*' (*'ānān*) appears

---

2. For further reading on the ark and the cherubim see Davies, 'Ark', pp. 51–61; Mowinckel, *Psalms*, vol. 1, pp. 174–177; Cross, *Canaanite*, pp. 91–111; Seow, 'Ark'; Clements, *God*, pp. 28–39; de Vaux, *Ancient*, pp. 297–302; Haran, *Temple*, pp. 246–259; von Rad, 'Tent', pp. 103–124. Especially enlightening from an archaeological perspective on the cherubim as a throne and the ark as a footstool are Mettinger, *In Search*, pp. 127–131; Keel, *Symbolism*, pp. 166–171.

over 'the ark'. In the Deuteronomic account the ark's sole purpose is to serve as a receptacle for the two stone tablets (Deut. 10:2, 5), and it is thus designated as 'the ark of the covenant' in the Deuteronomistic History.

The wilderness period

In the wilderness the ark served to *lead* the people (Num. 10:33). At the beginning of each stage of the journey Moses invoked what is commonly called 'the song of the ark': '*Arise* [*qûmâ*], O LORD, let your enemies be scattered, and your foes flee before you' (v. 35). Similarly, whenever the ark 'came to rest' (*nwḥ*), Yahweh is implored to 'return' (*šûbâ*). The scattering of enemies and flight of foes associates the ark with *battle*. This is confirmed later in Num. 14:44, which presupposes that the ark must precede the people in the conquest of the land. Also related to the ark is 'the *cloud* of the LORD', which led them on their journey. We should note that this wilderness passage makes no explicit mention of the cherubim.

Jericho

Prior to the conquest of Jericho the ark leads Israel's armed men in repeated *processions* (*hlk*) around the city. Priests carry '*trumpets* of rams' horns before the ark' (Josh. 6:4, 6, 7, 13), blowing them during the procession (v. 9). After the final procession the priests give a prolonged 'sound of the trumpet' and all the people '*shout* with a great shout' (vv. 5, 16, 20), after which the city walls collapse.

The ark narrative

In ways similar to *Raiders of the Lost Ark*, this passage exhibits the popular belief that the ark would give success in *battle* (1 Sam. 4:3). The full name of this sacred object is stated as 'the ark of the covenant of *the LORD of hosts*, who is *enthroned* on the cherubim' (4:4). When the ark approaches, 'all Israel gave a mighty *shout*'. The child named Ichabod (*'î-kābôd*) makes a clear connection between the ark and Yahweh's *glory* (*kābôd*, 4:21–22). Though the ark does not magically guarantee military victory, it brings dire consequences to those failing to treat it properly (5:1–12; 6:19, see NRSV margin). The response of the citizens of Beth Shemesh (6:20) is similar to the questions opening the temple entry liturgies found in Pss. 15:1 and 24:3: 'Who is able to stand before the LORD, this *holy* God?' The men of Kiriath Jearim then *'took up'* (*'lh*) the ark.

Later in 2 Samuel Uriah implies that the ark accompanied Israel's armies in their *battles*. At the battle front, 'the ark and Israel and Judah remain in booths . . . camping in the open field' (11:11). These 'booths' (or 'huts', *sukkôt*) are clearly not related to the 'tent' (*'ōhel*) of 2 Sam. 6:17 or the 'tent curtain' (*yerî'â*) of 2 Sam. 7:2.

David brings the ark into Jerusalem

Similar to 1 Sam. 4:4, the ark is here specified as 'the ark of God over which is called the name, the name *Yahweh of hosts* who is *enthroned* on the cherubim' (2 Sam. 6:2, translation mine). This designation may well imply that there was a ritual of calling the name 'Yahweh of hosts' over the ark (cf. the invoking of God's 'name' in Num. 6:22–27; Exod. 20:7, 24). The verb describing its transport to Jerusalem is 'to *bring up*' (*'lh*, hiphil, vv. 2, 12, 15). Uzzah's sudden death emphasizes the fearful consequences of mishandling the ark. On the other hand, the second, successful attempt to bring the ark into Jerusalem is done 'with *shouting*, and with the sound of the *trumpet*' (v. 15).

Solomon brings the ark into the temple

The room prepared for the ark was the 'inner sanctuary' (*debîr*, 1 Kgs 6:19), where there was a pair of cherubim (6:23–28). Each of their outer *wings* touched the opposite wall, and their inner wings 'toward the centre of the house were touching wing to wing' (6:27). Cherubim were carved elsewhere in 'the nave' (or 'the temple/palace', *hêkāl*, 6:29, 31–35; 7:29, 36). Again the verb describing the transfer of the ark into the sanctuary is 'to *bring up*' (*'lh*, hiphil, 8:1, 4). After sacrifice is offered before it (8:3, 5), 'the priests brought the ark of the covenant of the LORD to its place, in the inner sanctuary of the house, in the most *holy* place, underneath the *wings* of the cherubim. For the cherubim spread out their wings over the place of the ark, so that the cherubim made a covering [*skk*] above the ark and its poles' (vv. 6–7). Once the priests withdrew from the holy place, 'a *cloud* filled the house of the LORD' (8:10), which exhibited 'the *glory* of the LORD'.

Consistent with the description of the ark in Deut. 10:1–9, its chief purpose here is to house the symbols of the covenant: 'There was nothing in the ark except the two tablets of stone that Moses had placed there at Horeb, where the LORD made a covenant with the Israelites' (8:9, also v. 21). The description of the carrying poles as 'there to this day' (8:8) implies the ark did not move from this place during the writer's lifetime.

The chronicler's interpretations

In the narrative of David's transport of the ark into Jerusalem (1 Chr. 13 – 16), the most striking variation in the chronicler's account is the inclusion of a lengthy psalm, comprised of selections from three separate psalms from the Psalter: 105:1–15; 96:1–13; and 106:1, 47–48 (1 Chr. 16:8–36). Thus, in the chronicler's view the singing of psalms served as fitting accompaniment to the ritual procession of the ark. Here David calls the leaders of the Levites to appoint 'singers to play on musical instruments, on harps and lyres and cymbals' (15:16) – the very instruments that accompany psalms. The names of the three chief Levites appointed as singers are also found in psalm superscriptions: Heman (88), Asaph (50, 73 – 83) and Ethan (89). The technical musical terms 'alamoth' and 'sheminith' are found only here (15:20–21) and in psalm headings (6; 12; 46). David appointed Levites as 'ministers before the ark of the LORD, to invoke, to thank, and to praise the LORD, the God of Israel' (16:4). Asaph is made their 'chief', and they play harps, lyres, cymbals, and *trumpets* 'regularly, before the ark of the covenant of God' (16:5–6, also v. 37).

In material unique to the chronicler, David calls the temple 'a house of *rest* for the ark of the covenant of the LORD, for the *footstool* of our God' (1 Chr. 28:2). The conjunction of the three terms 'rest', 'ark' and 'footstool' implies that the chronicler takes his lead from Ps. 132:7–8, which he later quotes in 2 Chr. 6:41 as an addition to Solomon's prayer of dedication. David gave Solomon 'his plan for the golden *chariot* of the cherubim that spread their wings and covered the ark of the covenant of the LORD' (1 Chr. 28:18). This chapter thus spells out the symbolism of both the cherubim and the ark, which represent Yahweh's 'chariot' and 'footstool' respectively.

In a command also unique to Chronicles, Josiah 'said to the Levites . . . "Put the *holy* ark in the house that Solomon son of David, king of Israel, built; you need no longer carry it on your shoulders. Now serve the LORD your God and his people Israel"' (2 Chr. 35:3). If Josiah were referring to a singular return of the ark after its conjectured removal in Manasseh's reign, the phrasing of this command is certainly odd. The verse in fact suggests that at that moment the ark was not inside the temple and that the Levites had been transporting it on a regular basis. This implies that it was from this point that the ark took permanent residence inside the temple. The Levites are therefore given a new commission.

The prophets

The ark's only explicit mention in the prophets comes in a prose oracle about 'those days', which refer to the post-exilic restoration and reunification of Israel and Judah (Jer. 3:16–18). Though not explicitly identified as a *throne* or with Yahweh's presence, the ark was clearly associated with them.

In Ezekiel's remarkable opening *chariot* vision there are four living creatures, later identified as 'cherubim' (10:15, 20, 22). In this case, the throne is above the cherubim; they do not form it themselves (1:26; 10:1). And 'the *glory* of the LORD' is not restricted to the cherubim-throne (10:4, 18), though it is usually located above them (10:19–20). This vision includes various theophanic elements, namely *wind, cloud, fire* and *lightning*.

Summary

This survey reveals a number of terms that are closely associated with the cherubim-ark. Some of them point to rituals: processions, ascent shouting and trumpets. The cherubim-ark is considered to symbolize Yahweh's throne, chariot and footstool. The divine name most closely associated with it is 'Yahweh of hosts', and the divine attributes most often connected with it are Yahweh's glory and holiness. A divine imperative linked to the ark is 'arise/rise up'. Some passages mention its use in contexts of battle. Finally, the cherubim-ark is commonly related to Yahweh's very presence, to such an extent that the phrase 'before the LORD' means before the cherubim-ark.[3]

The cherubim-ark in the Psalms

Explicit mention of the ark

Psalm 132

The Psalter's only explicit mention of the ark refers to it as 'the ark of your might' (or 'strength', *ʿōz*, v. 8), probably because of its associations with Yahweh war. The phrasing 'you and the ark of your might' makes clear that Yahweh is not to be identified with this cultic object. The parallelism with the preceding verse suggests that the ark symbolizes Yahweh's 'footstool'. This was the interpretation of the chronicler (1 Chr. 28:2; 2 Chr. 6:41). The imperative 'rise up' (*qwm*), addressed to Yahweh, and the mention of 'your resting place' echo 'the song of the ark' in Num. 10:35–36. The appropriate response to this symbol of divine presence is to 'worship' (*hištaḥăwah*, lit. 'bow down'). Yahweh himself announces that Zion will be his 'resting place', where he will 'reside' (or 'sit' enthroned, *yšb*). This psalm, while probably post-exilic in its final form, cites pre-exilic tradition, reflecting the events narrated in 2 Sam. 6 – 7, where David brings the ark into Jerusalem and is then promised a dynasty by Yahweh.[4] Verses 6–8 appear to re-enact ritually David's procession with the ark from Kiriath Jearim (2 Sam. 6:21 – 7:2) to its final 'resting place' in Zion (Ps. 132:13–14).

The ark as Yahweh's 'strength'

Psalm 78

In this historical psalm the claim that Yahweh 'delivered his power [or strength, *ʿōz*] to captivity, his glory [or 'splendour', *tip'eret*] to

---

3. See Fowler, 'Meaning', pp. 384–390.

4. Broyles, *Psalms*, p. 471.

the hand of the foe' (v. 61) is theologically problematic until we recognize that this verse refers to the events recounted in 1 Sam. 4, when the Philistines took the ark in battle. This allusion shows how closely the ark came to symbolize Yahweh's strength, so much so that explicit use of the term 'ark' was unnecessary. This divine attribute was probably singled out because of the ark's use in the context of warfare. The term used in parallel, 'his splendour', brings to light another characteristic closely associated with the ark, this one pointing to a royal attribute. This reference to the ark is simply a historical one – it does not point to a ritual enactment accompanying the psalm's performance.

Psalm 105

The opening imperative, 'Seek the Lord and his strength [ʿōz]; seek his presence [pānîm, lit. 'face'] continually' (v. 4), could point to more than simply a divine attribute. The reference to Yahweh's strength may indicate that the symbol of the ark was visible to the congregation. It is otherwise difficult to account for the inclusion of this psalm in the chronicler's account of David's bringing the ark into Jerusalem (1 Chr. 16:8–22 // Ps. 105:1–15), apart from this allusion to the ark.

Psalm 96

In this psalm of Yahweh's kingship the ascription of praise, 'Honour and majesty are before him; strength [ʿōz] and beauty [tipʾeret] are in his sanctuary' (v. 6), uses terms that we have just seen are closely associated with the ark. The localizing of these attributes to 'his sanctuary' also points to this physical symbol.[5] Since both 'strength' and 'beauty' identify the ark, we should read this phrase as a hendiadys (i.e. 'beautiful strength'). Parallel to 'strength and beauty' are the terms 'honour and majesty', which are thus further royal attributes associated with the ark. The symbolism of sacred space and ritual is further evidenced in vv. 7–9 immediately following, where the nations are to acknowledge by

---

5. The claim that the ark is 'in his sanctuary' need not indicate that it was hidden from view in the holy of holies. Cf. Ps. 68:24.

confession and ritual the royal attributes of 'glory' and 'strength' symbolized at the temple. As seen above, the appropriate response to the symbol of the ark is to 'worship' or 'bow down' (*hištaḥăwah*, v. 9). Other psalms celebrating Yahweh's kingship point to a procession whereby the ark 'ascended' into the sanctuary (Pss. 47; 68; 97, on which see below). This psalm may indicate the climax of that ritual with the announcement that 'strength and beauty are [i.e. have now arrived] in his sanctuary'.

Explicit mention of the cherubim

Psalm 99

The parallelism of the opening verse suggests that the acclamation 'the LORD is king' is reinforced by the physical symbol of the cherubim throne – 'he sits enthroned upon the cherubim'. The subsequent imperative, 'worship [or 'bow down'] at his footstool' (v. 5b), is virtually identical to the directive we saw in Ps. 132:7, where the congregation prostrates itself before the ark. Thus, in the same psalm we hear reference to both the cherubim-throne and the ark-footstool. Corresponding to the congregation's prostration before the ark is their exaltation of Yahweh: 'Extol [or 'exalt', *rwm*, polel] the LORD our God; worship at his footstool. Holy is he!' (v. 5a). This imperative directs the worshippers to enact ritually what is already considered a reality, as claimed earlier: 'The LORD . . . is exalted [*rwm*] over all the peoples' (v. 2). This state of exaltation of the one 'enthroned upon the cherubim' is probably the result of Yahweh's 'ascent' (*ʿlh*), as symbolized by the ark's ascent celebrated in two other psalms of Yahweh's kingship to be discussed below. The mention of Samuel along with Moses and Aaron as those to whom Yahweh spoke 'in the pillar of cloud' (vv. 6–7) might seem problematic until we recognize that elsewhere the Bible locates the cloud at the ark (Num. 10:33–35; Lev. 16:2; 1 Kgs 8:6–12). Of course, Samuel was raised at the Shiloh sanctuary, 'where the ark of God was' (1 Sam. 3:3).

Psalm 80

Among the opening petitions, Yahweh, who is 'enthroned upon the cherubim', is stirred to exercise his warrior 'strength' (here

gĕbûrâ, not ʿōz) as in the tribal days. This appeal is reminiscent of
the ark's function in leading the tribes in the wilderness and scattering the enemies, as commemorated in 'the song of the ark'
(Num. 10:33–36). The name of God repeated in the psalm's
refrain, '(Yahweh) God of hosts' (vv. 3–4, 7, 19, also v. 14), was the
divine title to be invoked over the ark, according to 1 Sam. 4:4 and
2 Sam. 6:2. Also contained in this refrain is the petition 'let your
face shine', which echoes the Aaronic benediction, another ancient
tradition found in Numbers (6:25). Other traditions concerning
the exodus, wilderness and conquest period are central to this
psalm's appeal (vv. 8–11). The divine titles (the one 'enthroned on
the cherubim' and 'Yahweh of hosts') and petitions associated
with them ('see', 'give ear' and 'save') are very similar to those
found in Hezekiah's prayer when he 'went up to the house of
the LORD' and spread Sennacherib's threatening letter 'before the
LORD' (Isa. 37:14–19 // 2 Kgs 19:14–19). Both texts imply these
prayers were recited directly before, or at least in close proximity
to, Yahweh's presence symbolized at the cherubim-ark.

The song of the ark

Psalm 68
The unity and development of Ps. 68 cannot be discerned on literary or theological grounds alone. But once we recognize the
allusions to the cherubim-ark, its integrity and sequence begin to
make sense in light of a ritual procession. The psalm not only
makes explicit reference to a procession (hălîkâ, 'Your solemn processions are seen, O God, the processions of my God, my King,
into the sanctuary', v. 24), it is described as visibly present (vv.
25–27). The allusions to the ark are several and throughout the
psalm. First, the procession commences with 'the song of the ark'
(with slight variation) as recorded in Num. 10:35. Second, a historical recital begins and ends with allusions to the ark. The opening
confession, 'O God, when you went out before your people, when
you marched through the wilderness' (v. 7), calls to mind God's
leading his people by means of the symbol of the ark. The closing
confession, 'You ascended [ʿlh] the high mount, leading captives in
your train and receiving gifts from people . . .' (v. 18), was probably

signified by the ark's ascent into the sanctuary, as will be confirmed by Ps. 47 below.[6] Third, Yahweh is celebrated as 'him who rides upon the clouds' (v. 4),[7] and as the 'rider in the heavens/skies' (v. 33). According to the thunderstorm theophany in Ps. 18, Yahweh 'rode' in the skies 'on a cherub' (vv. 9–10). As the earthly temple symbolized its counterpart in the heavens, so the cherubim above the ark symbolized the cherub figure of the skies. A fourth allusion appears in the closing section of the psalm, which repeatedly appeals to and celebrates God's 'strength/might/power' (various NRSV translations for $\'\bar{o}z$ in vv. 28, 33, 34 twice, 35) in close connection with the title 'rider in the heavens'. As noted above, this is the divine attribute most closely associated with the ark. Thus the symbolism of the cherubim-ark is not only the thread that ties the psalm together as a literary unit. It is also the thread that unites the psalm's various theological portrayals: Yahweh as the leader of the wilderness march (v. 7), the warrior who takes captives (v. 18), the rider of the clouds/skies (vv. 4, 33) and Israel's 'king' (v. 24). Each of these roles is represented by the versatile symbol of the cherubim-ark.

Yahweh's 'throne' and 'ascent'

Psalm 47
The claim that 'God sits [*yšb*] on his holy throne' (v. 8) may have been more than an imaginative metaphor for the congregation; it may have been visually symbolized by the cherubim-throne. It is similar to the claim that 'he sits enthroned [*yšb*] upon the cherubim' (99:1), and both expressions are paralleled by the familiar acclamation, 'God/the LORD is king' (*mālak*). Verse 5 refers to

---

6. When David and Solomon have the ark transported into Jerusalem and the temple respectively, they 'bring it up' (*'lh*, 2 Sam. 6:2, 12, 15; 1 Kgs 8:1, 4).

7. The later comparable expression, 'rider in the heavens' (v. 33), implies that we should understand *rōkēb bā'ărābôt* in a way analogous to Baal's title, 'rider on the clouds' (*rkb 'rpt*, *CTA* 2.IV.8; 19.i.43–44). Ugaritic and Hebrew *p* and *b* are sometimes interchanged.

God's ascent as a completed action: 'God has gone up [*ālâ*] with a *shout*, the LORD with *the sound of a trumpet*' (emphasis mine). The verb implies that God's presence is conceived as localized to particular space or symbol. Since the opening verse commands, 'Clap your hands, all you peoples; *shout* to God with loud songs of joy' (emphasis mine), v. 5 appears to report that the ritual enactment initiated in v. 1 has been performed. When 'David and all the house of Israel brought up [*ʿlh*] the ark of the LORD' into Jerusalem, they did so 'with *shouting*, and with *the sound of the trumpet*' (2 Sam. 6:15, emphasis mine, cf. vv. 2, 12). As noted above, Ps. 68 also refers to God's ascent, and both texts do so in connection with God's subjugation of opponents (47:3–5; 68:18). The verse closing Ps. 47 also connects God's ascent with his possession of the earthly powers he has vanquished: 'The princes of the peoples gather as the people of the God of Abraham. For the shields of the earth belong to God; he is highly exalted' (lit. 'ascended', *naʿālâ*, v. 9). This constellation of connections implies that God's ascent was symbolized by a victory procession of the cherubim-ark into the inner sanctuary.

Psalm 97

Like Ps. 47, this psalm declares that Yahweh/God 'is king' (*mālak*, v. 1), that he is 'exalted' (lit. 'ascended', *naʿālêtā*, v. 9), and refers to his 'throne' (v. 2). This psalm may thus belong to the same complex of psalms sung during the processional ascent of the cherubim-ark. But this time the throne itself is described: 'righteousness and justice [*mišpāṭ*] are the foundation of his throne' (v. 2). Since the twin cherubim form the throne itself, 'righteousness' and 'justice' appear to have been personified in the cherubim figures. A description of Yahweh's throne amidst a description of a thunderstorm theophany might seem puzzling unless we take our lead from Ps. 68, where the cherubim above the ark symbolize the cherub figure that Yahweh rides in the skies. It is these two attributes of righteousness and justice that are later revealed from the heavens to the earth. 'The heavens proclaim his righteousness', with the result that 'all the peoples behold his glory' (v. 6), another divine attribute associated with the cherubim-ark. And so Zion rejoices because of Yahweh's 'judgments' (*mišpāṭ*, v. 8). There is another case where the earthly temple corresponds to and symbolizes Yahweh's dwelling in the heavens/skies. Parallel to the description of this 'throne' under Yahweh is mention of 'clouds and thick darkness' (*'ānān wa'ărāpel*) that 'are all around him' (v. 2). Both these very elements – also described as 'the glory of the LORD' – had filled Solomon's temple after the ark's instalment (1 Kgs 8:10–13). Finally we should note that once again the imperative 'bow down' (*hištaḥăwah*, v. 7; cf. 96:9; 99:5; 132:7) appears in connection with the cherubim-ark, but here it is addressed to the 'gods'.

Psalm 89

While Ps. 89 in its final form laments the demise of the Davidic covenant (vv. 38–51), vv. 1–37 probably formed an originally independent unit celebrating Yahweh's kingship and the establishment of David's kingship as part of a regularly observed festival.[8] Verses 13–17 contain a concentration of terms associated with cherubim-ark. The expression 'righteousness and justice are the foundation of your throne' is identical to that found in 97:2. The next verse refers to 'the festal shout' (*terû'â*) during a procession (*hlk*, cf. Josh. 6:8, 9, 13; Ps. 68:24) 'in the light of your countenance' (lit. 'face'). In vv. 13 and 17 reference is also made to Yahweh's might/strength (*gĕbûrâ* and *'ōz*), exaltation (*rwm*) and glory/splendour (*tip'eret*). Thus 89:1–37 in its original usage should probably be seen as another psalm connected with (or at least referring to) the ritual procession of the cherubim-ark.[9]

---

8. See Broyles, *Psalms*, pp. 355–358.

9. Parallel to the expression 'righteousness and justice are the foundation of your throne' is 'steadfast love and faithfulness go before you' (or 'approach your face'; see under *qdm* in *HALOT*). If the twin cherubim forming the throne symbolize the former pair of attributes, one wonders if the latter pair had also been symbolized in the procession. Elsewhere in the Psalms 'steadfast love and faithfulness' appear to be personified as guardians or emissaries sent by Yahweh (40:11; 57:3; 61:7; 85:10; cf. 43:3). It may not be mere coincidence that Ezekiel's vision of Yahweh's cherubim-throne counts four cherubim (Ezek. 1:5; 10:9).

Psalm 24

The presence of the ark in Ps. 24 is not self-evident, but several features indicate that its use is presupposed. First, in vv. 7–10 gates are commanded to open 'that the King of glory may come in'. The depiction of Yahweh passing through gates indicates that his presence is localized in some form and may be transported past some point in space. This indicates a physical symbol. Second, the title 'King of glory' points both to the royal role depicted by the cherubim-throne and the ark-footstool and to the divine quality of 'glory' associated with the ark elsewhere. Third, the reply to the gatekeepers' question, 'Who is this King of glory?' is simply 'the LORD of hosts', which was the special name invoked over the ark (1 Sam. 4:4; 2 Sam. 6:2). Fourth, Yahweh is described as 'strong' (*'izzûz*), which is an attribute embodied by the ark, and 'mighty in battle' (lit. 'a warrior of war', v. 8). In Israel's early history the ark played a leading role in Yahweh war (esp. Num. 10:35; Josh. 6:4–13). Fifth, the worshippers who 'ascend [*'lh*] the hill of the LORD' (v. 3) must do so following the entry of 'the King of glory' through the gates. This may reflect the ark's 'ascent' through the gates of Jerusalem or the temple (note the use of *'lh* in Pss. 47:5, 9; 68:18; 97:9; 2 Sam. 6:2, 12, 15; 1 Kgs 8:1, 4). Ps. 24 may have been sung regularly to commemorate David's bringing the ark into Jerusalem. Finally, 'seeking the face of God' has special connections to the ark in certain passages (e.g. 105:4).

'Refuge' under Yahweh's 'wings'

Psalm 63

It is possible to read the phrase 'in the shadow of your wings I sing for joy' (v. 7b) as simply an imaginative metaphor for Yahweh's protection. But the earlier claim, 'so I have looked upon you in the sanctuary, beholding your power [*'ōz*] and glory' (v. 2), locates the speaker at the temple. To interpret this remarkable claim of seeing God appropriately we must remember our context is not that of prophets and their visions but that of liturgies and temple symbolism. In poetic parallelism the second colon often specifies the first. In the parallel phrase the objects of 'beholding' are two terms that are clearly associated with and sometimes even denote the cherubim-ark (cf. 78:61). Thus, it is possible that this psalm was to be recited in direct vision of the cherubim-ark. Another possibility is to understand the claim of v. 2, where the Hebrew perfect verb is used, as a reference to a past experience during a festival procession of the cherubim-ark, and the claim of v. 7b, where the Hebrew imperfect verb is used, as a present action. (The verb tenses in the NRSV are consistent with this reading, though we should be cautious of pressing verbal aspect in Hebrew poetry too far.)

Psalm 36

In the verse following the claim that 'all people may take refuge in the shadow of your wings' (v. 7), an allusion is made to the temple and its ritual sacrifices. 'They feast on the abundance of your house' (v. 8) is not merely a metaphor for a rich banquet but points to the symbolism of the 'thanksgiving' or 'fellowship offerings', portions of which were to be eaten by the worshippers themselves (Lev. 3; 7:11–36). In the verses immediately preceding and following there appear key terms also found in the description of the ark's procession in Ps. 89. Verses 5–6 mention the same two word pairs that served as the foundation of Yahweh's throne ('righteousness' and 'judgments/justice', 89:14) and as his escorts ('steadfast love' and 'faithfulness', 89:14). Both psalms also celebrate Yahweh's 'light' (36:9; 89:15), which may have had its symbolic counterpart in the ritual worship. In Ps. 36 the cosmic dimensions of these attributes are emphasized, especially with reference to the heavens. The connection between the heavens and Yahweh's 'house' becomes apparent when we recall that the cherubim figures symbolized Yahweh as 'rider in the heavens' (68:33–34).

Psalm 61

In this psalm of pilgrimage[10] the wish that the speaker may 'find refuge under the shelter of your wings' is paralleled by the wish that he may 'abide in your tent for ever' (v. 4). This juxtaposition

---

10. See Broyles, *Psalms*, pp. 255–256.

locates Yahweh's 'wings' at the sanctuary. In addition, the word pair 'steadfast love and faithfulness' is personified as the king's guardians (v. 7).

Psalm 57

This prayer psalm of the individual appears to have several internal inconsistencies. How do we explain the transition from lament motifs in the first half (vv. 1–4) to hymnic motifs in the second (vv. 5–11)? How do we explain that the concerns of an individual seeking protection become overshadowed by concerns for God's international (vv. 9–10) and cosmic manifestation (vv. 5, 11)? And how do we explain the spatial discrepancy that the speaker takes refuge 'in the shadow of your wings' (v. 1), and yet God 'will send from heaven and save me' (v. 3)? Could these inconsistencies be explained by an editorial splicing together of originally separate texts? This possibility gains some validity after we observe that vv. 7–11 are virtually identical to 108:1–5, a psalm which is itself composite (108:6–13 is identical to 60:5–12).

On the other hand, the cherubim-ark may help explain the broadening of horizons from the individual to the international and cosmic spheres, and thus support the psalm's integrity. An allusion may be found in the expression 'in the shadow of your wings I will take refuge' (v. 1). Especially by means of this symbol, Israel perceived a unity between God's earthly and heavenly temples (as noted e.g. in Ps. 68; see above). Hence, the speaker may take refuge 'in the shadow of your wings' at the temple, and simultaneously God 'will send from heaven and save me' (cf. Ps. 11). This symbol also helps us to make sense of the petition repeated in vv. 5 and 11. As the cherubim-ark 'ascended' into the temple (see on Pss. 47; 68), so God was envisaged as ascending above the heavens (cf. 18:10). Also associated with the cherubim-throne was Yahweh's royal 'glory', which was seen to fill the earth (cf. Isa. 6:1–3). Moreover, the earthly audience for this 'ascent' was not merely the residents of Jerusalem but also the nations (cf. 47:8–9; 99:1–2) – hence the international audience for the speaker's praises (v. 9). Another possible connection to the cherubim-ark may be found in the word pair 'love and faithfulness'. In v. 3 they are dispatched as guardians from heaven. And v. 10 emphasizes the cosmic setting of these attributes and is thus very similar in wording to 36:5, noted above.[11]

Concluding remarks

If the cherubim-ark was so prominent in Israel's pre-exilic festival worship, then why is this not more self-evident from the psalms themselves? The book of Psalms in its final form is a post-exilic collection, and the ark, of course, vanished from the time of the Babylonian destruction of Jerusalem in 587 BCE. Moreover, several lines of evidence indicate that the cherubim-ark ceased to be used in ritual performance from the time of Josiah's reform. First, this interpretation is most consistent with a straightforward reading of 2 Chr. 35:3, where Josiah instructs the Levites to install the ark in Solomon's temple and, instead of carrying it about, to serve Yahweh. Second, the claim that the poles used to carry the ark could be 'seen from the holy place in front of the inner sanctuary . . . to this day' (1 Kgs 8:8) implies that the ark did not move from this inner sanctum during the writer's lifetime. Since 1 and 2 Kings have clearly been written from the perspective of Deuteronomy, a form of which was 'the book of the law' discovered in Josiah's reform (2 Kgs 22:8, 11; cf. 23:24), the writer and 'this day' were probably contemporary to Josiah. Third, in the Deuteronomistic History the sole function stated for the ark is to house the tablets of the covenant (Deut. 10:1–9; 1 Kgs 8:9, 21). No ritual function is evident. Josiah's reasons for terminating the use of the ark in ritual processions and locking it up in the inner sanctuary probably stem from the avoidance of anything smacking of divination or magic, which is an inclination evident in his reform and in the book of Deuteronomy.

With the termination of the ritual processions of the cherubim-ark and its permanent installation in the holy of holies, its function

---

11. Another possible allusion to the cherubim-ark may be found in Ps. 17, a prayer of the individual. After the request 'hide me in the shadow of your wings' (v. 8), there follows the imperative familiar from the song of the ark in Num. 10:35, 'rise up' (v. 13).

as the symbolic throne and footstool of the divine King faded into the background, and its function as the repository of the two tablets of the Ten Words emerged in the foreground. It became 'the ark of the covenant' (as in the Deuteronomistic History) and 'the ark of the testimony' (as in the priestly strands of the Pentateuch). As a result, the depiction of God also changed: from the dynamic 'Rider on the Clouds' and cosmic King 'enthroned on the cherubim' to the more static notion of the God of covenant or legal treaty. However, the prophet Jeremiah, a contemporary of Josiah's reform, appears to have held these two notions in tension (14:21–22). In poetic parallelism Jeremiah appeals to Yahweh's 'name',[12] 'the throne of your glory' (lit.) and his 'covenant' – three terms which together allude to the cherubim-ark. In the very next verse he acknowledges that it is Yahweh alone, as God of the skies, who can 'bring rain' and 'give showers'.

In our efforts to retain 'the whole counsel of God' (Acts 20:27, lit.), as the apostle Paul puts it, we must recognize that older traditions, metaphors and symbols in the Bible do not thereby become obsolete. This essay has, in part, been an attempt to recover from the final form of the Scriptures an earlier phase of God's revelation, one that still retains validity and indeed offers an important perspective of our dynamic God.

There is another theological implication that follows from the analysis above, and it relates to theological method. Instead of constructing theology on the basis of ideas, concepts and themes, it becomes apparent that the psalms – as liturgies – often presented their theology by means of visual symbols, rituals and their associated traditions. Rather than merely describing Yahweh in terms of attributes, the psalms sometimes dramatize him in symbol and ritual as the warring storm-god in his cherubim-chariot and as the king on his cherubim-throne.

---

12. The name 'Yahweh of hosts' is more frequent in Jeremiah (81 times) than elsewhere in the Old Testament (281 times altogether). This, of course, was the name to be invoked over the ark.

© Craig C. Broyles, 2005.

C. THE PSALMS AND INTERPRETATION ISSUES

8. THE TEACHING OF THE PSALMS

David G. Firth

Psalm studies and the teaching of the psalms

By the middle of the twentieth century, it might almost have seemed incongruous to speak of the teaching of the psalms. The form-critical method that was so effectively pioneered in Gunkel's *Introduction*, even though challenged and refined in various ways by scholars such as Mowinckel,[1] had become the dominant approach to the study of the Psalter. Given that an overriding aim of this method was to place the various psalms in the appropriate *Sitz im Leben*, and that the particular emphasis of most of the psalms as prayers addressed to God was highlighted, it seemed that there was little to be said about the teaching of the psalms. Moreover, if human words addressed to God were seen in their appropriate role, then those engaged in the teaching of the psalms in the context of worship were left with little that they

---

1. See especially Mowinckel, *Psalms*, vol. 1, pp. 23–41, for his own summary.

could use. Indeed, Gowan argues that attention to the original function of the psalms as prayers means that, although worshippers might wish to use them in prayer, they should not normally be the texts chosen for preaching and teaching.[2] Where Dietrich Bonhoeffer had pondered the question of how it was that human words to God became God's word to us in the psalms,[3] form criticism's answer was that this change did not happen. The psalms were always human words to God, and as such their teaching function was limited to the wisdom psalms, and the more important questions were really to do with the access that they gave to the cult.[4]

A significant change in the ways in which the psalms have been interpreted came with the work of Brevard Childs.[5] Although many aspects of his programme have not been followed through, the study of the Psalter is one point where his canonical approach has been of abiding significance. Childs recognized the importance of the form-critical method, and did not wish to lose its essential insights, but he was also keen to recover the Psalter's function as scripture, and hence to stress its instructional role. Consistent with the approach he had developed, Childs sought to examine the canonical shape of the book, and to uncover its significance for the way in which psalms continued to function.[6] Although he recognized a degree of redactional complexity across the Psalter as a whole, he still sought to demonstrate that there was an intentional shape to the book. This shape was particularly evident in the role assigned to Ps. 1 as the introduction to

---

2. Gowan, *Reclaiming*, pp. 145–146.

3. Cf. Childs, *Introduction*, p. 513; Miller, 'Dietrich Bonhoeffer'.

4. E.g. Johnson, *Sacral Kingship*, examines the so-called 'royal' and 'enthronement' psalms purely in terms of the role played by the king in the ancient Israelite cult. But note the very different analysis of much the same material offered by Starbuck, *Court Oracles*.

5. Childs, *Introduction*, pp. 504–525. Note, however, the seldom recognized contribution of Scott, *Psalms*, pp. 71–88, which raises some of the questions with which Childs would wrestle.

6. Childs, *Introduction*, p. 513.

the book of Psalms. We cannot review the whole of Childs's programme here, but his attempt to recover a theological emphasis in
which the psalms continued to speak to the worshipping community has been of continuing significance. This is especially seen in
the work of his student Gerald Wilson on the final shape of the
Psalter, and the positions taken by various scholars in the dialogue
generated by Wilson's work.[7] Wilson's proposals have been largely
adopted by McCann as a central element in recovering the
instructional role of the Psalter,[8] while Whybray has forcefully
rejected the idea of an ordered arrangement in the book of
Psalms as a whole. However, Whybray does not exclude the possibility that the final form of the Psalter was used for instructional
purposes.[9] What is clear is that the instructional role of the
psalms has come to the forefront of recent study, though the
exact means by which they instruct has not been resolved.
Nevertheless, certain broad principles can be noted, principles
that can also assist those who are themselves called to teach the
psalms, and to these we now turn.

Levels of teaching

The heart of the debate between Whybray and Wilson revolves
around the question of whether or not one can speak of an intentional arrangement of the individual psalms so that they contribute
to the instruction offered by the Psalms as a book. Although their
answers to this question are seemingly opposite, they share a
degree of common ground in that both accept the possibility that
there was an editorial process involved in the selection of the

---

7. Wilson, *Editing*. For a brief overview of his position, see ch. 12 in this
   volume; also 'Shape', pp. 129–142. See also his *Psalms*.
8. McCann, 'Psalms as Instruction', pp. 117–128. This is more fully worked
   out in his *Theological*, pp. 25–50. See also his 'Psalms'.
9. Whybray, *Reading*, p. 119. Later, pp. 121–122, he allows the possibility of a
   more limited programme, such as that offered by Brueggemann,
   'Bounded', pp. 63–92, but still sees problems in the approach.

various psalms, and that this basic level of editorial engagement suggests at least some degree of didactic intention in the book. Where they differ is that Whybray is largely sceptical of the ability of exegesis to recover this process, particularly in terms of reading the Psalter as a structurally intentional book, whilst Wilson's proposals obviously assume that this is possible. To avoid unnecessary complications, this paper will seek to demonstrate that even a minimalist approach, which does not detect overarching structural themes, can still recognize the importance of understanding the instructional function of the Psalms as a book. This is because the very process of canonical collection means that the 150 psalms now gathered together are seen as playing a special role within the life of Israel. Their place within the canon also means that they have a further role beyond the issues studied by the form-critical approach. That is, their very status as scripture means that they now have a teaching role. Even if it is not possible to recover the editorial process in full, it can still be argued that the psalms are indeed intended to teach.

This means that it becomes necessary to investigate the didactic levels at which the various psalms now function. Each psalm has a primary teaching role of its own, though it is also possible to investigate the ways in which this didactic function might contribute to the larger message of the Psalms. Such a function is not necessarily ascertained through a structured reading strategy (though it may be), but can be achieved by recognizing elements of theological consistency across a range of issues. That is to say, the editorial process may have ensured that only psalms that operated within a given set of theological assumptions remained within the collection, whilst those variations that remain are themselves an intentional element within the instruction of the book. This second-level instructional function within the book as a whole would not be in contradiction to the primary teaching of the individual psalm, but it can provide a nuanced interpretation of it. The instruction of any given psalm is thus shaped by its place within the larger book. We can therefore explore the teaching of the Psalter at the level of each psalm individually, but we can also do so at the level of the Psalms as a whole. It is possible that some psalms may have had a wider range of functions in the course of the editing of the Psalter.[10] But since the two editorial points that we can recognize with certainty are the creation of a psalm as an individual text and the book of Psalms as a whole, it seems more appropriate to remain with them as the points within which the investigation can be controlled. Therefore we now consider the didactic function of individual psalms, before considering the didactic function of the book as a whole.

The teaching of individual psalms

Although individual psalms have a teaching function because of their place within the canonical text, we should not imagine that all will operate in the same way. It is not possible to survey all of the instructional methods employed by various psalms, but it is important to note at the outset that every psalm is at least a model of prayer or praise in practice, which functions to teach those gathered in worship. That is to say, through the compilation of the canon every psalm is in some sense mimetic, in that it has an underlying truth or insight that it seeks to communicate. At the most basic level, the majority of psalms offer instruction on how to pray, simply because they are examples of prayer in action. So we need to extend Miller's insight that how one prays and what one prays indicates what one believes about prayer.[11] The editors of the Psalter have already done this through the compilation process, so that their underlying beliefs about the nature of prayer and praise are now taught through the modelling that is offered by each psalm individually. It is possible that some psalms, such as those traditionally known as 'wisdom psalms', were intentionally composed with a specific instructional purpose. Others, such as

10. It may be possible to trace the editorial approach of a given book within the Psalms, such as in Zenger, 'Composition', pp. 77–102, and Miller, 'End', pp. 103–110. Smaller collections have also been analysed, e.g. Zenger, 'alles Fleisch', pp. 1–27. The function of Ps. 73 as an individual psalm within the canon is examined by Brueggemann and Miller, 'Psalm 73', pp. 45–56.

11. Miller, *They Cried*, p. 1.

the complaints, most likely were not. However, the fact that it will be possible to trace a clear didactic intent across a range of form-critical genres might suggest that 'wisdom psalm' is not a heuristically helpful category. It will also become clear that the didactic function of a given psalm will not depend upon its traditional form-critical categorization.

If we survey only those psalms which seem to have had a didactic intent in their composition, rather than those which have inherited it through their canonical status, then we can still identify three key teaching strategies that are employed – testimony, admonition and observation. Although we will focus on psalms that use only one of these methods, other psalms (e.g. Ps. 37) combine several, with the learning goal shaped by the methods employed. What should be stressed is that the choice of a dominant teaching strategy will itself affect the means by which a learning outcome is reached, since the adoption of the different strategies leads the reader to respond in different ways.[12] What is also clear is that each method represents an experience-based learning strategy – each invokes experience, whether that of the speaker or the learner, as a basis for teaching. This experience-centred model of teaching is also important in that it highlights the fact that all three methods are directed towards the shaping of character among those who read and pray these psalms.[13]

Testimony

An important, but frequently overlooked means by which a given psalm's teaching function can be developed is through testimony.

---

12. In speech-act terms, we can say that each of these psalms is a locution, but the teaching method adopted represents a different illocutionary force, and that the perlocution will thus vary. On the application of speech-act theory to biblical interpretation generally, see Briggs, *Words*. Speech-act theory, with its emphasis on illocutionary force and perlocutions, is a valuable aid to understanding the teaching intent of individual psalms. On psalms and speech-acts see Irsigler, 'Psalm-Rede'.

13. Estes, *Hear*, p. 14, suggests that 'formation' is the key educational goal in Prov. 1 – 9. Something similar can be suggested for these psalms.

We can highlight the instructional intent of testimony by defining it as the reciting of past experience, either that of an individual or group, through first-person verbs, to provide the community with a new insight into a situation. That is to say, the very nature of testimony is that it is directed towards others so that they may respond to it, and the new insight towards which it works is its didactic goal. Testimony does not guarantee an answer to a specific problem for those who hear it, but as a strongly self-involved medium it seeks to challenge those encountering it to work towards the same insight in their experience. Such an approach seems to have been especially appropriate for what we might describe as counter-faith experiences, points where something other than the blessing of the righteous is experienced. Testimonies provide a mechanism of instruction in these circumstances that suggest that the resolution of seemingly intractable problems is possible. Some samples of this will demonstrate the differing ways in which this is achieved.[14]

Ps. 73 represents a clear example of testimony, and in particular demonstrates the ability of testimony to address counter-faith experiences. Here the psalmist speaks to the community at a period when the issue of the prosperity of the wicked had been so powerfully negative that orthodox faith in God seems to be failing (73:1–11). Thus, an assertion of orthodox faith (73:1) becomes the foundation for describing an apparently counter-faith experience, as the psalmist explains that the wicked were the ones who prospered while denying that God had any interest in what they were doing (73:11). In the face of overwhelming personal anguish the psalmist had remained silent, knowing that to have spoken would have been negative for the community as a whole (73:12–15). The goal of this testimony lies in its resolution in 73:16–28, where an experience of worship is first described. After this, the focus of the psalm moves more clearly from the

---

14. A fuller treatment of this theme can be found in Firth, 'Psalms', pp. 440–454; 'Testimony', pp. 12–22. Other psalms which employ this method include 18; 32; 34; 40; 116; 124; 138. Cf. Gous, 'Reason', pp. 455–467.

community to God,[15] as the psalmist focuses on the hope that God provides. Nevertheless, the community continues to overhear, so that the language of prayer into which the psalm moves is itself a part of the testimony. A direct answer to the problem of the prosperity of the wicked is not given, perhaps because to do so would simply create a new oppression when this answer was found to have limits too. But those who now encounter this testimony through the book of Psalms are continually reminded of the fact that the experience of worship is the point at which resolution of the problem is found, even if the answer is not capable of exact articulation. Those who encounter this testimony are thus challenged to work through towards their own resolution of the problem that it opens up.

Ps. 30 represents a very different kind of testimony from Ps. 73. Here, the psalmist speaks as one who has been delivered from a difficult situation, presumably a life-threatening illness (30:3), which might be thought to be inconsistent with the blessing of the righteous. However, in common with most thanksgiving psalms, the exact context is not well defined, and the background situation could be understood differently. However, it is clearly not an intellectual challenge, as was the case in Ps. 73. Where this psalm is like Ps. 73 is that it once again has two sets of listeners in view, so that vv. 1–3 (the opening assertion of the reason for praise) and vv. 6–12 (the record of the previous complaint and its resolution) are addressed as a testimony of thanksgiving to Yahweh, whereas vv. 4–5 are addressed in the plural to the congregation. The psalm is thus a testimony directed towards Yahweh, which the worshipping congregation is meant not only to overhear but also to learn from so that they can join with the psalmist in singing praise to Yahweh. The instructional function of the psalm is not reduced to the announcement that Yahweh works on behalf of his saints, though it is a concrete example of that, because the testimony involves the congregation in other respects. An important element of the testimony is that it also reflects on the experience of the psalmist prior to deliverance. Here, the psalmist confesses to a period of hubris:

---

15. 73:15 is also addressed directly to God.

As for me, I said in my prosperity,
'I shall never be moved.' (30:6)

This language evokes the promise to the righteous found in Ps.
15:5, but the psalmist's testimony is that personal prosperity was
not the measure of righteousness before Yahweh. As such, the testimony functions not only to assure the community that Yahweh
acts on behalf of his saints, but also to ask the community to
reassess their own relationship with Yahweh. Thus, testimony not
only functions to reassure the community that Yahweh does
indeed act, it also probes its members as to the nature of their
relationship to him.

Admonition

A second form of instruction in specific psalms is admonition.
Given the frequency of this form in the wisdom literature, it is
perhaps surprising that it plays a relatively minor role in the
instructional model of individual psalms. In part, this derives
from the fact that admonition depends upon evidence being available towards which a psalm can point the reader and urge for an
appropriate response. These psalms are marked by a direct appeal
made in the second person, even in the case of self-admonition
(e.g. 103:1). Most commonly, admonition is an element found
within psalms that employ testimony or observation, but which
then make an appeal for a response based on the evidence provided. This is somewhat different from psalms which are almost
entirely invitation (e.g. Pss. 96; 100; 150), since these do not necessarily seek to provide a justification for their summons. Although
it goes too far to say that such psalms offer praise without
reason,[16] it is true to say that the content that lies behind their
invitation is provided more by the rest of the Psalter than by these
psalms on their own.

Admonition is a teaching form that is most appropriate where
the goal is the shaping of behaviour, and in particular when there
is some urgency that requires an immediate response. Although all

16. So Brueggemann, *Israel's Praise*, pp. 89–122.

three teaching methods ultimately seek behavioural and cognitive changes, it is the change itself rather than the information that is the dominant concern with admonition.[17]

Due to the comparative scarcity of this teaching strategy, we will consider Ps. 130 as our only example. Although the bulk of this psalm is an individual complaint, the whole of it builds towards the conclusion of the closing verse, in which the nation as a whole is summoned to wait for Yahweh. Indeed, there is a close structural relationship between the affirmation of Yahweh as one who forgives (vv. 3–4) and the closing admonition.[18] Moreover, the structure of the psalm as a whole gradually builds towards the summons to Israel. Moving from direct address to Yahweh in vv. 1–4, through to comments about why the psalmist waits for Yahweh in vv. 5–6, the focus gradually shifts towards the nation in anticipation of the final summons. The admonition thus transforms the initial plea into a form of testimony of prayer, and this is borne out by the fact that, although vv. 3–4 are addressed to Yahweh, they actually lay an instructional basis for what follows. Admonition, however, suggests that the psalmist does not believe that Israel currently acts in the way requested, which is why the climax in vv. 7–8 contains both the admonition proper and additional reasons why Israel should decide to express such hope. A range of instructional forms are thus applied to the specific task of changing the behaviour of the nation.

Observation
In testimony it is the resolution that provides the teaching goal of the psalm, whilst admonition seeks to introduce certain behavioural and attitudinal changes. But another important goal is the formation of character along certain lines, and it is here that observation becomes an important teaching strategy adopted by a number of psalms. This method is marked by third-person verbs which are essentially descriptive, though the very process of

---

17. Other psalms for which this is an important technique include 37; 49; 115; 136.

18. Prinsloo, 'Psalm 130', pp. 453–469.

description is part of the rhetoric of instruction. It involves a psalm pointing towards either certain types of behaviour and their outcomes or key theological concepts as a means of guiding towards appropriate behaviour. As a teaching method, it refrains from actually appealing for this behaviour. Rather, it describes certain realities and then leaves it to the reader to decide how to respond. These psalms remain predominantly descriptive rather than prescriptive. Observation as a teaching technique thus requires that there be at least a general trend of supporting experiential evidence, and that this evidence can be accessed by the readers. Once again, it is best to access this teaching method through some examples, where we will recognize that it also transcends the dominant form-critical categories.[19]

Any consideration of the teaching techniques of the psalms will inevitably consider Ps. 1.[20] Its description of the life of the righteous and wicked is a classic exposition of the 'two ways' theme, and thus draws on the classical wisdom literature. It is, of course, somewhat reductive to insist that there are only two ways and that they can be so simply separated, but from the perspective of the psalm a choice needs to be made to follow one of them, and the nature of the choice needs to be clearly indicated. The observational approach that is adopted here focuses alternately on the righteous (vv. 1–3) and the wicked (vv. 4–5), before bringing the two together in the climactic comparison in the closing verse. Nevertheless, the process adopted is purely descriptive, so that those who read the psalm might begin to make the same observations. To some extent, verse 3 could be said to be a deduction from the preceding observations rather than something intrinsically observable, but no appeal is made on the basis of this. Rather, the process of description is meant to entice a response, a possibility that gains force through the closing summary statement of Yahweh's engagement with the righteous and the certainty of the destruction of the wicked. Teaching is

---

19. Other psalms employing this method include 8; 14; 19; 24; 46; 65; 78; 84; 87; 91; 103; 105; 106; 107; 111; 112; 113; 121; 127; 128; 133; 147.

20. Lombaard, 'By Implication', pp. 506–514.

thus directed towards the formation of character that is centred on the torah, but only through pointing the reader to observable phenomena.

Although traditionally included with the enthronement psalms, Ps. 93 also makes use of the technique of observation, even though the observations themselves move into credal affirmations. The structure of the psalm is fairly simple, operating around a paired set of statements about Yahweh as king in vv. 1–2,[21] followed by two more paired statements about the waters, in which it is affirmed that Yahweh is mighty on high (vv. 3–4). The conclusion (v. 5), however, is somewhat surprising, in that the association of Yahweh's reign and authority over the chaos waters of creation is applied to his decrees and the appropriateness of holiness in the temple. As is common, the language moves between direct address to Yahweh and speech about Yahweh. In either case, the language is purely descriptive, and yet is still presented in a way that offers a form of intentional instruction to which the reader is indirectly called to respond. This is achieved through the use of a number of motifs that are common in Ancient Near Eastern mythology, notably the threatening sea and uncontrollable power of the floods, as well as the sky god. These concepts, however, are brought beneath the overarching concept of the reign of Yahweh. All threatening forces are thus shown to be subject to Yahweh's reign, so that the trustworthiness of his decrees and holiness of the temple are seen to be entirely appropriate. Nevertheless, this is not a conclusion that is presented directly. Rather, by presenting these as observable phenomena, albeit phenomena outside the realm of measurable experience, the psalm invites readers to respond by accepting the reign of Yahweh and thereby make its conclusion their own. Thus the approach seeks to shape the character of the reader through the recognition of what is described, but not through directive instruction.

---

21. The complex questions surrounding the translation of *yhwh mlk*, whether 'Yahweh has become king', 'Yahweh reigns' or 'Yahweh is king', can be set aside for our purposes.

The teaching of the book of Psalms

Although many psalms had an intentional teaching function at the level of composition, it is also true that all psalms now have a new status through their place within the canonical book. As a result, the immediate context for the interpretation of a given psalm is provided by the rest of the book, in much the same way as the context for a given saying within the book of Proverbs is provided by the remaining proverbs. Two clear strategies appear to be applied in the book at this canonical level: thematic modelling through the accumulation of psalms on a given topic, and the creation of an intratextual dialogue within the book.

Thematic modelling

Thematic modelling is a teaching strategy in which the editors of the Psalter present a selection of psalms that develop a theologically consistent attitude to a particular issue, even though these psalms did not necessarily have this teaching intent at the compositional level. Teaching under this model occurs through repeated exposure to patterns of prayer and behaviour, so that the instruction is inculcated indirectly through repetition. This is particularly useful with the complaint psalms, since their nature as petitions means that they tend not to have a clear teaching strategy of their own. However, by the accumulation of a number of prayers which present a similar attitude in related contexts, these psalms now take on a teaching function in that they model to the reader attitudes and responses that the editors of the Psalter deem appropriate. In the same way as students learn through the repeated demonstration of certain approaches, even when those approaches are not directly articulated, so also the repetition associated with these themes provides a form of instruction.

This teaching method implies that the editors had the right to exclude certain psalms because of the theological responses they demonstrated. Although this may have happened over an extended period, it still creates an overall theological consistency that can be demonstrated across the Psalter as a whole. For example, it is possible to note that a number of individual complaint psalms deal with the issue of the threat of violence and response to it.[22] We can break these down further into prayers of the accused (Pss. 7; 17; 109; 139), prayers for protection (Pss. 3; 27; 55; 56; 64; 143) and prayers of the sick (Pss. 38; 69). Given the nature of these psalms as prayers, it is not surprising that they do not set out to offer reasoned instruction as to how one should respond to the threat of violence, nor to the psychological distress that it causes. Moreover, it is still possible that these psalms individually raise other matters of instruction, as for example in the opening eighteen verses of Ps. 139 which emphasize the absolute certainty with which Yahweh knows the psalmist. So it is possible to have different didactic goals for a given psalm at the individual and canonical levels, though there must also be a correlation between them.

Returning to the theme of the response to violence, although each of these psalms represents a quite different *Sitz im Leben*, it is striking that they all model essentially the same response, one in which the right to retribution is surrendered to Yahweh. In addition, although a number of them move over into imprecation in which Yahweh is specifically asked to act with violence against the offender,[23] the request never exceeds either the *lex talionis* or the penalty that would have applied under the law of the unjust accusation (Deut. 19:15–21). Without providing any direct teaching on the subject, the consistent thematic modelling provided by the collection offers its own form of instruction at the level of the book as a whole. As canon, they therefore also provide a model for the way in which worship can continue to be constructed so as to deal with such issues.[24]

Intratextual dialogue
The Psalter as a whole also sets up a dialogue within itself such that the various psalms can provide both commentary on and

---

22. Cf. Firth, 'Responses', pp. 317–328; 'Context', pp. 86–96; *Complaint Psalms*, ch. 2–4.

23. Cf. Zenger, *God of Vengeance*, on the relevance of these psalms for contemporary belief.

24. Mays, *Lord Reigns*, p. 5.

specification of the application of other psalms. The way in which this operates can best be understood through a modification of Brueggemann's *orientation – disorientation – new orientation* scheme.[25] Although his concern was to link the psalms to human experience, such a strategy can also indicate the ways in which the intratextual dialogue can function. One weakness of Brueggemann's system is his exclusion of the so-called royal psalms, which means that he misses the eschatological dimension in the Psalter. Through this, the Psalms always retain a level of hope beyond any point of new orientation that is reached.[26]

Recognizing this limitation, we can note the teaching strategy it supports. For example, in examining the role of observation, the apparently over-simple worldview of Ps. 1 was noted. This is one which is untroubled precisely because it wants the reader to choose the path of the righteous. Taken on its own, this psalm might not seem to be true to actual experience since many righteous people have indeed suffered – one need look no further than Job to recognize this. But the book of Psalms knows that this orientation can be problematic when it becomes simplistic rather than simple, as becomes abundantly clear by the third psalm. Here, there are innumerable enemies and the threat of considerable violence. The orientation given by Ps. 1 has become disoriented within the Psalter itself. This functions, however, to refine the understanding of the blessing of the righteous, so that blessing cannot mean the avoidance of any form of suffering. In this way, the subsequent psalms begin the process of redefining the life of blessedness. Other texts, such as Ps. 18, insist that the threat of violence is not the end, and Yahweh does act on behalf of his people and deliver them from such threats. This then provides a context for both Pss. 1 and 3 – blessing is not the absence of struggle, but neither does the presence of struggle mean the failure of the observations of Ps. 1.

A new orientation is reached, an orientation that is consistent with experience, in which it is understood that the blessings

25. Brueggemann, *Message*, pp. 15–23.
26. Firth, 'Stages', p. 8.

promised by Ps. 1 are ultimate, though may not represent the experience of any individual at a given point. However, the fact that the royal psalms (including Ps. 18) were retained in the post-exilic setting when the Psalter was finally edited points to an eschatological edge that takes this dialogue further, looking with messianic hope beyond all forms of current experience. No new orientation is final, even those which seem to resolve earlier complaints, and there remains the hope of something more. In this way, the intratextual dialogue continues to form its own model of teaching within the Psalter, and may in fact represent one of the best reasons for reading through the Psalter in sequence.

Conclusion

Teaching therefore needs to be understood as a central concern both of individual psalms and of the Psalter as a whole. When we consider the different forms of teaching that individual psalms employ, we can see that many more psalms than those traditionally identified as 'wisdom' texts have a distinct teaching goal. All psalms now function to teach within the structure of the book as a whole, due to the process of canonization and the editorial work that lies behind it. Once this teaching strategy is appreciated, it becomes possible for those whose calling today is to teach the psalms to continue this process. They need to be attentive to the range of teaching strategies employed by individual psalms, as well as to the ways in which the Psalter as a whole offers instruction. Those who are creative enough to recognize these strategies can then utilize them in their own instruction, and even highlight those points where a given psalm has multiple functions in its individual and canonical roles.

© David G. Firth, 2005.

9. THE ETHICS OF THE PSALMS

Gordon J. Wenham

Introduction

I do not know what hymnbook you use at church, but I should like to quote you a few lines from ours. From Graham Kendrick:

> This is our God, the Servant King,
> he calls us now to follow him,
> to bring our lives as a daily offering
> of worship to the Servant King.
> *The Servant King* by Graham Kendrick
> Copyright © 1983 Thankyou Music*

Or Charles Wesley:

> O thou who camest from above
> the fire celestial to impart,
> kindle a flame of sacred love
> on the mean altar of my heart.

Or John Bunyan:

> He who would true valour see,
> let him come hither.

Or, even more militantly, George Duffield:

> Stand up, stand up for Jesus,
> ye soldiers of the cross!
> Lift high his royal banner,
> it must not suffer loss.
> From victory unto victory
> his army he shall lead
> till every foe is vanquished
> and Christ is Lord indeed.

These hymns are prayers set to music that God will work within us to make us what the hymn-writer thinks we ought to be like. They are implicitly teaching us what to believe and how to behave. When we sing them, we declare our commitment to these views and we encourage our fellow worshippers to do the same.

This is sometimes recognized. Recently I came across a hymn-book, *Hymns Old and New*, whose introduction I skimmed. It explained that some ancient hymns were unsuitable for modern worship, because they put over some ideas incompatible with modern thought. It was not just unfeminist ideas that the compilers disliked, but the militarism of some hymns.[1] Consequently, 'Stand up, stand up for Jesus' was completely rewritten, while 'Onward Christian soldiers' has become 'Onward Christian pilgrims'! But 'Dear Lord and Father of mankind' did survive, despite its quasi-Buddhist lines:

> Breathe through the heats of our desire
> thy coolness and thy balm.
> Let sense be dumb, let flesh retire . . .

---

1. Their reasons are set out in the introduction, Moore, *Hymns*, p. 3.

And of course the prayer of St Francis, 'Make me a channel of your peace', was included.

Now though I do not endorse the compilers' principles of selection, I do think they are right to notice the teaching function of hymns and indeed liturgy in general. I remember my tutor on Early Christian Doctrine stressing *lex orandi, lex credendi*, i.e. worshippers' central beliefs are expressed in their prayers. A study of the Lord's Prayer may be just as informative about Christian theology as the much longer Apostles' Creed, for it is in prayer that people give utterance to their deepest and most fundamental convictions. Thus the words hymn-writers and liturgists put on our lips in worship affect us profoundly: they teach us what to think and feel, the more effectively when they are put to music, so we can hum them to ourselves whenever we are inclined.

Particularly influential in this regard are the psalms, which have been at the heart of Jewish and Christian worship for the best part of three millennia.[2] Sung first in the temple, then in the apostolic churches, the psalms constituted the core diet of the monastic tradition on the one hand and the reformed tradition on the other. It is only a relatively recent phenomenon that hymns have displaced the psalms as the mainspring of Christian worship. If the *lex orandi, lex credendi* principle is correct, the psalms must have had the most profound effect on Christian theology and ethics.

Though the theology of the psalms has often been discussed,[3] very little work is devoted to their ethics. For instance, three recent works on Old Testament ethics more or less overlook the contribution of the psalms. Eckhart Otto's *Theologische Ethik des Alten Testaments* (1994) has just thirteen references to the Psalms compared with forty to Proverbs and seventy-eight to Deuteronomy, although the book of Psalms is about three times as long as Proverbs or Deuteronomy. A similar disproportion is noticeable in Cyril S. Rodd's *Glimpses of a Strange Land: Studies in Old Testament Ethics* (2001), which has double the number of references to Deuteronomy and to Proverbs as it has to the Psalms. A slight

---

2. See Holladay, *Psalms*.

3. E.g. Kraus, *Theology*.

improvement is visible in Christopher Wright's *Old Testament Ethics for the People of God* (2004), but still there are 50% more references to Deuteronomy than to the Psalms.

This scholarly blind spot is the more surprising in that the Psalter begins with Ps. 1, which invites the reader to meditate on the law day and night. Careful examination of the psalm suggests that the law the psalmist had in mind is not just the law of Moses, but the Psalter itself, which probably has been deliberately divided into five books to mimic the Pentateuch.[4] That the law is so important is underlined by the presence of Ps. 119, the longest psalm in the Psalter with its repeated refrain 'Teach me your statutes' (vv. 12, 26, 64, 68, 124, 135, 171) and similar prayers (vv. 29: law; 33: way of your statutes; 66: good judgment and knowledge; 108: rules). While some commentators have noted these phenomena, there has been a tendency to downplay them, ascribing them to a later wisdom redactor, who, because of alleged lateness, is *ipso facto* unimportant. This paper seeks to start to remedy this neglect by drawing out the pervasiveness of ethical concern in the Psalter and making a preliminary evaluation of its potential for Old Testament ethics.

But it should be stressed that this seems to be virgin scholarly territory. Not only is the topic rarely touched on in works on Old Testament ethics, but I have been able to find very few articles that discuss our topic. Discussion rarely gets beyond the entrance liturgies of Pss. 15 and 24, the imprecatory psalms, or the ideals of kingship in Ps. 72.[5] So how should we proceed?

If the Ten Commandments are the quintessence of biblical ethics, then an appropriate departure point is to see when and where they are alluded to or quoted. Are there any direct quotes? Which topics in the Decalogue are most often mentioned in the Psalms, and which are omitted? From an examination of the rules

---

4. In the Hebrew Bible it is striking that, right at the beginning of both the Prophets (Josh. 1:8) and the Writings (Ps. 1:2–3), there is explicit encouragement to meditate on the law. The latter seems clearly to allude to the former.

5. See Houston, 'King's'; Clements, 'Worship'; Zenger, *God of Vengeance*.

endorsed by the Psalms, we shall turn to the lifestyle they commend. What should the righteous be like? How may their character be defined in terms of virtues, and what are the typical vices of the wicked?

The Psalms are first and foremost prayers, so they constantly bring God into the picture, not least in their ethical statements. God's character is constantly appealed to as the guarantor of the ethical system: he will ensure that the wicked are punished and the righteous are rewarded. But more than that, God's actions are often seen as a model for human behaviour. His care for the downtrodden and oppressed, his hatred of duplicity, should inspire all his human subjects in their attitudes to others.

The Psalms and the Decalogue

Though the law in general (see Pss. 1; 19; 119) and individual laws in particular are so important in the Psalter, it is surprising how rarely the law-giving at Sinai is mentioned. In fact, in the long psalms reciting Israel's history it is usually omitted. The plagues of Egypt are mentioned, as are the exodus, wilderness wanderings and the conquest of Canaan, but the law-giving is notable by its absence (Pss. 78; 105; 106; 107; 114). Sinai is only explicitly named in Ps. 68 (vv. 8, 17) and Horeb in Ps. 106:19. However, though the law-giving may not be mentioned at the most appropriate place in the historical sequence, it clearly is presupposed. Ps. 78 essentially demonstrates how Israel has persistently neglected the law they were given and told to teach to their children:[6]

> He established a testimony in Jacob
> and appointed a law in Israel,
> which he commanded our fathers
> to teach to their children,
> that the next generation might know them,
> the children yet unborn,

---

6. All biblical quotations in this chapter are from the ESV.

> and arise and tell them to their children,
> so that they should set their hope in God
> and not forget the works of God,
> but keep his commandments;
> and that they should not be like their fathers,
> a stubborn and rebellious generation,
> a generation whose heart was not steadfast,
> whose spirit was not faithful to God. (78:5–8)

Similarly, though Ps. 105 says nothing about the law-giving in its historical review, it ends:

> And he gave them the lands of the nations,
> and they took possession of the fruit of the peoples' toil,
> that they might keep his statutes
> and observe his laws.
> Praise the LORD! (105:44–45)

These reviews of Israel's past are thus designed to produce a sense of gratitude and therefore willingness to observe the law (Ps. 105), or to highlight Israel's treachery in failing to keep it (Ps. 78).

Ps. 81, a much shorter history psalm, is different. It quotes the prologue to the Ten Commandments:

> I am the LORD your God,
> who brought you up[7] out of the land of Egypt. (81:10)

It also paraphrases the first two commandments:

> There shall be no strange god among you;
> you shall not bow down to a foreign god. (81:9)

Compare Exod. 20:3–5:

---

7. Exod. 20:2 has 'brought out' ($y\dot{s}$ ', hiphil), whereas Ps. 81:9 has 'brought up' ($'lh$, hiphil).

> You shall have no other gods before me. You shall not make for yourself
> a carved image, or any likeness of anything that is in heaven above, or
> that is in the earth beneath, or that is in the water under the earth. You
> shall not bow down to them or serve them.

I have not noted any other close quotation of the first commandment, but the stress on God's uniqueness and/or supremacy over
other gods is frequent. For example:

> There is none like you among the gods, O Lord,
> nor are there any works like yours . . .
> For you are great and do wondrous things;
> you alone are God. (86:8, 10)[8]

Another approach to affirming the first commandment comes
in the declarations affirming one's complete dependence on the
one God.

The second commandment banning idolatry is reaffirmed
strongly too. Ps. 24:3–4 reads:

> Who shall ascend the hill of the LORD?
> And who shall stand in his holy place?
> He who has clean hands and a pure heart,
> who does not lift up his soul to what is false
> and does not swear deceitfully.

'What is false' ($\check{s}w$') is usually supposed to be a reference to idola-
try,[9] though the phraseology is closer to the third commandment:
'You shall not take the name of the LORD your God in vain, for the
LORD will not hold him guiltless who takes his name in vain'
(Exod. 20:7).

However, there is no mistaking the robust assault on idolatry
in Ps. 115:

---

8. Cf. 95:3; 96:4; 97:9.

9. E.g. Kirkpatrick, *Psalms*; Kraus, *Psalms*; Ravasi, *Salmi*; Terrien, *Psalms*. But
   Seybold, *Psalmen*, prefers to connect it to Exod. 20:7.

Why should the nations say,
'Where is their God?'
Our God is in the heavens;
he does all that he pleases.
Their idols are silver and gold,
the work of human hands.
They have mouths, but do not speak;
eyes, but do not see.
They have ears, but do not hear;
noses, but do not smell.
They have hands, but do not feel;
feet, but do not walk;
and they do not make a sound in their throat.
Those who make them become like them;
so do all who trust in them. (115:2–8; cf. 135:15–18)

Ps. 31:6 sums up the attitude of the Psalter:

I hate those who pay regard to worthless idols,
but I trust in the LORD.[10]

The third commandment in Exod. 20:7, 'You shall not take the
name of the LORD your God in vain', is not directly quoted in the
Psalms unless 24:4 is an allusion to it, but the proper use of his
name is frequently celebrated.[11] Ps. 8 is devoted to this topic.

O LORD, our Lord,
how majestic is your name in all the earth! (8:1, 9)

Other typical sentiments in the Psalms are:

Ascribe to the LORD the glory due his name;
bring an offering, and come into his courts! (96:8)

---

10. See also 44:20; 81:9; 97:7; 106:36.
11. *THAT* 2.937 gives 106 uses in the Psalms out of 778 in the whole Old
Testament.

Let them praise your great and awesome name!
Holy is he! (99:3)

The psalms underline the importance of the proper use of the
name by illustrating how it ought to be used, not by banning its
misuse. If God's name were honoured in the way the psalms do,
there would be no question of taking it in vain.

The only commandment that seems to be completely ignored
by the psalms is the fourth: 'Remember the Sabbath day, to keep it
holy' (Exod. 20:8). There is one psalm (92) whose heading is 'A
song for the Sabbath',[12] and Ps. 81:3 urges:

Blow the trumpet at the new moon,
at the full moon, on our feast day.

But nowhere else is there a mention of the obligation to
remember the Sabbath. Ps. 95:7, 'Today, if you hear his voice',
and Ps. 118:24, 'This is the day that the LORD has made', clearly
refer to the day on which these psalms are being sung, which
could be the Sabbath. Given the importance of the Sabbath in
the pre-exilic era, when most of the psalms were composed, and
in the post-exilic era, when they were collected (Amos 8:5; Isa.
1:13; Neh. 13:15–22), the celebration of the Sabbath must be
presupposed by the Psalter. But there is no obvious reason for
this lack of reference. Possibly it is assumed that the psalms
were for use on the Sabbath by worshippers in the temple, so
they did not need reminding. Alternatively the Psalms may
reflect a popular lay piety, which encouraged their use anywhere
and at any time.

The fifth commandment, 'Honour your father and your
mother, that your days may be long in the land that the LORD your
God is giving you' (Exod. 20:12), is another that at first sight
seems not to matter in the psalms. However, the gift of children
and the privilege of parenthood are very much celebrated in the

---

12. Ps. 38 is said in the Septuagint (LXX 37) to be 'for the memorial offering
of the Sabbath'.

Psalter, not to mention the land promise. Just as the name of God is celebrated and its profanation barely mentioned, so the psalms celebrate the family dimension of life.

God is the archetypal father: this in itself implies that earthly fathers should be honoured. For example:

> He shall cry to me, 'You are my Father,
> my God, and the Rock of my salvation.' (89:26)

God's blessing is shown in the gift of children: a big family is to be treasured.

> Behold, children are a heritage from the LORD,
> the fruit of the womb a reward. (127:3)

If the fourth and fifth commandments are relatively underplayed in the Psalter, the sixth prohibiting murder is quite frequently alluded to, even if some remarks do not imply literal killing so much as depriving someone of his livelihood.

Enemies are compared to savage lions or dogs rending their prey (7:2; 17:12; 22:13, 16; 35:17), or to bulls (22:12), or to a highwayman (10:8) who watches for the righteous and seeks to put him to death (37:32; cf. 54:3; 70:2). The wicked also kill the widow and the sojourner, and murder the fatherless (94:6). These accusations are mostly embedded in laments, pleas to God to prevent or avenge such crimes.

Adultery, the focus of the seventh commandment, is mentioned explicitly only once in the Psalms:[13]

> But to the wicked God says:
> 'What right have you to recite my statutes
> or take my covenant on your lips?
> For you hate discipline,
> and you cast my words behind you.

---

13. Whereas the prophets frequently speak of Israel 'whoring' (*znh*) after other gods, the Psalms only use this image twice (73:27; 106:39).

If you see a thief, you are pleased with him,
and you keep company with adulterers.
You give your mouth free rein for evil,
and your tongue frames deceit.' (50:16–19)

The condemnation of adultery is here linked to a rejection of
God's statutes, covenant and 'words' – the Hebrew term for the
Decalogue is the 'Ten Words' (Exod. 34:28) – and the string of
offences (theft, adultery and false witness) makes it clear that the
psalmist is consciously recalling the Ten Commandments.

Although this is the only explicit reference to adultery in the
Psalter, it stands next to Ps. 51, the most moving of all the penitential psalms, which is entitled, 'To the choirmaster. A Psalm of
David, when Nathan the prophet went to him, after he had gone
in to Bathsheba.' It begins:

Have mercy on me, O God,
according to your steadfast love;
according to your abundant mercy
blot out my transgressions. (51:1)

Whatever may be the origin of the psalm and its heading, readings
which take seriously the canonical status of the headings cannot
fail to observe what a powerful statement Ps. 51 is about the sin of
adultery.

Theft and coveting, addressed in the eighth and tenth commandments, are also frequently bemoaned in the Psalms. We have
already noted the string of theft, adultery and lying in 50:18. But
stealing, especially from the poor, is condemned often elsewhere.

For the wicked boasts of the desires of his soul,
and the one greedy for gain curses and renounces the LORD . . .
he lurks in ambush like a lion in his thicket;
he lurks that he may seize the poor;
he seizes the poor when he draws him into his net. (10:3, 9)

'Because the poor are plundered, because the needy groan,
  I will now arise,' says the LORD;
'I will place him in the safety for which he longs.' (12:5)[14]

But of all the sins in the Decalogue it is surely that of the ninth
commandment which receives the fullest treatment: 'You shall not
bear false witness against your neighbour' (Exod. 20:16). Verse
after verse condemns the misuse of the tongue.

O men, how long shall my honour be turned into shame?
  How long will you love vain words and seek after lies? (4:2)

You destroy those who speak lies;
  the LORD abhors the bloodthirsty and deceitful man . . .
For there is no truth in their mouth;
  their inmost self is destruction;
  their throat is an open grave;
  they flatter with their tongue. (5:6, 9)

His mouth is filled with cursing and deceit and oppression;
  under his tongue are mischief and iniquity. (10:7)

Everyone utters lies to his neighbour;
  with flattering lips and a double heart they speak. (12:2)

He who walks blamelessly and does what is right
  and speaks truth in his heart;
who does not slander with his tongue
  and does no evil to his neighbour,
  nor takes up a reproach against his friend;
in whose eyes a vile person is despised,
  but who honours those who fear the LORD;
who swears to his own hurt and does not change. (15:2–4)[15]

_____

14. See also 14:4; 22:18; 26:4, 10; 69:4.
15. See also: 27:12; 28:3; 34:13; 35:11, 20; 50:19–20; 52:2–5; 56:9–11, 21; 59:12;
    64:3–5; 66:13–14; 69:4; 73:8–9; 101:5; 109:2; 120:2–3; 140:3; 144:11.

The abundance of passages on this topic is a surprise. Why should it be so important, whereas the Sabbath is so neglected? It is not clear, but three observations may put this feature in perspective. First, the book of Proverbs also frequently highlights the use and abuse of speech. Second, the Psalms are most concerned about interpersonal behaviour, about honesty, integrity and good neighbourliness, all of which may be destroyed by ill-considered words. Third, the Psalms themselves are examples of the positive use of the tongue for the praise of God. This makes its negative use to destroy other people especially reprehensible. As James puts it: 'With it we bless our Lord and Father, and with it we curse people who are made in the likeness of God. From the same mouth come blessing and cursing. My brothers, these things ought not to be so' (Jas 3:9–10).

The righteous and the wicked

So far I have only tried to show how the Psalter supports the principles of the Decalogue. This is only one string to its ethical bow. Indeed, I think it is secondary to its chief approach to presenting ethics, which is through the description of the righteous and the wicked. The two ways of the righteous and the wicked are presented in the very first psalm.

> Blessed is the man
> who walks not in the counsel of the wicked,
> nor stands in the way of sinners,
> nor sits in the seat of scoffers;
> but his delight is in the law of the LORD,
> and on his law he meditates day and night.
> He is like a tree
> planted by streams of water
> that yields its fruit in its season,
> and its leaf does not wither.
> In all that he does, he prospers.
> The wicked are not so,
> but are like chaff that the wind drives away.

> Therefore the wicked will not stand in the judgment,
> nor sinners in the congregation of the righteous;
> for the LORD knows the way of the righteous,
> but the way of the wicked will perish.

There are two types of people, two types of life, and two conclusions. 'Which will you choose to follow?' is the question posed by Ps. 1. Its own answer is clear, but the following psalms develop this contrast between the wicked and righteous very fully. Time and again the psalms declare that the righteous enjoy God's favour (5:12; 7:9; 14:5; 34:15; 37:17, 29; 112:6). He answers their prayers (34:15, 17) and delivers them from the plots of the wicked (37:39).

But apart from meditating on the law and avoiding the wicked, what characterizes the righteous? Ps. 112 amplifies the picture:

> Praise the LORD!
> Blessed is the man who fears the LORD,
> who greatly delights in his commandments!
> Light dawns in the darkness for the upright;
> he is gracious, merciful, and righteous.
> It is well with the man who deals generously and lends;
> who conducts his affairs with justice.
> For the righteous will never be moved;
> he will be remembered forever.
> He is not afraid of bad news;
> his heart is firm, trusting in the LORD.
> His heart is steady; he will not be afraid,
> until he looks in triumph on his adversaries.
> He has distributed freely; he has given to the poor;
> his righteousness endures forever;
> his horn is exalted in honour. (112:1, 4–9)

Though study of the law is one aspect of the righteous person's character, this passage also highlights both his trust in God (vv. 1, 7–8) and his generosity (vv. 5, 9).

It is important to note that, though the righteous enjoy ultimate prosperity and vindication, they may well have to suffer in the short term. The many laments in the Psalter are prayers of the righteous, who are suffering from illness, oppression and persecution (e.g. Pss. 3 – 7).

The wicked, on the other hand, are the converse of the righteous. The psalms emphasize that they will ultimately perish (1:6; 3:7; 9:5, 16, 17; 34:21; 68:2; 101:8; 146:9; 147:6). In the short term the wicked may appear to flourish, but that is misleading.

> For I was envious of the arrogant
> when I saw the prosperity of the wicked.
> For they have no pangs until death;
> their bodies are fat and sleek.
> They are not in trouble as others are;
> they are not stricken like the rest of mankind.
> Therefore pride is their necklace;
> violence covers them as a garment.
> Their eyes swell out through fatness;
> their hearts overflow with follies.
> They scoff and speak with malice;
> loftily they threaten oppression.
> They set their mouths against the heavens,
> and their tongue struts through the earth.
> Therefore his people turn back to them,
> and find no fault in them.
> And they say, 'How can God know?
> Is there knowledge in the Most High?'
> Behold, these are the wicked;
> always at ease, they increase in riches . . .
> Truly you set them in slippery places;
> you make them fall to ruin.
> How they are destroyed in a moment,
> swept away utterly by terrors! (73:3–12, 18–19)

Whereas the righteous fear God, the wicked mock him. Whereas the righteous are generous to the poor, the wicked exploit the poor, impoverishing them further.

> The wicked draw the sword and bend their bows
> to bring down the poor and needy,
> to slay those whose way is upright . . .
> The wicked borrows but does not pay back,
> but the righteous is generous and gives . . .
> The wicked watches for the righteous
> and seeks to put him to death . . .
> I have seen a wicked, ruthless man,
> spreading himself like a green laurel tree.
> But he passed away, and behold, he was no more;
> though I sought him, he could not be found. (37:14, 21, 32, 35–36)

The wicked pay lip service to God's law but do not practise it (50:16). Indeed, they are boastful, scheming and bear grudges (75:4; 64:2; 55:3).

God as guarantor of judgment

The psalms are direct address to God. They are prayers of faith expressing the psalmists' conviction that God reigns, that he is the ultimate judge. Even the laments, which start in despair, end in hope. The kingship psalms, 93 – 100, which celebrate the fact that the Lord reigns, often end with the affirmation that God will judge the earth and that this is cause for celebration.

> Let the heavens be glad, and let the earth rejoice,
> let the sea roar, and all that fills it;
> let the field exult, and everything in it!
> Then shall all the trees of the forest sing for joy
> before the LORD,
> for he comes to judge the earth.
> He will judge the world in righteousness,
> and the peoples in his faithfulness. (96:11–13)

This is rarely our reaction to the thought of God coming in judgment, but it recurs frequently throughout the Psalter. As Zenger has pointed out, that God will be the universal judge is a message of hope in a world of oppression and injustice.[16] The Psalms look forward to a universal judgment, but also to a more immediate judgment on the wicked and their activities.

Ps. 1:6 declares that the way of the wicked will perish. In Ps. 2 the kings of the earth plot against the Lord and his anointed, but God will dash them in pieces like a potter's vessel (2:1–9). Ps. 3:7 affirms that 'you break the teeth of the wicked'. Ps. 5:6 affirms:

> You destroy those who speak lies;
> the LORD abhors the bloodthirsty and deceitful man.

Ps. 6 ends with the triumphant cry of faith:

> The LORD has heard my plea;
> the LORD accepts my prayer.
> All my enemies shall be ashamed and greatly troubled;
> they shall turn back and be put to shame in a moment. (6:9–10)

Ps. 7 pictures the wicked catching himself out:

> He makes a pit, digging it out,
> and falls into the hole that he has made.
> His mischief returns upon his own head,
> and on his own skull his violence descends. (7:15–16)

This sounds like nasty vindictiveness, *Schadenfreude*, celebrating your enemies suffering their comeuppance. But if we look at it through the eyes of the sufferers, we might feel this is an over-harsh judgment. Commenting on one of the harshest imprecatory psalms, McCann says:

> Psalm 109 not only tells it like it is with us, but it also tells us how it is with the world. The psalmist had been victimized; and when persons become victims, they are bound to react with rage . . . When persons are treated unjustly, we can expect them to lash out; we can expect them to

---

16. Zenger, *God of Vengeance*, pp. 63–86.

express vehemently the desire for an end to the violence that has made
them a victim.[17]

But we could see these remarks as making a moral statement to the
person uttering them, in a more subtle fashion than some of the
hymns quoted at the beginning. Those who rejoice in the fact that
God will dash the wicked in pieces like a potter's vessel are implicitly putting themselves firmly on God's side and committing
themselves not to do anything that would put them in the class of
the wicked.[18] The moral implications of reciting these remarks
about divine judgment are thus immense. To rejoice in God's judgment on sin is to turn the spotlight on one's own life and
behaviour: will I pass muster with God? Such questions become
particularly acute when reciting Ps. 14 with its stress on the univer-
sality of sin, or in singing Ps. 139 with its recognition that we are
often unaware that we are sinning. Is this perhaps why traditional
Christians, who used the psalms so much, lived in such awe of the
Last Judgment?

The imitation of God as a principle of the Psalms

In many ways, though not in all, the righteous are supposed to
imitate God, who himself is often called righteous (e.g. 11:7;
116:5). God is the one who is the righteous judge: he intervenes to
save the oppressed, something the righteous should do if they can.

> He raises the poor from the dust
> and lifts the needy from the ash heap,

---

17. McCann, *Theological*, p. 114.
18. Thiselton, *New Horizons*, p. 299, points out that in worship many
    statements are performative speech-acts. To say 'I give thanks to you, O
    Lord, with my whole heart' is not merely informing God about one's
    feelings, but an act of thanksgiving in itself. This observation, though
    based on modern speech-act theory, is not new. Athanasius discusses it in
    his letter to Marcellinus, cf. Gregg, *Athanasius*, pp. 101–129.

to make them sit with princes,
with the princes of his people.
He gives the barren woman a home,
making her the joyous mother of children. (113:7–9)

Those in the best position to promote righteousness are the kings, and they are called on to exercise godlike qualities of justice.

Give the king your justice, O God,
and your righteousness to the royal son!
May he judge your people with righteousness,
and your poor with justice . . .
May he defend the cause of the poor of the people,
give deliverance to the children of the needy,
and crush the oppressor! (72:1–4)

In Ps. 101 King David promises that he will indeed act in a godly way and insist that all his servants will have to meet God's standards. He insists on integrity, loyalty, no backbiting or arrogance, and so on.

. . . he who walks in the way that is blameless
shall minister to me.
No one who practises deceit
shall dwell in my house;
no one who utters lies
shall continue before my eyes.
Morning by morning I will destroy
all the wicked in the land,
cutting off all the evildoers
from the city of the LORD. (Ps. 101:6–8)

The king is thus expected to identify with God's standards by promoting the righteous and demoting the wicked. But this identification with the divine standpoint extends to everyone who prays the Psalms. This emerges in the very first verse of the Psalter (quoted above). The psalmists also recite back to God what God thinks, e.g. in Ps. 5:

> For you are not a God who delights in wickedness;
> evil may not dwell with you.
> The boastful shall not stand before your eyes;
> you hate all evildoers.
> You destroy those who speak lies;
> the Lord abhors the bloodthirsty and deceitful man. (5:4–6)

Running through the Psalms there is an identification of God's standpoint with that of the righteous plaintiff: this is why the psalmist anticipates that God will heed his pleas.[19]

Conclusion

This essay has begun an exploration of the ethics inculcated by the Psalms, an area that seems to have been largely overlooked by recent biblical scholarship. It has drawn attention to the self-involving language of worship, the relationship of the Psalms to the Decalogue, and to their models of behaviour in righteousness and steadfast love. But these are only preliminary observations. They need refining and correcting if this potentially important area is to be fully exploited in the study of biblical ethics.

---

19. Cf. 7:3–5, 9–10; 9:10; 10:12–14; 11:7; 14:5.

© Gordon J. Wenham, 2005.

10. BODY IDIOMS AND THE PSALMS

Andy L. Warren-Rothlin

Introduction

A first-draft translation of Ps. 1:1 into one northern Nigerian language read, 'Blessed is the man who . . . does not obstruct sinners.' The translator defended his rendering on the basis of the traditional English wording, 'nor stands in the way of sinners' (RSV, NIV). He had quite understandably read 'stand in the way of' in its idiomatic sense of 'obstruct'. This was clearly a bad translation on the part of the RSV, both because it is an over-literal rendering of the Hebrew and because the phrase has a quite different idiomatic meaning in English. It was noticeably dropped in the NRSV.

Similarly, a draft of Gen. 22:13 had the ram hanging by its horns from a high tree! When questioned, the translator referred to the RSV, 'Abraham lifted up his eyes and looked.' He had, again understandably, read this as meaning 'looked upwards' (so NRSV).

The Church of Jesus Christ of Latter-Day Saints ('Mormons') teaches that God the Father (specifically, 'Elohim') 'has a body of flesh and bones as tangible as a man's' (*Doctrine and Covenants*

130:22). I am not aware of any published work of theology claiming that God also has wings (following Ps. 17:8, etc.), but it could well exist! The irony is that those who would argue such things would not expect anyone else to come to the same conclusion about their own daughter when they describe her as an 'angel'!

Feminist theologians claim that biblical imagery referring to God in terms of female body parts or bodily functions (e.g. Matt. 23:37; Ps. 131:2; Isa. 42:14) demonstrates that God is not 'male'. I am not aware whether such logic has ever been applied to an understanding of the kings at whose breasts God's people will suckle (Isa. 60:16).

These are all examples of how figurative language is misunderstood. However much we may be amused at the more extreme examples, we have to admit that literal Bible translations, which form English expressions from Hebrew idioms, potentially do a great disservice to the uninitiated reader,[1] and that those most committed to the reliability of the biblical texts have often been the least reliable interpreters of their meaning.

Linguistics

Linguistic studies are conventionally considered at various 'levels', from phonetics and phonology, up to syntax (language structure) and semantics (language meaning).[2] Above clausal semantics are the fields of 'discourse' (relations within a text) and 'pragmatics' (relations to the real world).[3] Discourse studies of biblical Hebrew have received considerable attention in the last decade or so, largely driven by the work of Bible translators. The pragmatics of biblical Hebrew has received much less attention, though it is also a major concern for Bible translators. The study of idiom lies at the interface of semantics and pragmatics.

Etymologically, the term 'idiom' is derived from the Greek *idios*

---

1. So also Lübbe, 'Idioms', pp. 59–61.

2. See Lyons, *Semantics*; and Lakoff, *Women*. For application to biblical studies, see Barr, *Semantics*; *Comparative*; etc.

3. See Levinson, *Pragmatics*; 'Three'.

in the sense of 'distinctive language', and modern linguists still define an idiom as any expression which cannot usually be translated word for word into other languages.[4] This definition corresponds to the broader, generic term 'idiom' (as in 'idiomatic language'), including the language of *politeness*,[5] *speech-acts*,[6] most *literary tropes* and other *figures of speech*,[7] i.e. what may otherwise be termed 'social communication',[8] 'pragmatics' or 'rhetoric'.

A special subclass of 'idiom' is formed by those expressions frequently referred to as *idioms*, most commonly defined as expressions in which 'the meaning of the whole is not the meaning of the sum total of the parts'[9] – where the 'idiomatic meaning' is different from the 'literal meaning'.[10] This subclass includes special collocations of the names for body parts, bodily functions and senses, colours, verbs of motion, etc., as well as special categories such as English phrasal verbs (e.g. 'put up' for 'accommodate', 'put down' for 'kill', 'put up with' for 'tolerate'). These are usually discussed in dictionaries just as distinct collocations of a headword.

Psalms

The distinctive language of the Psalms has received special attention, including a general survey,[11] a grammar,[12] studies on the verbal system,[13] a study of its syntax,[14] a study of formulaic language[15]

---

4. Babut, *Idiomatic*, p. 13.

5. See Brown and Levinson, *Politeness*.

6. See Austin, *How*, and the several subsequent works by Searle.

7. See Lakoff and Johnson, *Metaphors*.

8. See Halliday, 'Language'.

9. Nida, cited in Babut, *Idiomatic*, p. 15.

10. Babut refers to 'transparent'/'endocentric' meaning versus 'global'/'exocentric' meaning.

11. Tsevat, *Study*.

12. Dahood and Penar, 'Grammar'.

13. Michel, *Tempora*; Zuber, *Tempussystem*; Warren, *Modality*.

14. Sappan, *Typical*.

15. Culley, *Oral*.

and studies in pragmatics.[16] In addition, there are the standard works on biblical poetry, which usually focus on literary forms, though also deal to some extent with figurative language.[17] Nevertheless, there are many new insights gained from recent work in pragmatics, the Hebrew verbal system, translation theory and translation practice.[18]

In the following, we will first survey idiomatic language and idioms in biblical Hebrew in general, and then turn to body idioms in particular. Though we will need to consider data from outside the Psalter, where literal and idiomatic uses can be more easily identified, we will draw implications throughout for the interpretation of the Psalms.

Idiomatic language

There have been a few important general works on idiomatic language in biblical Hebrew,[19] though none yet to my knowledge from a technical linguistic standpoint.

Politeness forms[20] can be seen at all levels in biblical Hebrew. The verbal system has one volitional form which is only used in requests by humans to God (the 'precative perfect', occurring most frequently in the Psalms)[21] and one which is only used in commands by God to humans (the 'preceptive imperfect').[22] Among particles, we find *nāʿ* and *bî*, which are often thought to mean 'please', though are probably dependent on context for their pragmatic force.[23]

---

16. E.g. Warren, *Modality*.

17. Watson, *Classical*; O'Connor, *Hebrew*.

18. The West African languages cited as examples in this chapter are all Niger-Congo and Chadic languages of Ghana or Nigeria.

19. König, *Stilistik*; Muraoka, *Emphatic*.

20. Lande, *Formelhafte*; Warren, 'Some Linguistic'; Dahood and Penar, 'Grammar', pp. 374–375.

21. Dahood and Penar, 'Grammar'; Buttenwieser, 'Grammatical'.

22. Warren, *Modality*, pp. 87–92.

23. Ibid., pp. 155–162.

Then there are phrases such as 'If I have found favour in your eyes'[24] and 'As surely as the king lives'. Perhaps most interesting is the verb *bārāk*, which has several meanings including 'to bless' (an inferior), 'to praise' (God, especially in the Psalms), 'to greet' and 'to thank'.[25] The function of this term in context is often misunderstood. Boaz uses *bārāk* to *greet* his reapers (Ruth 2:4) and to *thank* Ruth (Ruth 3:10), and we understand the difference from the context, but when this is translated directly into languages which only use 'blessing' for *leave-taking* (as often in West Africa), it sounds as if he's dismissing them all! When we find *bārāk* used for *praising* God in the Psalms, we need to consider whether this might be a way of *greeting* God or *thanking* him.[26]

Speech-acts or 'performative utterances' in biblical Hebrew have received much attention in recent years.[27] A typical English speech-act might be 'I hereby pronounce you man and wife'. The key formal elements are a first-person subject, an active verb in the perfect aspect and an adverbial marker (e.g. English 'hereby'; Hebrew 'behold', 'and now'), and the key functional issue is that an action (e.g. marriage) is performed *by means of* the words. Thus, in the Psalms, 'I hereby put my trust in you . . . I hereby declare you to be my God' (31:14, a.t.) makes a covenant, 'I hereby pour out' (2:6, a.t.) appoints to an office, and 'I hereby sire you' (2:7, a.t.) adopts a son. Even some recent Bible translations fail to realize that these are performative utterances and so mistranslate the verb form as past (e.g. 'today have I fathered you' NJB).

---

24. Lande, *Formelhafte*, pp. 95–97; Babut, *Idiomatic*, pp. 149–192.

25. See similarly German *grüssen/Grüß Gott/Grüezi*, 'to greet'/'May God bless you', Birifor *puor*, 'to bless, greet, thank', and Waali *baraka*, 'thank you' (derived via Hausa from the Arabic cognate of Hebrew *bārāk*).

26. Contrast the claim by Westermann, *Praise and Lament*, that there is no true 'thanking' in the Psalms; he renames the 'Psalms of thanksgiving' as 'declarative praise'.

27. White, *Speech Act*; Macky, *Biblical*; Hillers, 'Delocutive', 'Performative'; Tigay, 'Some more'; Wagner, *Sprechakte*; 'Bedeutung'; 'Stellung'; Warren, *Modality*.

Literary tropes and other figures of speech have also received attention in biblical studies. *Similes* are expressions of explicit comparison, usually involving in English the terms 'like' or 'as', and in Hebrew the particle *kĕ*. They may be nominal, introducing a noun (e.g. 'like water . . . like wax . . . like a potsherd', 22:14–15), or predicative, introducing a phrase (e.g. 'As a hart longs . . .', 42:1).

Metaphors may often be described as 'implicit similes', but it is doubtful whether such a description rightly reflects the mental processes involved in their interpretation,[28] and it is often now thought that metaphors are in fact the more 'primitive' form of language.[29] Following Aristotle they were usually considered as involving *substitution* of one term for another, though in fact a metaphor usually stands not for an equivalent term but for a whole bundle of semantic features. For example, 'I am a worm' (22:7) means more than just 'I am a wretch' – it means 'I am of low value, ritually unclean, powerless', etc. Like similes, they may be nominal ('I am a worm'; 'The LORD is my rock, and my fortress', 18:2) or predicative ('I am poured out', 22:14; 'The LORD will swallow them', 21:9).[30]

Metonymy is often considered a subtype of metaphor (or vice versa), but a useful distinction can be made by saying that metaphor involves substitution *between* semantic domains (in the above examples, worms and water come from different semantic domains from that of humans), whilst metonymy involves substitution *within* a semantic domain. This may mean substitution of concrete for abstract, e.g. 'thrones for judgment' for 'justice' (122:5), 'smooth their tongue' for 'smooth their words' (5:9, cf. Prov. 2:16); or abstract for concrete, e.g. 'all wickedness' (107:42) for 'all wicked people'. It may be substitution of a part for the whole (called 'synecdoche'), e.g. 'the works of your fingers' (8:2) for 'your works'; or of the whole for a part, e.g. 'my anointed one(s)' for 'my prophets' (105:15) and for 'David' (132:17). Or it may be another type such as cause for effect, effect for cause (e.g. 'clean teeth' for 'hunger', Amos 4:6), etc.

---

28. Glucksberg, *Understanding*, p. 10.

29. Bühlmann and Scherer, *Stilfiguren*, s.v. 'Metapher'.

30. On animal metaphors in Psalms, see Dahood and Penar, 'Grammar', pp. 383–384.

Other important figures of speech include: *paranomasia* (word-play),[31] such as in Samson's riddle (Judg. 14:14), Amos's 'basket of summer fruit' (Amos 8:1), or many plays on personal and place names; *euphemism*,[32] as in Rachel's reference to 'the way of women' (Gen. 31:35), the frequent use of 'to go in to (a woman)' to refer to sexual intercourse, the Seraphim's covering of their 'feet' (Isa. 6:2) and other uses of 'foot' and 'hand' for 'genitalia'.[33]

Idioms

Whilst metaphors ('I am a worm') usually have an *absurd* literal meaning, making them easily identifiable as not intended literally, idioms ('hide the face', 'make mouths')[34] usually have an *opaque* literal meaning,[35] such that the brain has to consider a range of factors in the process of interpretation.[36] They may involve multiple metaphorization – of first a noun and then the whole phrase – and are often derived from culture-specific symbolic acts which may have since died out, leaving traces in archaic words ('a dab hand') or words with archaic meanings ('to lend a hand').

Let us consider an example in English. In previous generations most British men wore hats, and would acknowledge a social superior's status by lifting or 'doffing' their hat [Stage 1: symbolic

---

31. Casanowicz, *Paranomasia*; Rendsburg, 'Word Play'; Lunn, 'Paranomastic'.

32. Parry, 'Word' (and the references in his first footnote); de Waard, 'Do you'; Schorch, *Euphemismen*; Paul, 'Euphemistically'.

33. Cf. also the *tiqqune sopherim*, many of the Massoretes' special *qere* readings such as *šākab*, 'to sleep (with)' for *šāgal*, 'to have sex' (probably a crudity; Deut. 28:30; Isa. 13:16; Zech. 14:2; Jer. 3:2), the perpetual *qere* for the tetragrammaton, and distinctive readings in special textual traditions such as the Dead Sea Scrolls (see Warren, 'Trisagion').

34. Babut lists some 138 expressions and studies several in detail, e.g. 'to speak on the heart', 'his ears will ring', 'stiffen the neck', 'If I have found favour'.

35. Glucksberg, *Understanding*, p. v.

36. Ibid., p. 10; I. Wilson, 'Merely', pp. 17–19.

action]. Later this was also done to a peer for some particular achievement – a metaphorical adaptation of the symbolic act, with the meaning 'congratulation' [Stage 2: metaphorical adaptation]. In time the expression 'he took his hat off to him' gradually lost its literal reference and became increasingly idiomatized [Stage 3: idiomatization]. As a result, now that most British men no longer wear hats, the same social act can be performed linguistically by saying, 'I take my hat off to you!' [Stage 4: expression as a speech-act], optionally reinforced with a mimed removal of a hat. The meaning is little more than 'well done'.

Understanding idiomatization as a process of at least these four stages is essential for proper interpretation of biblical idioms. A biblical example similar to the above might be 'I can throw my sandal on' (Ps. 60:8), which – since we do not think of God as literally wearing sandals – is an expression of disdain, perhaps based on a symbolic act of claiming territory by placing one's foot on it, or on a taboo on placing footwear on something respected. Whatever the derivation, the metaphor is dead, so that the idiom here simply means 'Edom is nothing to me!'

Certain types of terms tend to occur in idioms. The most common, body parts, are considered in detail below. Also common are items of clothing, such as hat (English) and sandal (Hebrew).

Bodily functions and senses, such as 'to look', 'to hear', 'to eat', 'to stand' and 'to say', often occur together with a range of different nouns in idioms. For instance, in Birifor, 'to eat' occurs frequently, e.g. 'eat testimony' (bear witness), 'eat oil' (have fun), 'eat one's head' (prosper), 'eat patience' (be patient), 'eat chief' (become chief). In Hebrew, 'to stand' has a similarly wide range of meanings: 'who could stand?' (survive, 76:7; 130:3), 'stand in Yahweh's house' (serve Yahweh, 134:1), 'stand at the right hand of' (defend, 109:31), 'stand to eternity' (last for ever, 111:3).

Colours may often have figurative associations in idioms, in conjunction with body parts: 'red-handed', 'green-fingered' (English), 'white-livered' (happy, Berom), 'red-eyed' (serious or angry, Birifor), 'blackness' (youth, Hebrew, Eccl. 11:10).

Verbs of motion and phrasal verbs may also have special idiomatic uses: 'go in' (die, German), 'enter a room' (give birth, Birifor), 'go in to' (have sex with, Hebrew, Gen. 39:14).

Idioms are studied from a variety of angles. Linguists may be interested in how lexical meaning relates to idiomatic meaning synchronically, or how lexical words undergo processes of idiomatization and grammaticalization diachronically. Pragmaticists may be interested in how idioms relate to politeness strategies, indirectness and conversation structure. Psychologists may be interested in the mental processing of literal and idiomatic language. Philosophers may be interested in truth conditions and the logical analysis of idioms.[37] And computational linguists may be interested in how computers can be programmed to read and translate idioms correctly.[38] Biblical scholars need to focus on the cultural environment and symbolic acts which produce such idioms, while Bible translators need to know the appropriate cultural equivalents in their target language.

Body idioms

Body idioms are by far the most common type of idiom in most languages, largely because of the role of body parts in symbolic social communication and the range of associations attached to body part terms.

Literature

A range of standard works discuss the body and its associations.[39] In recent years, body language has also received much attention from theologically minded scholars, motivated by a reaction against Gnostic and Augustinian Platonic dualist theology, which saw the body as fundamentally bad, and by feminist interests,

---

37. e.g. Glucksberg, *Understanding*.

38. e.g. Fass, et al., *Proceeding*; such work is also being done on biblical Hebrew, especially by E. Talstra in Amsterdam and W. Richter in Munich.

39. E.g. Pedersen's *Israel*; Koehler's *Hebrew Man*; Wolff's *Anthropology*; and reference works such as *TDOT* and *NIDOTTE*. The linguistic terminology is also treated in Caird, *Language*. For the key terms 'heart' (*lēb*), 'soul' (*nepeš*) and 'spirit' (*rûaḥ*) to refer to emotions, see Lauha's *Psychophysischer*.

often focusing on anthropomorphic language about God. Particularly worthy of mention in this connection is Schroer and Staubli's beautifully illustrated *Die Körpersymbolik der Bibel*.[40]

Actual Hebrew body idioms are approached in different ways by different authors. Babut approaches them in terms of componential analysis of meaning, starting his analysis from the verb rather than the body part itself. Lübbe's approach is structural, and he shows how much flexibility is possible in the linguistic form of idioms by considering the interaction of the verb 'to lift' (*nāśā'*) with various body parts. Gillmayr-Bucher's approach is psycholinguistic, as she considers how body imagery in general contributes to the vividness of Psalm language. Our approach here is semantic, considering the relationship between 'idiomatic meaning' and 'literal meaning', together with the symbolic acts and social context which have produced the idiom.[41]

Body part terms

Body part terms are some of the most productive nouns in many languages.[42] That is to say, they contribute to a language much more than physical reference alone. Most importantly, their semantic range may be greatly enlarged by the culturally defined associations of the respective body parts, such as, in a range of cultures:

Spatial associations: 'heart', 'stomach', 'eye' for centre; 'head' for up; 'hand' for side; 'lip' for edge; 'foot' for down; 'face' for front or forwards.

Functional associations: 'hand' for acting, working, taking responsibility, owning; 'mouth' for speaking; 'eyes' for seeing.

Psychophysical associations:[43] 'heart' for feelings, love, thought; 'head'

---

40. See also the literature cited there and in Gillmayr-Bucher, 'Body Images'.

41. Similarly, Wilson, 'Merely'.

42. Certainly those of Europe, West Africa and the Middle East, with which I am most familiar.

43. See the frontplates in Schroer and Staubli, *Körpersymbolik*; Lauha, *Psychophysischer*.

for thought; 'throat' for personhood; 'liver' for joy, courage; 'guts', 'semen' for courage; 'womb' for compassion; 'kidneys' for moral stature.

Superstitious associations: 'right hand' for good, true, justice; 'left hand' for bad, sinister.

It is especially on the basis of these associations that body part terms come to have metaphorical meanings and idiomatic collocations.

In the Psalms, body part terms account for 5.7% of the lexical stock, occurring in all but seven Psalms.[44] However, only very few of these occurrences constitute literal reference to body parts. Some represent semantically redundant use with sensory verbs for vivid effect (e.g. 'see with the eyes', 'hear with the ears'), but most uses are in grammaticalization, literary tropes, proverbs, or body idioms.

Grammaticalization is a process whereby a lexical word (noun, verb, etc.) takes on the function of a grammatical word (preposition, conjunction, pronoun, etc.). Body part terms are often grammaticalized by means of spatial associations into adpositional phrases[45] (expressions of temporal, spatial or logical relations); this is usually done in conjunction with any existing true adpositions or grammatical cases, e.g. at the foot of, at the mouth of, in the heart of (English), 'the ground's head' (on the ground, Birifor), 'the back of the meeting' (after the meeting, Birifor), 'his stomach's stomach' (in his stomach, Hausa), 'in the intestines of your temple' (inside your temple, Ps. 48:10).

Body part terms may also be grammaticalized into verbs (by means of functional or psychophysical associations), e.g. to hand to/over/down/out/in (English). So in Hebrew: 'to hand' (acknowledge, thank, *yādâ*, e.g. 136:1, etc.), 'to nose' (be angry, 2:12), 'to ear' (listen, 80:2), 'to tongue' (slander, 101:5).

Literary tropes of various types may use body part terms, including metaphor (e.g. 'Absalom's hand' for Absalom's monument,

---

44. Gillmayr-Bucher, 'Body Images', p. 301.

45. This is a collective term for prepositional and postpositional phrases.

2 Sam. 18:18), euphemistic metonymy (e.g. 'hand' or 'foot' for genitalia) and merism (e.g. 'throat . . . flesh' for the whole person, Ps.
63:2). In the Psalms, we frequently find body part terms in part-for-
whole metonymy,[46] referring to one of the three primary parties in
the Psalms – God, the psalmists and the enemies, e.g. 'May your
hearts live for ever!' (22:26), 'You bring down raised eyes' (18:27),
'return on the head . . . land on the skull' (7:16).

True body idioms are expressions in which a term for a body
part collocates with other words to form an expression with a new,
distinct meaning.[47]

Form of body idioms

A huge number of body part terms can occur in idioms. A recent
English list cites 92 body part terms, the most frequently occurring
being hand, heart, head and eye (in 78, 55, 52 and 42 idioms
respectively);[48] my own Niger-Congo list cites 23, and my biblical
Hebrew list[49] cites 59, the most common being head, face, eye,
mouth, heart and hand. By contrast, the governing verbs or
qualifiers come from a restricted list; in Hebrew, the most frequent
include 'be strong', 'be hard', 'hide/uncover' and 'lift'.

As for the structures involved, contrary to the frequent assertion that idioms have 'limited syntactic flexibility',[50] there may in
fact be a lot of stylistic and syntactic flexibility in the form of an
idiom.[51]

Meaning of body idioms

There is no simple one-to-one correspondence between an idiom
and a meaning. This should be obvious, since it is also true of

---

46. Gillmayr-Bucher, 'Body Images', especially pp. 315, 321–323.

47. Babut, *Idiomatic*, p. 17.

48. Fuller, *Body Idioms*.

49. Supplemented by those of Gillmayr-Bucher, 'Body Images'; Jenni,
    'Verba', etc.

50. Wilson, 'Merely', pp. 17–18; Babut, *Idiomatic*, pp. 21–25.

51. E.g. presence of the accusative marker, status as adverbial or
    independent, passivization; Lübbe, 'Idioms', p. 50.

single lexical words; however, it is often forgotten by biblical scholars and translators.[52]

There may be a 'one-to-many' correspondence, with one expression having several different idiomatic meanings (polysemy), e.g. in English, 'to give someone a hand' can mean to applaud or to help; in Hebrew, 'to lift face' can mean to show partiality (Ps. 82:2), to spare (Deut. 28:50), to grant a request (Gen. 19:21), to be confident (Job 11:15), or to show favour (Ps. 4:6);[53] 'to lift head' can mean to count (Num. 1:2), or to rebel (Ps. 83:2); 'to lift one's hand'[54] can mean to bless people (Lev. 9:22), to bless God (Neh. 8:6; Ps. 63:5), to entreat, pray (Ps. 28:2), to respect (Ps. 119:48), to rebel against, attack (2 Sam. 18:28), to exercise power (Ps. 10:12), or to swear an oath (Deut. 32:40); 'to open one's mouth' can mean to long for (Ps. 119:131), to be greedy (Isa. 5:14), or to threaten (Ps. 22:14). It is clear from these examples that the polysemy of body idioms derives from the range of associations, the diversity of the symbolic acts and the range of contexts. An error frequently made by biblical scholars is to assume that a given expression has just one basic meaning from which all others are derived according to context.

There may be a 'many-to-one' correspondence, with different expressions having one idiomatic meaning (synonymy). These may differ either in the verb or in the body part term: e.g. 'to lift' or 'to raise' one's head (be confident, Job 10:15; Ps. 110:7); to lift one's 'hand' or 'head' (to rebel, 2 Sam. 18:28; Ps. 83:2). Biblical scholars often fail to see that synonymy is a normal feature of language. Though there may be no such thing as perfect synonymy in some technical sense, it would be wrong to try to see significant distinctions in meaning here.

Similarly, expressions with the same literal meaning may have different or even opposite idiomatic meanings; expressions with

---

52. See the works by Barr referred to above.

53. Following a widely accepted textual emendation.

54. Lübbe, 'Idioms', p. 50; Gelander, 'Convention', p. 305, comments that a 'wider range of meanings . . . possibly reflects a later stage of development or a later transmutation of the language'.

different or even opposite literal meanings may have the same idiomatic meaning; and expressions with opposite literal meanings may not have opposite idiomatic meanings. Finally, one expression may have a literal, metaphorical or idiomatic meaning, and we will go on to consider this after looking at the derivation of body idioms.

Derivation of body idioms

As has been discussed above, body idioms may be based on psychophysical associations of particular body parts, e.g. 'open one's heart', 'wear one's heart on one's sleeve', 'take heart', 'take to heart' (English); 'have a white liver' (be happy, Berom); 'put one's heart to' (consider well, Ps. 48:14); 'close one's flab' (be callous, 17:10); grind one's teeth against' (mock, 35:16).

They may be based on natural functional associations: 'give/lend someone a hand', 'have a lot on one's hands', 'wash one's hands of', 'take the law into one's own hands' (English); 'widen one's mouth over' (mock, 35:21), 'send one's hand against' (attack, 55:20).

They may also indicate the natural and instinctive functions of sensory organs: 'expose the ear' (inform, 1 Sam. 9:15), 'close one's lips tightly' (plan evil, Prov. 16:30).

Most distinctive of body idioms, however, is their derivation from symbolic functional associations, as in the hat-doffing and sandal-throwing examples mentioned above. In the Psalms, symbolic functional associations, particularly those relating to temple ritual acts and the formal relationships between the three main parties, yield a number of important body idioms. As we consider them, it is important to remember the dictum that *the meaning of a word or expression is its use in a language system*, not its derivation from different times, places or languages.[55]

---

55. See the recent vigorous discussions of the role of etymological data in Hebrew lexical semantics, centred on the new dictionaries, *HALOT* (Köhler-Baumgartner), *DCH* (Sheffield/Clines) and *DBHE* (Alonso-Schökel).

Distinguishing literal and idiomatic meanings

Rightly interpreting and using idioms is perhaps the 'final frontier' in learning a foreign language; even more so when interpreting texts from a great geographic, historical, cultural and linguistic distance. A naïve approach to language seeks to interpret words, and a naïve Bible translation translates words. A more sophisticated approach interprets whole phrases, and such Bible translations render phrasal meanings in 'dynamic' or 'functional' equivalents. In this particular sense, Psalms scholarship has tended to be naïve in its understanding of body idioms.

The point is that symbolic acts such as cap-doffing do sometimes die out, leaving dead metaphors and dead idioms – fossilized linguistic traces with only a functional meaning and no literal referent. Just as a Swiss atheist uses *Grüezi* (derived from 'God bless you'), and a Christian talks about *disasters* (derived from 'ill-starred event'), so too I can 'give someone a hand' by phone or email, or 'have a hand in' a great soccer victory without my hand touching the ball. Similarly, in Birifor, one can disagree with someone face to face and be angry with one's eyes closed, though the words used are 'I turn my back to you' and 'I have red eyes'; and toothless old women can make fun of others, though the expression is 'to open mouth to reveal teeth'. In all these cases the derivation, however recent, has been lost, leaving only a linguistic trace with little or no original meaning.

As already noted, idiomatization is a process, and a given idiom may be at any point along the road to full fossilization. Hence a hatless British man may still touch his forehead when saying, 'I take my hat off to you.' Similarly, a Joseph can use the idiomatic meaning of 'lift your head', i.e. restore to former position, for the cupbearer (Gen. 40:13) and then also the literal meaning of 'lift your head', i.e. off your shoulders, for the baker (Gen. 40:19). Most cultures like to exploit such linguistic ambiguity in poetic and humorous wordplay, threatening insinuation, erotic *double entendre* and obfuscating half-truths. And the biblical genre of prophetic revelation often uses it, from Joseph's dream interpretation to Amos's 'basket of summer fruit' (Amos 8:1–2) to many other instances. So how do we determine how far along the road to fossilization an idiom has travelled?

It is safe to assume idiomatic meaning when the person concerned does not possess the body parts referred to, such as David's
horn (Ps. 89:24) or God's wings (91:4), just as with God's sandal
above (60:8). However, these are special examples. The raised horn
may derive its idiomatic meaning of success and social status from
confident stags and bulls holding their heads high, or from victorious soldiers blowing horns. And wings may derive their idiomatic
meaning of protection and closeness to God from Canaanite
winged deities, adult birds covering their young, the cherubim on
the ark of the covenant, the side-flaps of the tent of meeting, or
the sleeping-cloths of potential husbands such as Boaz.[56]

Idiomatic meaning can similarly be assumed in the case of a
divine possessor or subject, since the Old Testament consistently
portrays God as having no physical form. This applies to 'The
LORD says . . . "Sit at my right hand"' (110:1). But then, if God
can say 'I hereby raise my hand' (Ezek. 36:7; 44:12) without suggesting a physical action, could Abraham use the same phrase
before the king of Sodom without literally raising his hand (Gen.
14:22)? Perhaps the millennium or more between Abraham and
Ezekiel was the time needed for full idiomatization. As idioms,
such expressions when used of God should not be considered
anthropomorphisms.

Idiomatic meaning may also be suggested by a divine object, as
in 'they have raised their heads [against God]' (Ps. 83:2), that is,
they have rebelled. The idiom may well be based on the usual
requirement to bow before a king, though there is no evidence
that there was ever any tradition of non-Israelites bowing towards
the ark, even though it was considered to be the divine King's
throne.

Idiomatic meaning is present in the case of 'big vision' generali-
zations, such as the anointed king 'lifting his head' (110:7),[57] and
when moral abstractions give the interpretation, as in 'I have washed
my hands in innocence' (73:13). Similarly, idiomatic meaning is

---

56. Gelander, 'Convention', pp. 309–310.

57. Also, incidentally, his 'drinking from the brook', though the meaning of
   this idiom is less clear.

usually present in nominalizations, such as 'my head-lifter' for my
Saviour (3:3) and 'a head-nodding' for a byword (44:14).

Literal and idiomatic meanings can often be distinguished by
other information in the text which indicates whether a symbolic
act took place. For example, when Ruth asks Boaz, 'spread your
wing over your maidservant' (Ruth 3:9), his response, 'I'll do what
you've asked' (v. 11), shows that he understood she did not simply
want a share of his blanket, and he did not even perform this symbolic act. Instead, in the next chapter he redeems her. It is
tempting to consider whether he might have legally done so by
saying 'I hereby spread my wing over' (without, of course, any
symbolic action, since Ruth was not present) instead of 'I hereby
buy' (Ruth 4:9). On the other hand, Abraham's servant did in fact
put his hand under his master's thigh to seal his oath (Gen. 24:2,
9), so here we can understand the expression literally. Later,
though, when Jacob asks the same of Joseph, he receives the same
reply as Ruth: 'I'll do what you've asked' (Gen. 47:29–31), suggesting perhaps that Joseph already understood the expression as an
idiom. Indeed, we may wonder if, when required to swear (v. 31),
he could have performed the act by saying, 'I hereby put my hand
under your thigh.'

Of particular interest are body idioms relating to cultic ritual
acts. There are several expressions in the Psalms meaning
'stretch/lift the hand(s) to' (Pss. 28:2; 68:31; 77:3; 134:2), and it
seems clear that this is an expression of prayer, with no reason to
doubt that it was accompanied by the act. However, such an
expression in performative form ('I hereby . . .', 143:6) invites an
idiomatic interpretation, since this is a speech-act – the act is in the
words; if the act were concomitant with the words, we might
expect a participle form ('I am spreading') rather than the *qāṭal*
(traditionally 'perfect') form. There is one example where an
idiomatic interpretation is suggested by the context: 'If we had . . .
spread forth our hands to a strange god, would not God discover
this? For he knows the secrets of the heart' (44:20–21) – if the
idolatry had been in the form of an act, God could have seen it in
their hands, without having to search their hearts!

Similarly, we might interpret 'I lift up my eyes to the hills'
(121:1) as literal, referring perhaps to the higher hills surrounding

Jerusalem. But when we then encounter 'I hereby lift my eyes to you' (123:1), the performative form suggests an idiomatic interpretation such as 'I hereby look to you for help', which should then be read through the entire psalm. If this is right, and if these two psalms come from a similar linguistic milieu, we may look back to Ps. 121 and reconsider an idiomatic reading such as 'If I look to the hills/hill deities for help, what good will that do me?'[58]

This all still leaves many unresolved cases, e.g. '[they] mock at me, they make mouths at me, they wag their heads' (22:7, RSV), 'let them not wink the eye' (35:19, RSV). In such cases, scholars discuss possibilities whilst translators have to make choices between: translating the words, even if they have no meaning in the target language (RSV here), or a wrong meaning (1:1, RSV); translating the symbolic meaning, and so losing reference to the act involved, e.g. '[everyone] . . . makes fun' (22:7, CEV); or substituting a culturally equivalent symbolic act, e.g. 'they stick out their tongues', 'Don't let [them] smirk with delight' (22:7; 35:19, GNB).

Conclusion

As discussed elsewhere in this volume, most twentieth-century Psalms scholarship focused either on literary genres (following Gunkel) or on cultic *Sitz im Leben* (following Mowinckel). As in so many fields of Old Testament studies, the results of such work need to be drastically reconsidered for the twenty-first century in the light of modern linguistics, especially pragmatics. The verbal system and its special functions, speech-act theory and the study of idioms are promising fields of study from which Psalms scholarship can expect to gain new insights.

---

58. Gunkel, *Psalmen*, ad loc.

11. TORAH-MEDITATION AND THE PSALMS: THE INVITATION OF PSALM 1

Michael LeFebvre

It is widely acknowledged that Psalms scholarship is in transition. In particular, scholarly interest is moving away from the genre of individual psalms toward the 'shape' of the Psalter as a whole.[1] In few places is the impact of this transition so pronounced as in how Ps. 1 is understood.

Within genre studies, Ps. 1 was among the 'problem children' of the Psalter (to borrow Mays's affectionate term).[2] Other psalms – penitential psalms, community lament psalms, thanksgiving psalms, etc. – received primary attention. Psalms of clearly definable genres set the framework for the study of those less easy to categorize. Ps. 1 was among the hard-to-categorize 'leftovers' in past approaches to Psalms scholarship. Suddenly, however, with the rising dominance of 'shape' studies, Ps. 1 has been exalted to a place of primacy in Psalms scholarship.[3] With emerging interest in

---

1. See Howard's article in ch. 1 of this volume.
2. Mays, 'Place', p. 128.
3. For an overview of Ps. 1 in recent studies: Nasuti, *Defining*, pp. 165–208.

the Psalter as a collection, Ps. 1 is now seen as an introduction to the whole book. Ps. 1 now provides the framework by which the rest of the psalms are received. This 'problem child' of the Psalter has suddenly taken the 'lead role'. Nowhere else in the Psalter has the present transition in scholarship had so dramatic an impact as in relation to how Ps. 1 is viewed.

Oddly, however, little fresh attention has been given to what this psalm actually says. Now that Ps. 1 has achieved a place of such importance, so that the way it is read influences how all the psalms are received, it seems a critical issue on the scholarly agenda to conduct a fresh examination of its message.

In this paper, I hope to contribute toward such a reassessment. In what follows, one fundamental question will be explored – namely, 'What is torah-meditation in 1:2?' Some explanation of why this question is important should first be offered.

The problem of genre

Ps. 1 has generally been classified as a 'wisdom psalm' or a 'torah psalm'. Though such designations highlight certain of its features, it is debatable whether they capture the main point of the psalm. As Nasuti has recently pointed out, identifying a psalm's genre is an important aspect of its interpretation and can hardly be ignored. Yet, when peripheral details of a psalm become the basis of its classification, a distorted reading results. Nasuti illustrates this through the so-called 'penitential psalms': '[this designation] emphasized the penitential aspects of these seven psalms, with the result that their other aspects were seen in a "penitential" light.'[4]

This same problem seems to have arisen in the handling of Ps. 1. Certain features of the psalm which sound similar to wisdom writings led to the view that Ps. 1 also arose in wisdom circles. However, other features of the psalm have often been forced to fit this wisdom classification.

---

4. Ibid., p. 195.

For example, because a wisdom text is supposed to deal with issues outside the cultus,[5] the imagery in v. 5 of Yahweh's court and 'the congregation of the righteous' has often been interpreted non-culticly. Eaton observes such a conclusion in Gunkel's handling of v. 5: 'He classified the psalm as a "Wisdom Song",' and concluded that 'the "judgment" of 1.5 is . . . as generally in Wisdom teaching, the constant acting of God.'[6] In other words, *because* this is 'wisdom teaching', *therefore* the cultic-sounding scene in v. 5 must be metaphorical: it is the daily consequences of sin, not an actual expectation of judgment in God's house, that is perceived. Untangling the debate about the meaning of v. 5 is beyond the scope of this paper.[7] However, one must at least ask whether it is the *interpretation* of the psalm that is driving its classification or a presupposed *classification* that is driving its interpretation.

Until now the presumed wisdom nature of Ps. 1 has only affected how we read that single psalm. Once Ps. 1 is understood to guide the reception of the whole Psalter, however, the implications are dramatic. Some scholars now deduce that the editors of the Psalter belonged to the wisdom tradition and, consequently, that the original cultic concern of the rest of the psalms in the collection is neutralized by Ps. 1.[8]

This is a heavy burden for Ps. 1 to bear. It introduces a massive change in how the Psalms are viewed which, to be permitted, must be more firmly grounded by demonstrating the wisdom-interest of the Psalter's editors.[9] It seems more likely that the move to view

---

5. 'It is common . . . to relegate a Wisdom Psalm into the private sphere' (Gerstenberger, *Psalms I*, p. 43).

6. Eaton, *Psalms of the Way*, pp. 30–31.

7. See Eaton's survey of approaches, ibid., p. 48.

8. Mitchell notes Reindl's argument: 'the original cultic *Sitz im Leben* of individual psalms becomes insignificant in the face of the new *Sitz im Leben* that the Psalter has received' (Mitchell, *Message*, p. 59; cf. Reindl, 'Weisheitliche', p. 340).

9. Note Whybray's test of torah/wisdom interests in the Psalter: Whybray, *Reading*, pp. 42–87.

the Psalter as part of the wisdom tradition is a consequence of allowing a wisdom designation assigned to Ps. 1, primarily because it did not fit into other genre categories,[10] to carry over into its 'new' role. The designation of Ps. 1 as a 'wisdom psalm' seems unhelpful and ought to be dismissed.

The other traditional ascription for Ps. 1, 'torah psalm', also presents problems. This designation suggests that Ps. 1 is of the same cloth as other torah psalms (like 19 and 119). Grouping these into the same category presupposes that they share the same basic intent. But do they?

Pss. 19 and 119 state explicitly their concern for *obedience* to the many statutes, ordinances and judgments of God's law. Ps. 1 also speaks about God's law, but does not say anything about its precepts and never mentions obedience. Ps. 1 speaks about *delight* (1:2a). Delight may infer obedience, but is not necessarily the same thing.[11] It is often said that 'where there's smoke, there's fire', and one might suspect that 'where there is delight there will be obedience'. This does not mean that smoke and fire are the same thing, however, and neither are delight and obedience. Ps. 1 is not about obedience, yet when it is grouped with 19 and 119, the concern for obedience in the latter generally influences the interpretation of the former.

This is a matter of limited import when only Ps. 1 is in view, but it is now the whole Psalter that is impacted. For example, Brueggemann writes: 'Standing at the beginning of the Psalter, this psalm intends that all the psalms should be read through the prism of torah obedience.'[12] The life of faith is thus bounded by obedience (Ps. 1) and praise (Ps. 150). Brueggemann's basic insight

10. Some scholars are no longer sure what features distinguish a 'wisdom psalm'. For a discussion of the problems, see Crenshaw, *Psalms*, pp. 87–95.

11. Note also that v. 1 commends the 'happy one' (cf. 'delight'; v. 2) on the basis of the counsel and communion he follows. The dialectic behind 1:1–2 is not 'sinning vs obeying', but 'delight-in-sinful-counsel vs delight-in-torah'.

12. Brueggemann, 'Bounded' p. 64, reprint p. 190.

is probably correct. However, it should be asked whether *obedience* is actually the opening boundary. Ps. 1 seems to express *hope* in torah rather than obedience. The boundaries would therefore be better expressed as unrealized hope (the delight of Ps. 1) and fulfilled hope (the praise of Ps. 150).

The designation 'torah psalm' probably gets closer to the point of Ps. 1 than 'wisdom psalm'. However, it is not the same kind of torah psalm as Pss. 19 and 119 and needs to be carefully distinguished from them.

I propose that Ps. 1 be viewed as a 'torah-meditation psalm'. It is delight-nurturing meditation on torah, not torah itself, that Ps. 1 promotes: 'but this one's delight is in the law of the LORD, and on his law this one meditates day and night' (1:2, a.t.). In what follows, I hope to outline how an understanding of Ps. 1 as a 'torah-meditation psalm' might look, and to open the way toward perceiving its implications for the Psalter.

The meaning of 'meditation'

The Hebrew verb generally translated 'meditate' in 1:2 is *hagah*.[13] It is widely recognized among commentators, however, that 'meditate' is an awkward translation. In particular, the English word carries the connotation of something done silently,[14] yet the Hebrew verb is always *vocal*.[15] In Prov. 8:7, for example, *hagah* is used of Wisdom crying out in the streets. Here *hagah* is something vocal and declarative rather than silent and reflective. However, while the translation 'meditate' is imperfect, it is not a complete misfit as will shortly be seen. Nevertheless, certain features of the

---

13. For ease of reading, the frequently used Hebrew terms *hāgâ* ('to meditate') and *tôrâ* ('law') are used in their Anglicized forms, *hagah* and *torah*, in this paper.

14. The *Oxford English Dictionary* defines 'meditate' as 'to exercise the mind in thought or reflection'.

15. Negoiță and Ringgren, '*hāghāh*'; Van Pelt and Kaiser, '*hgh* I'. Cf. Sarna, *Book*, pp. 38–39.

Hebrew term that are not conveyed in the English translation must be brought sharply into focus.

First, as noted above, *hagah* denotes vocal activity, not silent thought. There are three ways in which commentators generally apply this to 1:2: (1) *reciting* something memorized;[16] (2) *reading* something written;[17] or (3) sounding *inarticulate* groans, sobs and murmurs in the midst of deeply emotional thoughts.[18] A fourth possibility that is rarely mentioned is *singing*. This is surprising, since three out of ten uses of *hagah* in the Psalter explicitly concern singing:[19]

> . . . my mouth praises you with joyful lips
> when I think of you on my bed,
> and *hagah* on you in the watches of the night . . .
> in the shadow of your wings I sing for joy. (63:5–7)

> I will also praise you with the harp . . .
> I will sing praises . . . with the lyre . . .
> My lips will shout for joy
> when I sing praises to you . . .
> All day long my tongue will *hagah* of your righteous help. (71:22–24)

> I remember my song in the night;
> with my heart I meditate [*síah*],
> and my spirit probes . . .
> I will *hagah* on all your work,
> and meditate [*síah*] on your mighty deeds. (77:6–12, a.t.)

---

16. E.g. Sarna, *Book*, p. 36; Davidson, *Vitality*, p. 11.
17. Even private reading in the ancient world was vocal. On 1:2 as instruction to read the torah, see e.g. Whybray, *Reading*, pp. 38–40. It has recently become common to speak of the whole Psalter as (part of) the torah here promoted for reading: e.g. Childs, *Introduction*, p. 513; Mays, 'Place', pp. 4–5; Wilson, *Psalms 1*, p. 96.
18. E.g. Terrien, *Psalms*, p. 73.
19. The ten appearances of *hagah* in the Psalter: Pss. 1:2; 2:1; 35:28; 37:30; 38:12; 63:6; 71:24; 77:12; 115:7; 143:5.

At least two of these texts refer to singing in private contemplation (63:6; 77:12), so that the lone individual in Ps. 1 could as readily be singing as reading, reciting or otherwise vocalizing thoughts.

Secondly, *hagah* indicates a quality of speech. The fact that *hagah* can be used for so many different kinds of enunciation – such as reading, reciting, groaning or singing – makes it clear that no one of them is *the* meaning of the term. If there is a specific kind of vocal activity in view, it is the context which must make this clear. On its own, *hagah* indicates a particular quality of speech rather than a particular kind.

Negoită provides the following clarification:

> . . . *haghah* is not a common word for speaking. Hebrew has other words for this, like *'āmar*, *dibber*, or *qārā'*. On the other hand, *haghah* is sometimes used to express the feelings of the human soul. With *siach* in particular, *haghah* means that a man 'is lost in his religion,' that he is filled with thoughts of God's deeds or his will.[20]

Other Hebrew terms of vocalization are more common than this one. When *hagah* is used rather than another speech-verb, it highlights that the speaker's wholehearted sentiments are being revealed.[21] This verb is like a transparency: it lends a certain colouring to the scene it overlays (the wholehearted character of the expression), but does not itself give shape to the action taking place (the kind of expression).

In Ps. 1, *hagah* emphasizes to us: (1) the vocal nature of the activity in view, and (2) the quality of that activity – it is a wholehearted enunciation of some sort. This might be confirmed by noting the verb's parallel in 1:2a – 'but this one's *delight* is in the law of the LORD, and on his law this one meditates . . .' (1:2, a.t.). It is an expression of innermost delight in torah that is revealed by the individual's *hagah*-speech.

---

20. Negoită and Ringgren, '*hāghāh*', p. 323.

21. 'The verb [*hagah*] describes the orientation of one's whole existence' (McCann, 'Psalms', p. 4.960).

This is why, although *hagah* does not always indicate meditation, when used of a solitary individual it does indicate 'talking to oneself' about one's deepest inner sentiments. Where used in soliloquy, 'meditate' is an appropriate translation, even if not perfect.[22] Unfortunately, no better translation seems to be available.

To summarize, then: the specific practice behind 1:2 is not made known by the verb *hagah*. This point should especially caution a common tendency in Psalter-shape studies which sees Ps. 1 promoting *reading* the Psalter.[23] All that *hagah* indicates is that the activity is vocal, and that it is reflective of the individual's innermost being. If a particular kind of vocalization is in view, this has to be supplied by the context.

The *hagah* of Ps. 1 does have a context, however: it is torah. Whether a particular kind of vocalization is expected when torah-meditation is promoted remains to be seen.

The meaning of 'torah'

Identifying the meaning of torah in 1:2 is probably more complicated than defining *hagah*. However, all that is necessary here is to note that the normal meaning of torah is 'law', with possible references being: (1) a certain, individual precept (*a* torah); (2) the whole Deuteronomic law collection (*the* Torah); or (3) the complete Pentateuch (also *the* Torah). Due to the definite nature of *the* torah in 1:2,[24] one of the latter two senses seems likely.

Traditionally, this is the way torah in Ps. 1 has been interpreted – as being the Mosaic law. More recently, however, it has become common to stress broader possibilities for the word, so that it might mean 'instruction' generally. In fact, Childs famously

---

22. Comparison with Josh. 1:8 supports the translation 'meditate' in 1:2. *Hagah* clearly expects contemplation in the Joshua passage (which is closely related to Ps. 1, as will be discussed below).

23. E.g., Wilson, *Editing*, pp. 206–207; *Psalms 1*, pp. 99–100.

24. Rendered definite by the construct relationship 'the torah of Yahweh' (1:2a), and by the possessive suffix 'his torah' (1:2b).

suggested that the Psalter itself might be part of the torah indicated by Ps. 1. According to him, the torah in Ps. 1 was originally the Mosaic law. However, 'the present editing of this original Torah psalm has provided the psalm with a new function.' In particular, 'Ps. 1 has assumed a highly significant function as a preface to the psalms which are to be read, studied, and meditated upon.'[25] In other words, the Psalms themselves become part of the torah commended for meditation in Ps. 1.

Building on Childs's suggestion, there has been a movement in Psalter shape scholarship to interpret the word torah in 1:2 as 'instruction' generally rather than 'law' specifically, and then to suggest that this instruction now refers to the Psalter itself.[26] This is not the place to address these studies extensively.[27] I simply note here that such shifts in understanding torah in Ps. 1 are not based on new insights into the psalm itself, but derive from a supposed relationship of Ps. 1 to the rest of the Psalter.

The supposition that Ps. 1 introduces the Psalter is appropriate. However, abandoning the normal translation of torah as 'law' seems more like an effort to justify Ps. 1's introductory role than an interpretation drawn from the text. The fact that the Psalter has been shaped as a five-book collection, mirroring the Pentateuch, should confirm the expectation that *the* Torah is indeed in view in Ps. 1.[28] So I will maintain the traditional translation of torah as 'law', a reference to the Mosaic law.[29]

---

25. Childs, *Introduction*, p. 513.

26. See note 19, above.

27. See essays by Howard and Wilson in this volume (chs. 1 and 12). These approaches have been questioned; cf. Whybray, *Reading*, pp. 38–42.

28. This view is ancient, cf. the rabbinic midrash on Ps. 1: 'As Moses gave five books of laws to Israel, so David gave five Books of Psalms to Israel...' (Braude, *Midrash*, p. 1.5).

29. Comparison with Josh. 1:8 also supports the translation of torah as 'law' for 1:2. The term certainly should be translated 'law' in Josh. 1:8, which is a close parallel to 1:2.

The meaning of 'torah-meditation'

The pieces are now in place to address the question, 'What is torah-meditation?' As one approach to answering this question, a look at the function assigned to the Mosaic song in Deut. 31 – 32 will be helpful.

Deut. 31 says that Moses composed two documents before his death: a book of law (v. 24) and a song (v. 22). Moses presented the torah-book to the priests and elders, but he taught the song orally to the whole congregation. These two texts, the law and the song, have so close a relationship in the account as to be seemingly confused at times. For example, both serve as a 'witness' against Israel (Deut. 31:19, 26). Furthermore, in Deut. 32:44–46, Moses recites 'all the words of *this song*' to the people, but upon doing so instructs them to 'observe all the words of *this law*'. In his study of this tightly integrated law-song relationship, Watts drew the following conclusion:

> The psalm . . . is taught to the whole people (31:19, 22, 30), whereas the law is transmitted to the Levites and the elders (31:9, 25, 28). This difference in the material's intended transmission depicts the psalm as a popular synopsis of the law, which by its poetic form is better able to transmit Deuteronomic notions to a large audience than the law book itself can . . . The emphasis on [the song's] oral as well as written transmission presents the psalm as a popularly accessible summary of Deuteronomy's theology and thus a counterpart to the law-book itself.[30]

Deut. 31 – 32 identifies law-contemplation with song-singing. It is the song which will be forever known by the people (Deut. 31:21), while the book is not accessible to them. According to Deuteronomy, the same Moses who appointed the written law also appointed song as an aid for common Israelites.[31] Watts suggests that this text offers an important insight into the function of

---

30. Watts, *Psalm*, p. 67.
31. Cf. McConville, *Deuteronomy*, p. 461; Miller, *Deuteronomy*, pp. 225–226.

psalmody in ancient Israel, and I agree.[32] Psalmody served as a means of torah-meditation.

It can now be proposed that, when torah-meditation is commended, *singing* may be particularly in view. The evidence from Deut. certainly says nothing about what Ps. 1:2 intends. However, there are certain features of Ps. 1 itself which suggest that a conscious link exists between the torah-contemplation-by-song idea of Deut. 31 and the torah-meditation commendation of Ps. 1.

The first of these features becomes clear when 1:2 is compared with Josh. 1:8. Scholars have long noted the nearly identical language of these two texts as indicating an intentional relationship between them:

> This book of the law [torah] shall not depart out of your mouth; you shall meditate [*hagah*] on it day and night . . . (Josh. 1:8)

> But this one's delight is in the law [torah] of the LORD, and on his law [torah] this one meditates [*hagah*] day and night.' (1:2, a.t.)

Both these texts idealize one who vocally meditates (*hagah*) on torah 'day and night'. Despite their overall similarity, there are also two rather significant dissimilarities. First, Josh. 1:8 is addressed to a specific person – Joshua.[33] Ps. 1, in contrast, exhorts the 'generic individual' (*'îš*; v. 1) to meditate on torah. How the ordinary Israelite could be expected to access the law, let alone read it, is problematic if it is the written law that Ps. 1 has in view. This, however, is the second distinction between the two texts. Ps. 1 does not say 'book of' torah, as does Josh. 1. Ps. 1 has no indication of a *written* torah. These two distinctions contrast the otherwise similar Joshua and Psalms torah-meditation texts. They seem to reflect deliberate coordination around the law-song paradigm of Deuteronomy, idealizing the leader's torah-meditation through

---

32. 'The narrative role of Deut. 32:1–43 provides evidence . . . of assumptions and expectations regarding psalmody in general' (Watts, *Psalm*, p. 80).

33. Cf. Deut. 17:18–20, which instructs Israel's king to have a copy of the law for daily study.

book-reading and the common Israelite's torah-meditation through unwritten means.

The verb *hagah* does not itself require 'singing' as the activity in view in Ps. 1. If one can *read* torah, then reading is appropriate. If one can *recite* torah, then recitation is fitting. Nevertheless, the features noted above suggest that the more popularly accessible means of torah-meditation must have been in view, of which *singing* is at least one demonstrable possibility.

A second observation from Ps. 1 can also be highlighted. It should be noted that vocalized meditation is not only *spoken about* in Ps. 1, but it is also *performed by* Ps. 1. Commentators have long discussed the adaptations of material from other contexts into this psalm. For example, the call to meditate in v. 2 is a restatement of Josh. 1:8, itself derived from a Torah injunction (Deut. 17:18–20). The tree imagery in v. 3 uses a common Ancient Near Eastern metaphor, possibly in some way related to Jeremiah's use of it (Jer. 17:8),[34] and possibly rooted ultimately in the Torah 'tree of life' tradition.[35] Even the judgment scene in v. 5 may draw upon an extant Torah tradition about the assembly (*ʿēdâ*) gathering at the sanctuary to receive God's judgment.[36] Ps. 1 presents a string of contemplations on existing claims of Israel's faith, including some rooted in *the* Torah.

This observation, if correct, is important. It means that Ps. 1 itself becomes a demonstration of what is envisioned in 1:2. It has occasionally been suggested that Ps. 1 is more properly regarded as prose rather than poetry; however, most scholars concur that Ps. 1 is indeed poetry. Ps. 1 is probably designed for memorization and recitation, and possibly even for singing.[37] To the extent that the function of Ps. 1 itself can be determined, the kind of activity envisioned in 1:2 can be further clarified.

Finally, whatever different activities might have been encompassed by torah-meditation when the psalm was composed, this

---

34. Holladay (*Psalms*, pp. 41–45) views Ps. 1:3 as the source of Jer. 17:8.
   Creach ('Like') sees Jer. 17:8 as the source of Ps. 1:3.

35. Cf. also Brown, *Seeing*, pp. 58–61; also Rev. 22:2.

36. Exod. 25:22; 29:43; 30:6, 36. Cf. Ps. 7:7.

37. E.g. Terrien, *Psalms*, p. 71.

commendation now appears in the context of psalmody. As noted earlier, the activity of *hagah* is determined by its context. As the introduction to a collection of songs, therefore, one might suspect that sung vocalization could have been particularly (though not necessarily exclusively) in mind for 1:2.

In summary: torah-meditation does not necessarily mean that the Mosaic Torah is the text being vocalized. Based on the paradigm in Deut. 31 – 32, it can be seen that Israel used surrogate texts for torah-contemplation, particularly songs. Ps. 1:2 may be promoting such contemplation of one's standing before the Torah through the vocalization of popularly accessible surrogates. By placing this psalm at the head of the Psalter, this collection would seem to be commended as a medium for this torah-meditation.

Conclusion

This paper has endeavoured to highlight the need for a fresh assessment of Ps. 1, and to contribute something toward that end. It is certainly not a complete study of the psalm, and its results are preliminary. Nevertheless, having considered the meaning of torah-meditation in 1:2, certain conclusions suggest themselves. The verb *hagah* is a generic word for wholehearted vocalization. In some instances, *singing* was a known means for popular contemplation on the Mosaic law (the Torah). There are hints that the Deuteronomy law-song paradigm may have influenced Ps. 1's shaping. It may be that it was this song-as-torah-surrogate ideal that the editors of the Psalter had in mind when they placed this psalm at the head of a book of songs. Now that Ps. 1 has become widely recognized as the entry point of the Psalter and the 'keynote' of the whole composition, a clearer understanding of what torah-meditation entails is an important question on the horizon of Psalms studies.

D. THE PSALMS AND INTERPRETATIVE TRADITIONS

12. THE STRUCTURE OF THE PSALTER

Gerald H. Wilson

In the last twenty years, research into the structure of the book of
Psalms, following earlier hints by Westermann and suggestions by
Childs,[1] has offered the community of biblical scholars new
avenues of approach to both psalms and Psalter. In contrast to the
predominantly negative conclusion of a preceding generation of
Psalms scholars that the canonical arrangement was largely
random and without a unifying editorial purpose, recent scholarship has convincingly demonstrated that the canonical Psalter is
the end result of a process of purposeful editorial arrangement of
psalms and collections of psalms producing a unified whole
marked by structures indicating editorial intent. Some of these
structural indicators include: the division of the Psalter into five
books marked by concluding doxologies; the existence of two
major stages of collection represented by the first three books
(Pss. 2 – 89) and the latter two (Pss. 90 – 145); the placement of
Pss. 1 and 146 – 150 as introduction and conclusion to the unified

---

1. Westermann, 'Sammlung', pp. 278–284; Childs, *Introduction*, pp. 512–513.

five-book collection; the placement of other significant psalms (some royal and 'wisdom' psalms) at strategic junctures of the canonical collection; more subtle distribution of thematic psalms and theologically significant phrases to suggest a particular hermeneutic for the reading of the collection in its final form.

Work to compare the shape of the canonical Hebrew Psalter with that of the related but distinctive LXX Psalter as well as the more radically divergent Qumran Psalter (11QPs[a]) has served to highlight the particular characteristics of the Hebrew collection and to offer insights into the intended effects of that arrangement on the reader. In addition, evidence from the Qumran Psalms manuscripts confirms the probability of the two-stage development of the final form of the Psalter and suggests a surprisingly late date for the conclusion of that process.

In what follows, I will first survey the evidence for the major editorially significant structures in the arrangement of the canonical Hebrew Psalter. I will then turn to a discussion of the theological implications that can be drawn from these structures and their effects on the attentive reader. I will conclude with a consideration of areas for continued research into the shape and shaping of the Psalter.

Indications of structure in the Psalter

The five-book division

Prior to the investigations of the last twenty years, the most widely recognized structural indicator in the Psalter was probably the division by doxologies into five 'books'. This division was known to the rabbis,[2] and was interpreted to imply a Davidic corpus of five books of psalms on a par with the five books of Moses. These five books are indicated by the presence of similar doxologies at the end of the first four books (Pss. 41; 72; 89; 106) and an

---

2. Braude, *Midrash*, vol. 1, p. 5. Dahood, *Psalms I*, p. xxxi, suggests that the fragmentary reference in 1Q30 to *sprym ḥmšym* may be 'the oldest explicit testimony to the fivefold partition of the Psalter'.

extended grouping of 'hallelujah' psalms (Pss. 146 – 150) at the conclusion of the fifth. The five-book structure may be intended to strengthen the authority of the Davidic collection by association with the Torah. It also highlights the theological significance of Torah, which is introduced at the beginning of the collection in Ps. 1 and reaffirmed by the massive presence of Ps. 119 in the final book.[3] I will return to this matter below.

Two groupings of books

The five-book division is only the most recognized structural indicator. These five segments are grouped into two distinct blocks of psalms characterized by distinct methods of arrangement and some thematic oppositions. The two blocks are composed of the first three books (Pss. 2 – 89) and the last two (Pss. 90 – 145). The first three books are dominated by psalms with author designations and genre terms in their superscripts, while very few psalms in the last two books include such indications. In addition, the first three books are composed primarily of individual lament psalms, while the last two contain predominantly communal thanksgiving and praise.

These distinctions suggest independent histories of development for these two sections of the Psalter. The likely conclusion is that the first three books came together at an earlier time than the last two and that the canonical collection is the result of a purposeful combination of these materials. This sequential development of the canonical Psalter is affirmed by the evidence from the thirty-plus Psalms manuscripts from the Dead Sea Scrolls. Investigation of the contents of these texts and their arrangement reveal no significant variations in the first three books. In contrast, the last two books demonstrate widespread differences in content and arrangement in manuscripts as late as the middle of the first century CE. As a result it seems certain that the canonical Psalter developed in two major stages: the first including Pss. 2 – 89 and completed by the mid-second century

---

3. See the development of this idea in the important works of Mays, in particular his *Lord Reigns*, pp. 128–135.

BCE; the second consisting of Pss. 90 – 145 brought together with the earlier collection some time by the mid-first century CE. The lack of any indication of variant manuscripts after this date indicates that the canonical arrangement won the day at that point and other arrangements faded from use.

A conclusion and an introduction

There is general agreement today that the final form of the canonical Psalter has been provided with a conclusion and an introduction. In the absence of a doxology at the end of the fifth book, a conclusion is supplied by the five hallelujah psalms (146 – 150) appended at the end of the Psalter.[4] A similar use of hallelujah psalms to conclude a segment is found at the end of the fourth book, where Ps. 106 exhibits the phrase *hallelujah* at beginning (v. 1) and end (v. 48) as well as a doxology (v. 48). The final *hallel* in Pss. 146 – 150 is precipitated by the concluding words of 145:21, 'My mouth will speak the praise of the LORD, and all flesh will bless his holy name for ever and ever.' Ps. 146, which is cast in the first person singular, represents David's fulfilment of the first half of 145:21, while in the remaining psalms the crescendo of praise increases in volume and participation, until 'everything that breathes' (150:6) joins in the final resounding 'Hallelujah!'

At the other end of the Psalter, it is increasingly clear that Ps. 1 stands intentionally positioned as an introduction to the whole Psalter. In many Psalter manuscripts, Ps. 1 is written without a number, or even in red ink – an indication that it was considered a preface or introduction to the book. This connects with the intriguing fact that in some Western New Testament manuscripts Acts 13:33 cites a passage from what is now known as Ps. 2:7 as coming from the *first* psalm.[5] This suggests that the author of those verses knew a manuscript in which Ps. 1 was not present, was left unnumbered as a preface, or had been combined with

---

4. A similar use of concluding praise and doxology is known from the Sumerian Temple Hymn Collection (Sjöberg and Bergmann, *Collection*, pp. 13–24).

5. The NA27 apparatus cites: Dgig, Or, Hil, Beda.

Ps. 2 as a single composition. A number of scholars claim that Pss. 1 and 2, while originally distinct compositions, have been editorially joined and positioned as a combined introduction to the final form of the canonical Psalter.[6] While it is true that in the final stages of editorial shaping of the Psalter Pss. 1 and 2 *have* been editorially reworked in order to serve together as a hermeneutical entrance point for reading the Psalter, those who espouse this view consistently fail to observe that Ps. 2 had already come to its position at an earlier stage (before Ps. 1 was introduced) in order to serve as introduction to the combined collection of Pss. 2 – 89.[7] This collection had eschatological overtones and sought to establish a strongly *messianic* reading of the first three books.[8] This collection – with Ps. 2 as its introduction – likely existed as an independent Psalter for some time, *before* Ps. 1 was added to preface an expanded collection that included the final two books (Pss. 90 – 145) and the concluding *hallel* (Pss. 146 – 150). It is likely that the placement of Ps. 1, with its emphasis on meditation and delight in God's torah (1:2), is connected to the division of the canonical collection into five books. I will comment further on the theological implications of this below.

Intersecting frames

Careful attention to the psalms occurring around the 'seams' of the five books – a place where editorial activity might reasonably be expected in order to 'stitch together' earlier groupings of psalms in a meaningful relationship – uncovers competing frames associated with the two larger segments (Pss. 2 – 89 and 90 – 145). A 'royal Davidic' frame is accomplished in the first three books by the placement of royal psalms at major seams: Pss. 2, 72 and 89.[9] The lack of a generally recognized royal psalm at the end of the first book (Ps. 41) may be explained by the apparent combination of the first two books into a collection of 'Prayers of David,

6. Cf. Willis, 'Psalm 1'; Sheppard, *Wisdom*, pp. 136–144.

7. Wilson, 'Psalms and Psalter'; 'Qumran'.

8. Mitchell, *Message*.

9. See Wilson, 'Use', pp. 85–94.

Son of Jesse', the end of which is indicated by the postscript to Ps. 72.[10]

Together these three psalms sketch out a thematic movement concerned to reflect on the rise, continuation and collapse of the hopes of the Davidic monarchy. Ps. 2 describes the inauguration of the Davidic dynasty in words reminiscent of 1 Samuel 7:1–17. At the end of the combined prayers of David, Ps. 72 (attributed 'to/for' Solomon) articulates the hope for successive Davidic monarchs to 'endure for ever . . . as long as the sun' (72:17). This happy hope of eternal blessing comes crashing down at the end of the third book. There Ps. 89, after beginning with the exalted expectations grounded in the inviolable word of God himself, turns swiftly to agonized confusion over the destruction of kingdom and monarch in the exile. God is called to task for his failure to protect his people as promised, and the psalm concludes with a demand that God remember his 'servant David' (cf. v. 20) and act to restore the kingdom (vv. 49–51). Mitchell suggests that the placement of royal psalms at the seams of the first three books was part of an eschatological programme with messianic interests characteristic of this earlier independent Psalter collection.

In contrast to the first three books, royal psalms do not stand at the seams of the last two books. Instead we observe the strategic placement of psalms and groups of psalms that have been tinged by apparent sapiential interests in order to provide a cohesive framework for the combined collection of five books.[11] These psalms include Pss. 1, 73, 90 and 107 and the grouping of 144 – 146. All of these psalms fall at the seams of the Psalter, while the first three (1; 73; 90) also stand adjacent to the royal psalms that provided shape to the earlier collection (Pss. 2 – 89). These wisdom-tinged psalms, along with the final *hallel* (Pss. 146 – 150), stand in their present positions as part of the cohesive framework that provides shape to the final form of the canonical Psalter.

---

10. Though Ps. 41 is not normally classified as royal, several elements accord
    with royal themes: concern for the poor, confidence in divine protection
    from enemies, hope for eternal security. See further my *Editing*, p. 208.

11. Wilson, 'Shaping', pp. 72–82.

The message of the final form

As I have indicated elsewhere, the elements just described combine in the final form of the Psalter to present an interpretative dialectic between the earlier Psalter (Pss. 2 – 89), with its focus on the demise of the Davidic monarchy, and the interpretative matrix provided by the final two books. I will now turn to a brief consideration of the conversation introduced by this movement to the canonical form of the Psalter.

A response to exilic agony

It is clear that *both* earlier and later segments of the Psalter are responses to the agony of loss in the exilic community. Psalms such as 74, 89 and 137 leave us no choice but to acknowledge that the final form of the Psalter reflects the period of exile. In response to the dislocation and crisis of identity associated with the demise of the Davidic monarchy, the loss of the ancestral land and the destruction of the Jerusalem temple, these two segments offer decidedly different perspectives. The earlier Psalter focuses hope on the Davidic monarchy, raises anguished questions over its demise, and provides a framework that both questions the purpose of God in allowing this destruction and finds hope in a future messianic restoration.

The reshaping of the earlier Psalter in the move to the final form suggests a different strategy in response to the same questions. This alternative strategy is reflected in new themes which are introduced particularly in the fourth and fifth books, but are also shared by the cohesive framework of the final form. Let me suggest just three shifts of perspective introduced in this later response.

Yahweh is king

The most obvious response to the agonized hopes raised at the end of Ps. 89 appears with the introduction of the *Yahweh Malak* psalms (93 – 99) in the heart of the fourth book. Following so closely on the anguished demand in Ps. 89 that God fulfil his covenant obligations and re-establish the Davidic monarchy, these psalms shift the focus of the reader away from human kingship to the eternal and just rule of Yahweh as king.

David is not

This redirection of focus is accompanied by a subtle but significant shift in the way that David is viewed in the last two books of the Psalter. In the first three books, the term *melek/mālak* ('king; be king') is employed as usual to describe: (a) kingship in general; (b) non-Israelite kings; (c) the kings of Israel/Judah; and (d) Yahweh as King. However, when we cross the boundary into the last two books, we discover that only three of these normal references survive; now *melek/mālak* is *never* used in relation to David or the kings of Israel/Judah. As in the first three books, David and his successors are spoken of as servant of Yahweh, anointed one, and even priest, but now never as *melek* ('king'). In these two books readers are encouraged to turn their hopes for rulership to Yahweh rather than to human kings who fail. Obviously the Davidic descendants do not simply disappear at this point, but are increasingly recognized as those anointed servants who usher in the kingdom of divine rule where Yahweh is King.

Delight in the Torah

Alongside this elevation of Yahweh to his rightful role of King over his people and the whole earth, the final shaping of the Psalter encourages a renewed allegiance to and even *delight* in Torah.[12] This attention to Torah is established by the placement of Ps. 1 (edited to link with Ps. 2) with its emphasis on constant meditation and delight on the torah of Yahweh (1:4) as the means of blessing (1:1) and the assurance of taking the right way – the way known by Yahweh (1:6). As Westermann and Mays (and others) have noted, this opening torah consciousness is balanced at the end of the Psalter by the inclusion of the massive acrostic Ps. 119 that is wholly a celebration of delight in and commitment to torah as the guiding force in the life of faith.[13]

---

12. See particularly the work of Mays, including *Lord Reigns*.

13. Westermann even posits the existence of an earlier form of the Psalter beginning with Ps. 1 and concluding with Ps. 119. See 'Sammlung', pp. 278–284.

The cohesive sapiential framework

Here let me sketch out in a brief form the effect of the cohesive sapiential framework I described above in light of the insights into the message of the final form just articulated. It is nearly impossible in such abbreviated space to provide more than suggestive comments in this regard, but some of this material has been developed more fully in other contexts and publications.

Psalms 1 and 2

As the introduction to the whole Psalter, Ps. 1 has now been edited in relation to Ps. 2 so that together the two introduce the major themes of delight in torah and reliance on Yahweh. Long ago the rabbis commented on the use of *'ašrê* ('blessed') at the beginning of Ps. 1 and the end of Ps. 2 and understood this double *'ašrê* as an indication that these compositions were to be read together. As we do so, it is interesting to note just where the emphasis of blessing falls. In Ps. 1, the singular addressee is *'ašrê* ('blessed') for delighting in God's torah and allowing it to guide their steps onto the way known and protected by God. Ps. 2 concludes with *'ašrê* ('blessing') on 'all who take refuge in him [Yahweh]' (2:12).[14] This tension between individual and community allows hope for the individual righteous person as well as the whole diaspora community seeking to understand what faithful living is when threatened by the overwhelmingly foreign environment of exile. These psalms then encourage the reader to approach the Psalms with this dual focus well and truly in mind: delight in torah and trust in Yahweh alone.

A pivotal psalm

Walter Brueggemann has espoused a pivotal role for Ps. 73 – a wisdom-tinged psalm standing adjacent to Ps. 72, just across the divide between the second and third books.[15] Brueggemann

---

14. In Ps. 2 it is sometimes difficult to determine who is described: God or the human king. This ambiguity encourages the reader to engage with the growing concern with Davidic kingship in the Psalter and with the shift to the kingship of Yahweh in the later books.

15. Brueggemann, 'Bounded', pp. 63–92. Others have noted the general shift

considers Ps. 73 to be the turning point in Israel's shift from obedience to praise, as suggested by the tension between the torah
obedience demanded in Ps. 1 and the universal call to praise with
which the Psalter ends (Ps. 150). Brueggemann claims that this
opening psalm of the third book 'stands distinctively and paradig-
matically in the difficult, demanding pilgrimage of Israel's faith
from obedience to praise . . . in the canonical structuring of the
Psalter, Psalm 73 stands at its center in a crucial role'. Ps. 73 is a
paradigm that Israel is called to follow and so mirrors the path
described in the Psalms, a 'path from obedience to praise, by way
of protest, candor and communion'.[16]

Brueggemann has observed a true phenomenon within the
shaping of the Psalter and he has offered helpful insights into
understanding one effect of this arrangement. His view is aligned
with that of Mays, who also emphasizes the importance of torah
to the editors of the canonical Psalter. However, as significant as
Brueggemann's insights are, they tend to oversimplify the message
of the final form. Ps. 73 is nevertheless an important psalm and its
position is significant.[17] It even represents a paradigm of sorts for
the believing community to follow, as Brueggemann suggests, but
it is a more nuanced paradigm than his treatment allows.

The third book of the Psalter (Pss. 73 – 89) is the place where
the collapse of the Davidic monarchy is most keenly felt. At the
end of this collection, Ps. 89 takes God to task for his failure to
respond in protective care according to his covenant obligations to
David. At the other end of this segment, Ps. 74 offers up an
equally confused cry of pain at the destruction of Zion and the
Jerusalem temple. These bookends set a tone of agonized

---

within the Psalter from individual lament to communal praise; e.g.
Gottwald, *Hebrew Bible*, p. 535.

16. Brueggemann, 'Bounded', pp. 81, 88.

17. It is particularly suggestive that, if the final *hallel* is omitted, Ps. 73 stands
at the exact centre of the remaining 145 psalm collection, with 72 psalms
both preceding and following it. Both 72 and 144 (72 + 72) are important
symbolic numbers in the Old Testament, which suggests that one should
look at the function and purpose of Ps. 73 more closely.

reflection and questioning as a consequence of the collapse of the Davidic monarchy and the subsequent experience of exile. How could God allow this to happen? And when will he respond in faithful fulfilment of his covenant responsibilities to re-establish the dynasty of David? These two psalms suggest a fitting conclusion for the eschatological programme that Mitchell describes as the message of Pss. 2 – 89.

But, in the final form of the Psalter, Ps. 73 stands just outside these bookends, and offers a contrasting way forward in response to the losses of the exile.[18] In opposition to the angry and demanding tone of Pss. 74 and 89, Ps. 73 models abandonment to the mysterious person and will of Yahweh. Rather than demanding a return to the past state of national identity, this psalm offers a new paradigm in which the inheritance (*ḥēleq*) of the faithful becomes Yahweh himself rather than the land. After a revelatory experience, the psalmist's soul-killing anger subsides, replaced by a reassurance based on knowing God himself. The psalmist surrenders:

> Whom have I in heaven but you?
> And there is nothing on earth that I desire other than you.
> My flesh and my heart may fail,
> but God is the strength of my heart
> and my portion forever.
> Indeed, those who are far from you will perish;
> you put an end to those who are false to you.
> But for me it is good to be near God;
> I have made the Lord GOD my refuge . . . (73:25–28)

Being near God is enough. God is a better portion than an inheritance of ancestral lands. Between Ps. 74 and its bracketing partner, the psalms of the third book offer mostly hopeful encouragement

---

18. Flint, *Dead Sea*, p. 48 n. 139, notes that Ps. 73 is one of only nineteen canonical psalms from the early collection of Pss. 2 – 89 for which no evidence has been discovered at Qumran. This is consistent with Ps. 73 having come to its current position in the last stage of Psalter redaction.

for those who remain loyal to Yahweh under the pressures of exile.[19]

A redirected response

In the last two books of psalms (90 – 145), key psalms tinged with wisdom interests stand at the seams of the books and provide assistance in redirecting a response to the anguished experience of exile and identity loss associated especially with Pss. 74 and 89. Ps. 90 reintroduces pre-monarchical Mosaic themes of reliance on Yahweh. Human strength is fragile and must turn to Yahweh as refuge, while acknowledging sin as the reason for divine wrath and judgment. This is a markedly different attitude from the demanding cries of Ps. 89, and prepares for the emphasis in the *Yahweh Malak* psalms (93; 95 – 99) on the kingship of Yahweh.

Ps. 107, at the beginning of the final book of the Psalter, describes a variety of exilic wanderers as they put their trust in God as the only hope for restoration. In the heart of this book, Ps. 119 celebrates the ongoing guidance provided by God's torah. At the end of the segment, the grouping of three psalms (144 – 146) – two *'ašrê* psalms surrounding a psalm of Yahweh's kingship – drives home once again the importance of placing trust in God's kingship rather than failing human princes. Ps. 144, attributed to David, celebrates God as the source of strength who gives victory and rescues those who trust in him. Ps. 145, also Davidic, proclaims Yahweh as the King whose kingdom is everlasting. Ps. 146 cautions not to trust in human princes who fail, but to rely on Yahweh who reigns for ever.[20]

Insights from Septuagint and Qumran Psalters

Elsewhere I explore in some detail a comparison of the

19. The primary exception to this hopeful tone is, of course, Ps. 88, which re-establishes the theme of deep despair over divine abandonment just before the questions of Ps. 89. On the arrangement of the third book, see further my *Psalms 2*.

20. On the arrangement of the fourth book, see further my *Psalms 2*.

arrangements of psalms in the Qumran, Masoretic and Septuagint Psalters.[21] I will mention here only the highlights of that research.

The LXX Psalter

In regards to the LXX Psalter, while the contents and arrangement of compositions remain essentially the same as in the Masoretic text,[22] a series of pluses in the psalms' headings give the sense of a more cohesive collection by filling out gaps in groupings of psalms with the same genre categories and author designations. By far the most significant addition in the LXX psalm headings is the attribution of additional psalms to David. The LXX adds such attributions to eleven psalms not so connected to David in the Masoretic collection. This tendency is especially strong in the fourth book (Pss. 90 – 106), where no less than nine compositions are supplied with Davidic attributions. This is particularly striking in that six of these nine psalms are the *Yahweh Malak* psalms (93; 95; 96; 97; 98; 99) that proclaim in the Masoretic Psalter the alternate vision of the kingship of Yahweh.[23] The addition of so many Davidic attributions changes the character of the fourth book from a segment in which David had receded into the background to a strongly Davidic collection.[24] Rather than shift emphasis from David to the kingship of Yahweh, the LXX heightens the profile and importance of David and the Davidic covenant. A similar emphasis on David is achieved by the addition in LXX of ten historical notices in the headings of Davidic psalms. While only four of these reflect specific events in David's life,[25] the effect is a further enhancement of the increasingly Davidic character of the LXX Psalter.

---

21. Wilson, 'Qumran'.

22. Note redivision: MT 9 & 10 = LXX 9; MT 114 & 115 = LXX 113; MT 116 = LXX 114 & 115; MT 147 = LXX 146 & 147.

23. The other three are 91; 94; 104.

24. David appears in only two of seventeen psalm headings in the Masoretic version of the fourth book.

25. Pss. 27; 97; 143; 144 (LXX 26; 96; 142; 143).

The Qumran Psalms Scroll (11QPsᵃ)

The Qumran Psalms Scroll offers a more radical alternative to the Masoretic collection than does the LXX Psalter. The Qumran Scroll is roughly parallel to the last two books and final *hallel* of the canonical Psalter (Pss. 90 – 150) and represents an alternative vision for completing the earlier collection of Pss. 2 – 89.[26] This scroll varies considerably from its Masoretic parallel by the omission of Masoretic psalms, the inclusion of non-Masoretic psalms, and a radically different arrangement.[27] Here is a brief summary of the most significant differences.

Omission of important groupings

The Qumran Psalms Scroll does not include several groups of psalms that form part of the thematic shaping of the canonical Psalter. These include: (a) the introductory psalms of the fourth book (90 – 92); (b) the editorial 'heart' of the Psalter including the *Yahweh Malak* psalms (94 – 100); (c) psalms marking the transition from the fourth to the fifth books (106 – 108); and (d) a group of wisdom-tinged hallelujah psalms (110 – 118). The omission of these important psalms radically changes the response of 11QPsᵃ to the agonized loss of the kingdom expressed in the third book. There can be no shift of focus to the kingship of Yahweh, because the requisite psalms to establish this theme are entirely missing.

In addition, the omission of the psalms that form the transition from Book IV to Book V reveals that the Qumran Scroll does not offer a five-book division like the canonical Psalter. As a result the canonical emphasis on delight in God's torah is undermined, even though Ps. 119 is included. This raises a question of whether the Psalter expanded by 11QPsᵃ would have included Ps. 1 – with its encouragement to delight in torah – as an introduction. And lastly, since the hallelujah psalms (110 – 117) reflect wisdom shading and introduce hope for a 'new exodus' from exile, their omission from

---

26. There is practically no evidence for variation in this earlier collection among the Qumran fragments. See Flint, *Dead Sea*; Wilson, Review of Flint, pp. 515–521.

27. See further Wilson, 'Qumran *Psalms Scroll*', pp. 448–464; 'Qumran'.

the Qumran Scroll eliminates these important themes that are part of the final shaping of the canonical Psalter.

Compositions not included in the Masoretic Psalter

A total of eleven compositions unknown to the canonical Psalter are included in the Qumran Psalms Scroll. Many of these works exhibit relationships to the sapiential tradition,[28] a fact that is not surprising given the common appearance of wisdom tinges in the final shaping of the canonical Psalter. In addition, these compositions add considerable emphasis on David. Toward the end of the scroll we find the last words of David from 2 Samuel 23, followed immediately by a prose piece describing David's compositions, and then the Davidic Ps. 140 known in the canon. Next comes the lone ascent psalm 134, then the scroll concludes with two new Davidic compositions (Pss. 151A and 151B). The scroll also adds Davidic attribution to Pss. 104 and 123. These additions, along with the elimination of many non-Davidic psalms, create a greatly heightened Davidic character for this collection.

11QPsᵃ as response to the complaint of Books I–III

Because of the elimination of the *Yahweh Malak* psalms, the response of the Qumran Psalms Scroll to the problem of Yahweh's rejection of the Davidic covenant in the exile revolves around two poles: desire for the restoration of Jerusalem and Zion associated with the nearly intact ascent psalm collection. The scroll laments the loss of Jerusalem and Zion (Ps. 137), but moves ultimately to assurance of restoration (the non-canonical Apostrophe to Zion). God will raise up a 'horn' for David through whom deliverance will be accomplished. In comparison to the canonical Psalter, the Davidic monarchy plays an elevated role in the Qumran Psalms Scroll.

Summary comparison

Examination of these three significantly different texts has highlighted the distinctive shape and vision of each in response to the

---

28. Particularly Ps. 154; Sirach 51; Hymn to the Creator; and the acrostic Apostrophe to Zion.

crushing experience of exile and the loss of the Davidic monarchy.
Comparison of these alternative responses provides insight into
the effect of the arrangement of the canonical Psalter. Perhaps the
most impressive discovery is the lack of any significant Davidic
presence in the third and fourth books of the canonical Psalter. In
the third book, as the monarchy is in collapse, we hear from David
only once in the prayer of desperate need in Ps. 86. David is similarly absent in the fourth book, where the foregrounding of the
Yahweh Malak psalms and the change in the use of the terms
melek/mālak point the reader away from dependence on the
Davidic monarchy to reliance on the kingship of Yahweh instead.

In contrast, the Qumran and LXX Psalters each respond in a way
that minimizes the power of the *Yahweh Malak* collection. In the
LXX, the distinctive voice of these psalms is muted by attributing
them to David and increasing the Davidic context of the book,
before and behind. This makes for a much more prominently
Davidic Psalter collection. In addition, the inclusion in LXX of attributions to the prophetic figures Jeremiah and Ezekiel (Pss. 65/64)
and four references to Haggai and Zechariah toward the end of the
Psalter (Pss. 146/145 – 148) creates a prophetic dimension to the
LXX Psalter that encourages even more an eschatological and messianic reading of David and the royal psalms.

11QPs[a] takes the more radical solution of eliminating the *Yahweh
Malak* psalms altogether, thus eradicating any strong acknowledg-
ment of Yahweh's kingship in tension with David. Instead, there is
heightened emphasis on David, celebrated in this collection as
prophet, sage and king, who leads the people into wise and diligent
obedience to torah as prelude to divine restoration.

Theological implications of shaping

While many theological implications of the shaping of the canonical Psalter have continuing impact on the believing reader of the
Psalms, there are still a few additional effects on interpretation that
have yet to be briefly stated.

The current shape of the final form of the canonical Psalter legit-
imates the continued use of the psalms as compositions intended

for the community of faith in worship of God. The superscriptions of the psalms recall the cultic origins of many of these compositions within the worship experience of Israel. The plural reference in many psalms intends to incorporate the whole worshipping community, and often even individual psalms have been supplied with an indication of adaptation to communal use. In addition, the liturgical structures present in many psalms invite communal performance of antiphony, refrains, liturgical question and response.

The shaping of the Psalter allows the continued individual appropriation of individual psalms as models of personal access to God in prayer. Obviously the individual reference in some psalms invites personal identification of individual readers. The historical references in some superscriptions interpret these compositions as responses to specific life-events. Elsewhere in Scripture the insertion of hymns in narrative texts confirms the use of psalms in this way (Jon. 2; Judg. 5; Hab. 3). These factors affirm the possibility that all psalms can be adopted as models of individual prayer.

The shape of the Psalter encourages an individual approach of meditation and study of the Psalter as a whole. The placement of Ps. 1 as introduction stresses individual diligence and continual study, gives admonition regarding the life and death significance of the enterprise, and links the Psalms to torah guidelines – a feature reaffirmed by the five-book division of the Psalter. The evidence for the careful and purposeful arrangement of psalms is only accessible to the kind of careful reflection and meditation envisioned by Ps. 1 – study that does not focus exclusively on individual psalms or their emotional content.

It is, in my opinion, pre-eminently in this careful shaping and arrangement of psalms and Psalter that these very human words *to* God have made the shift to become God's word to *us*. This is where biblical theology intersects with a historical-critical reading of the psalms. Reading the psalms from beginning to end forces us to set aside our own preconceptions and calls us to lay aside our own perceived needs as the driving force of our encounter with the psalms. Such openness allows God freedom to challenge, confront and ultimately transform us in ways we do not control or even expect.

The clear shift from dominant lament in the first half of the Psalter to predominant praise and thanksgiving in the last half indicates that we are called to live in a real world of undeniable suffering and pain. Yet lament is not God's final word. Thus it is appropriate that the Hebrew title of the Psalter is *Tehillim*, 'Praises'.

The shift from individual lament to communal praise/thanksgiving that takes place within the Psalter when read from beginning to end suggests that individuals faced with the pain of the real world find strength within the community of faith. Alone we are confronted with our weakness; within the community we hear testimony to God's strength and redeeming purposes. God continues to offer us refuge within the storm of life.

The emphasis of the final form is that Yahweh is King! Human sin and weakness cannot undermine the sovereignty of God, who counters human weakness with his power and continued provision, who confronts human sin and evil with his judgment and justice.[29]

---

29. See Wilson, 'Songs', pp. 231–243.

© Gerald H. Wilson, 2005.

13. QUMRAN AND THE PSALMS

Dwight D. Swanson

No volume on a biblical topic is complete without reference to the evidence of the Dead Sea Scrolls relating to that topic. Too often this is a token nod to the need to 'keep all the bases covered', while the rest of the book hardly notes the implications raised. This should not be the case in this instance, with more than one author conversant in the Psalms material from Qumran. The fact is, the evidence of the Dead Sea Scrolls regarding the Psalms touches on a wide variety of topics relating to biblical studies. The significant number of manuscripts and the plurality of texts represented provide important data for textual criticism and the history of the biblical text for Old Testament studies. The differing order of psalms in relation to the Masoretic Text, inclusion of otherwise unknown psalms, and whole manuscripts of non-canonical psalms, offer insight into the development of the corpus during the late Second Temple period. 'Commentaries' on some of the psalms add to our understanding of the interpretation of the Psalms in this period, and a high degree of citation of psalms in the New Testament makes the scrolls important for New Testament studies.

The goal of this essay is to describe the Psalms manuscripts among the Dead Sea Scrolls, and the state of the scholarly discussion regarding their significance, in order to emphasize the importance of the Psalms scrolls for the questions just raised.

The manuscripts

Statistical overviews

The manuscript evidence regarding the Psalms may be presented in a variety of ways. The first is to count the scrolls. By Peter Flint's count, there are thirty-nine Psalms scrolls from locations along the Dead Sea: thirty-six from the eleven Qumran caves, one from Nahal Hever, and two from Masada.[1]

The second is to place these numbers in some sort of context. The Qumran Psalms scrolls represent the largest number of manuscripts of any single biblical book at Qumran.[2] Three of these come from Cave 1, twenty-seven from Cave 4, one each from Caves 5, 6 and 8, and four from Cave 11. Two of the Cave 11 manuscripts are among those containing the largest extent of surviving text. Besides these manuscripts containing only psalms, there are seven other texts that include significant citations of the psalms. To place these numbers in perspective, some 200 of the estimated 900 manuscripts represented by the Qumran fragments are recognized as 'biblical' (reflecting the later Jewish and Christian canons).[3] Thus, the Psalms scrolls represent nearly 20% of biblical manuscripts found.

The significance of these numbers is that, even if allowance is made for the simple accident of preservation of some manuscripts as opposed to others through the centuries, their numbers relative to the survival rate of all biblical books serve as an indicator of the important place of the Psalms in the life of the

---

1. Flint, *Dead Sea*, pp. 257–264; 'Psalms Scrolls', pp. 287–290.
2. The next most copied are Deuteronomy with twenty-six and Isaiah with twenty-two; cf. Ulrich, 'Isaiah', p. 385; Duncan, 'Deuteronomy', p. 198.
3. VanderKam, *Dead Sea*, pp. 30–31.

community that copied and preserved them. Having said this, some caution needs to be maintained with regard to the extent of the original content of these manuscripts. Many of them are too fragmentary for us even to begin to speculate as to how many psalms were in the complete scroll. For example, 4QPs[j] consists of some twenty verses in one fragment of Ps. 48, two of Ps. 49, and one of Ps. 51;[4] 4QPs[k] contains a fragmentary column of Ps. 135 and another of Ps. 99 (in that apparent order); 4QPs[n] consists of one fragment of a portion of Ps. 42:5. Altogether, nineteen of the manuscripts are similarly minute, tempering any assumption that all represent a complete Psalter. In light of this count, the evidence for evaluating collections of psalms is limited to no more than twenty manuscripts.[5]

Collections

In light of this, it should be no surprise to learn that there is *no* scroll that contains all the biblical psalms, nor that not all the biblical psalms are extant (only some 126).[6] Even so, the evidence from what is present suggests that none of the manuscripts would ever have contained that many psalms. One simple reason is that such a scroll would have been very large and unwieldy. Flint spells this out: the Cave 11 Psalms Scroll (11QPs[a]), containing forty-nine psalms, is 5 m long; a full 150 psalms would mean a 15 m long scroll. In comparison, the Great Isaiah Scroll (1QIsa[a]) measures just over 7 m, and the Temple Scroll (11QT[a]) just over 8 m.[7] It is unlikely that any manuscript was ever that long.

---

4. By the Masoretic Text's versification.

5. By my own count. This does not imply that these fragmentary manuscripts do not contain important data for understanding the Psalms, as we shall see.

6. Flint, *Dead Sea*, p. 48. The use of the word 'biblical' refers to the later canonical 150 psalms, based on the Masoretic Text, and not necessarily to those which would be considered 'Scripture' by the community that preserved them. On this distinction, see Swanson, 'How Scriptural', pp. 407–408.

7. Ibid., pp. 40, 48.

Recognition of this practical factor raises some interesting questions regarding what is included in these shorter collections, such as what principles of inclusion were used. This aspect will be discussed more fully in the next section,[8] but we can begin to seek the answer to this question by surveying the contents of the manuscripts.

(1) The first notable feature is that most manuscripts appear to have contained psalms only from Pss. 1 – 89, while others only from beyond Ps. 90.[9] This has given birth to the theory that a corpus of Davidic psalms reached essentially their canonical shaping prior to this period, with the rest of the Psalter still in process of growth. This will be discussed more fully below.

(2) In light of this, it is useful to consider the evidence from those manuscripts that do overlap. 1QPs[a] consists of twenty-two fragments, only eleven of which can be identified. There are portions of Pss. 86, 92, 94, 95–96 and 119. Obviously little can be speculated upon as to how extensive this manuscript may have been. Yet, because these fragments come from psalms relatively close to each other, it is conceivable that they represent what is left of the end of a manuscript which concluded with Ps. 119.

4QPs[e] contains portions of psalms between 76 and 130, but without 119. Ps. 118 is followed immediately by 104 and 105, and then 120. On the other hand, 11QPs[b] (which begins with Pss. 77 – 78) includes Ps. 119, followed by 118 with verses in a different order from the MT. What has not commonly been observed of both these manuscripts is that, although they contain psalms earlier than Ps. 89 (in MT numbering), none is earlier than Ps. 72, which in the MT contains the note, 'The prayers of David son of Jesse are ended.' Thus, these may represent collections reflecting development beyond the fixing of Pss. 1 – 72.

One manuscript includes later psalms within a collection of earlier ones. 11QPs[d] contains fragments from Pss. 6 to 86 (though not in the MT order), with Pss. 81, 86, and 115 – 116 situated between portions of Ps. 78. Again, there is no way of knowing the original extent of this manuscript. But if the order of fragments is

---

8. And relates to Gerald Wilson's contribution in ch. 12 of this volume.

9. Flint, *Dead Sea*, notes only five manuscripts that overlap, p. 48.

correctly discerned, the insertion into the account of Israel's faith-lessness in Ps. 78 with psalms of supplication and thanksgiving gives this manuscript an exegetical or liturgical slant that is not seen in other manuscripts. Is this, then, a collection of psalms, or an exegetical text?

The manuscript least susceptible to explanation for overlap is 4QPs^f. Ten columns are reconstructed at Pss. 107 – 109, followed by three non-canonical psalms not known outside Qumran.[10] One fragment also survives, from Ps. 22. The editors believe Pss. 107 – 109 would have taken seven or, more likely, eight columns of the scroll.[11] They do not discuss the possible length of the scroll, but the relatively short width of columns leads one to believe this to be an excerpted manuscript (more on this below) rather than a full collection. If such is the case, then we must look for some other organizing principles for the inclusion of Ps. 22.

(3) The six fragments of 1QPs^b include portions of Pss. 126 – 128. Flint is cautious, but raises the possibility that this manuscript may have contained only the Songs of Ascents (Pss. 120 – 134). This would provide manuscript evidence for these as a separate unit prior to inclusion in the larger corpus of the Psalter, but the point cannot be pressed.

(4) If that is conjecture, then we probably find ourselves on even shakier ground in wondering what to make of the absence of some psalms from collections. 4QPs^b contains text of Pss. 91 – 118, and appears to have ended at Ps. 118. What surprises is that col. 25 ends with Ps. 103, and col. 26 picks up with Ps. 112. Were Pss. 104 – 111 not included? Or were they placed elsewhere? Whichever case, the editors wonder if this implies that these psalms once formed an independent unit.[12] Again, this is an attract-ive idea for the light it may shed on the formation of smaller collections. At the same time, it raises a new question as to why, if these were an existing collection, the MT split them across Books IV and V of its Psalter.

---

10. One of which is held in common with 11QPs^a and 11QPs^b.

11. Skehan, Ulrich and Flint, 'Psalms', p. 85.

12. Ibid, p. 23.

Excerpted texts

We have already hinted at the existence of scrolls consisting of selected psalms (4QPs^f), rather than of 'Psalters'. We have seen that large scrolls, up to 15 m in length, would be cumbersome for either study or quick reference, making their existence unlikely. Undoubtedly some scrolls were created for more ready access. Whereas we have speculated on a possible exegetical purpose for 4QPs^f, there are other potential purposes for such scrolls. One suggestion is that some psalms are 'excerpted' from a larger collection for particular purposes.[13] We look at some of these now.

(1) Ps. 119 seems to have held a place of importance amongst psalms at Qumran. Two manuscripts (4QPs^g and ^{h}) are likely to have consisted of only this one psalm.[14] The manuscript of 4QPs^g is only 8.4 cm high, and there are no more than eight lines per column. The text is written out in poetic form (stichometrically), with four lines per stanza; the whole would have been twenty-five columns long. 4QPs^h appears to begin with Ps. 119:1. The columns in this case contained twenty-one lines, so the scroll extended to nine columns.

It is not difficult to imagine the reason for multiple copies of this psalm existing in a community which lived to meditate upon and keep Torah, and who were called to a 'perfect walk'. The Community Rule affirms: '[The Master] shall admit into the Covenant of Grace all those who have freely devoted themselves to the observance of God's precepts, that they may be joined to the counsel of God and may live [lit.: walk] perfectly before him in accordance with all that has been revealed ...'[15] (cf. Ps. 119:1).

(2) 4QPs^l is a single fragment including text on two columns, both containing portions of Ps. 104. The wide right-hand margin before the beginning of the psalm confirms that this is the beginning of the scroll. Like the Ps. 119 manuscript, this is clearly a small scroll, with the text presented in stichometric lines little

---

13. Tov, 'Excerpted'.

14. Brooke, 'Psalms', p. 8; Skehan, Ulrich and Flint, 'Psalms', p. 107. Both include the possibility of 5QPs as another example.

15. 1QS 1; Vermes, *Complete*, pp. 98–99.

more than 4 cm long. This would make for six columns of text,[16] or a handy 35–40 cm of leather.

In discussion of 4QPs^e, above, we noted that Ps. 104 appears in a different setting from the MT. Further, in three of the five scrolls which include Ps. 104, the text differs in form from the biblical text. Ps. 104 seems to have important exegetical significance at Qumran. The opening, 'Bless, O my soul, the LORD', is the inspiration for another text found at Qumran of which five copies survive, *Barki Nafshi* (4Q434–437). The latter does not appear to be a sectarian text, that is, it does not originate with the Qumran community. However, one text which is considered a core sectarian text, the Thanksgiving Hymns (1QH), also shows affinity to Ps. 104. These factors point to a common strain of development from this psalm.

(3) A third manuscript of interest here is 4QPs^x (4Q98g),[17] which illustrates the indistinct territory between what is a 'biblical' text and what is something-else-but-not-quite-Bible. At its first publication this manuscript was described as a source for the canonical Ps. 89.[18] Patrick Skehan, the first editor of the Qumran Psalms manuscripts, disagreed, seeing it instead as based on the canonical psalm.[19] J. P. M. van der Ploeg viewed this as similar to early Christian *testimonia*, or collections of messianic proof-texts.[20]

The ambiguity arises from the arrangement of the psalm with different order[21] and possible Aramaic influences.[22] If it is the canonical psalm, it is a different version. The difficulty in deciding

---

16. Skehan, Ulrich and Flint, 'Psalms', p. 128.

17. Flint, *Dead Sea*, pp. 38 and 268, where it is discussed under the earlier designation 4QPs98/4Q236; Skehan, Ulrich and Flint, 'Psalms', renamed as here.

18. Milik, 'Fragment', pp. 94–104.

19. Skehan, 'Gleanings', p. 439. Flint, *Dead Sea*, p. 38, cites Skehan's description of the fragment as a 'practice page written from memory'. The rather irregular script does give credence to the suggestion (Plate XX).

20. Van der Ploeg, 'Le sens', p. 475.

21. Verses 20–22 are followed by vv. 26, 23, 27–28 and 31.

22. Skehan, 'Gleanings', pp. 441–442.

how this relates to the canonical Ps. 89 is further complicated by the early date given to this manuscript – dated palaeographically by J. T. Milik between 175 and 125 BCE – making it one of the oldest Psalms scrolls.[23] Ps. 89 would appear to be a firm part of the Davidic collection by this time, but the existence of this version indicates that the text itself was still fluid at least in the second century BCE.[24]

That each of these examples might be viewed as being excerpted from a collection for theological reasons has implications for our understanding of the role of the Psalms in the Second Temple period, and in their subsequent canonical shape – the various ways a single psalm is presented may differ from setting to setting, with a different theological function. Interpretation of a psalm cannot be divorced from the purpose of its setting.[25]

'Non-canonical' psalms

Thus far we have looked only at Qumran psalms in comparison to their canonical, 'biblical' counterparts. One of the significant aspects of these Psalms scrolls is the inclusion of 'non-canonical' or 'apocryphal' psalms in a significant number of manuscripts.

(1) The so-called apocryphal psalms are those previously known from Psalters besides the MT. The LXX includes a Ps. 151 with a superscription that clarifies it as supernumerary to the proper 150, although it is affirmed as being written by David himself. This psalm and four others also appear in Syriac manuscripts.[26] The Syriac translation of the Scriptures is a Christian version, clearly later in provenance than the LXX version, and has thus been regarded as a late witness to the Psalms tradition. As such, the psalms that are extra to the MT have been regarded as being of

---

23. Flint, *Dead Sea*, p. 38, on Milik, 'Fragment', p. 95.

24. Dahmen, *Psalmen*, attempts to address this issue in terms of analysis of the text form and composition of 11QPs[a].

25. Brooke makes this point with regard to the Qumran collections as an 'intermediate stage' of the formation of the complete collections, 'Psalms', p. 8.

26. Details may be found in Sanders, *Dead Sea*, p. 53.

later composition. All of these appear in the most complete Qumran Psalms scroll, 11QPs[a]. This factor has forced a re-evaluation of their pedigree, so that now the Syriac psalms are seen to be a faithful reflection of the Psalter extant in Palestine at the turn of the era.[27] These 'apocryphal' psalms must be seen as authentically authoritative texts for a significant portion of Second Temple Judaism and early Christianity prior to the fixing of the corpus at some point late in the process of canonization.

(2) The Cave 11 Psalter also includes two other previously known compositions. This scroll begins with the MT Ps. 101, and ends with LXX/Syriac Ps. 151, within twenty-eight extant columns. The psalms do not follow the MT order, and include Ps. 93. The chief divergence is seen following Ps. 145 in col. 17: Ps. 154 (Syriac equivalent) is followed by the 'Prayer for Deliverance', then Pss. 139:8–24, 137:1, 138:1–8, Sirach 51 (vv. 13–20, 30) and the 'Apostrophe to Zion'. The final two columns begin with the 'Last Words of David' from 2 Sam. 23, then a prose epilogue called 'David's compositions', followed by Pss. 140:1–5, 134:1–3 and 151.

(3) As noted above, the Qumran scrolls also include some hitherto unknown compositions. 11QPs[a] contains four of the six or seven unique psalms.[28] Two appear here only: the 'Hymn to the Creator' and 'David's Compositions'. The latter serves as the epilogue to this Psalter, and gives the total of David's psalms as 4,050. This is broken down into 3,600 psalms, plus other types of songs besides those set for the whole of the liturgical calendar. The purpose of this seems to be to plant the seal of David's authority firmly over all the compositions, and thus it serves to determine the context for interpreting them.

---

27. Brooke, 'Psalms', p. 9. Brooke, p. 11, also draws attention to Ps. 154 in 4Q448, a manuscript referring to King Jonathan, as indicative of the status of this psalm. The text is edited by Eshel and Eshel in '4Q448 and Prayer', with a fuller study in '4Q448, Psalm 154'.

28. Flint counts ten or eleven, including as non-MT pieces what he calls the 'catena-like' version of Ps. 118, in which only vv. 1, 15–16, 8, 9 and 29 appear.

Two other new Psalms, 'Apostrophe to Zion' and 'Plea for Deliverance', are shared with 11QPs[b], and the latter with 4QPs[f]. 4QPs[f] in turn contains a further two new psalms, one entitled 'Eschatological Hymn', and the other 'Apostrophe to Judah'.

While it is tempting to go into the contents of these psalms, it must suffice for this discussion to observe that they appear alongside texts common to other Psalters, and thus must be considered of the same importance or validity. They stand as evidence of the breadth of possibilities still open for collections beyond that known in the Masoretic tradition.

(4) The psalms discussed thus far in this section appear within collections of known canonical psalms. But there are manuscripts which contain psalms without the inclusion of any material known from the MT or LXX, yet are clearly 'Psalm-like'. 4Q380 is a fragmentary collection of compositions; a 'Zion Psalm', laments and wisdom psalms.[29] The one complete title reads 'Prayer of Obadiah' – whether this refers to the prophet or to another of that name is not clear. 4Q381, Eileen Schuller notes, is written with the same scribal practice as found in the Psalter texts,[30] and includes ascriptions to 'Manasseh', 'the man of God' and a 'king of Judah' whose name is lost in a lacuna.[31] Noting that these manuscripts have not been included in discussion of the Psalms thus far, George Brooke argues that they have to be included in any theory of the development of Psalter, not only at Qumran, but also before Qumran.[32]

This is a valid point, which must not be quickly dismissed. Because of scholarship's orientation towards the MT when discussing the Psalms, the manuscript evidence of non-canonical psalms is easily disregarded. The presence of non-canonical psalms *within* manuscripts containing 'canonical' psalms implies that non-canonical psalms scrolls such as 4Q380 and 381 must be recognized too. In a period when the collection is not yet fixed, the

---

29. Schuller, 'Non-Canonical', p. 77.

30. Ibid. p. 88.

31. Ibid. p. 90.

32. Brooke, 'Psalms', p. 12.

possibilities for inclusion are broader than has been commonly considered.[33]

The growth and editing of the Psalter

Growth of the Psalter(s)

The Cave 11 Psalms Scroll (11QPs^a), containing some forty-nine psalms beginning with the canonical Ps. 101, is dated to the middle of the first century CE. The existence of a version so different from the canonical Psalter, and so late in the Second Temple period, has opened a window on the process of the formation of the Psalter.

The significance of this manuscript has been contested since publication. James Sanders followed up his 1965 edition of the scroll with the thesis that this represented a genuine Psalter, showing that the 'canon' of the Psalms was not closed at this time. The process of fixing the text was already virtually complete for Pss. 1 – 100, but the rest were still capable of re-arrangement.[34] This scroll is one step along the way in a gradual process of growth.

Issue was taken with this thesis by Shemaryahu Talmon, who rejected the idea that these could be considered biblical psalms due to the inclusion of the prose 'David's Compositions'. He contended instead that they are intended for liturgical and homiletical purposes.[35]

The liturgical argument was picked up by Skehan, who further argued that the Cave 11 collection is based on knowledge of the canonical 150 psalms. The fact that eight non-canonical psalms appear amongst the last eleven canonical psalms indicates for him their late insertion into a fixed order.[36]

---

33. Beckwith, 'Early', is an example of the MT orientation in arguing that inclusion of a 'recent book' like Sirach in a collection could not be considered 'biblical text' (p. 22). He also ignores the evidence of the non-canonical psalms, using only the Thanksgiving Hymns (1QH) as a basis for comparison (p. 17).
34. Sanders, beginning with 'Variorum', and given fullest expression in *Dead Sea*.
35. See Talmon, 'Pisqeh'.
36. Skehan, 'Qumran', p. 169.

These arguments are based on the premise that the MT 150-psalm Psalter was already settled by the time of the translation of the LXX, presumed to have been complete by the second century BCE.[37] On this basis, a much later manuscript such as 11QPs^a must be seen as a derivative text without canonical pretensions. This could be argued as long as 11QPs^a was viewed as a one-off text. But the publication of the rest of the Qumran biblical manuscripts, with their evidence of the pluriformity of biblical texts into the first century CE,[38] and particularly the Psalms scrolls from Cave 4, has changed the landscape.

Peter Flint, who completed the editing of the Psalms scrolls begun by Skehan and Ulrich, has put forward the most comprehensive proposal for the relation of the various Psalters and Psalms collections to each other. His thesis is that there were three literary editions of the Psalter: Edition I consists of Pss. 1/2 – 89; Edition IIa is Edition I plus the 11QPs^a Psalter (also represented by 4QPs^e and some other Qumran manuscripts); Edition IIb is the MT Psalter, i.e. Edition I plus Pss. 90 – 150 (also represented at Masada in MasPs^b).[39] In other words, the Psalters took form in two parts.[40] First, Pss. 1 – 89, the first three books of the MT Psalter, were an established collection at an early date, based on Davidic authorship, most certainly preceding the formation of the Qumran community. Second, the Psalms collections continued to develop gradually over the course of one or two centuries, with great flexibility in contents and order of material. We have manuscript evidence of at least three Psalters existing simultaneously in late Second Temple Judaism: an MT-type, a Cave 11-type, and an LXX-type. It is not unreasonable to conclude that there could be even more options found within the Qumran scrolls, but these are difficult to discern due to the scrolls' fragmentary nature.[41]

---

37. As asserted by Beckwith, 'Early', p. 6. As with the other scholars, he does not show how he arrives at this dating.
38. See esp. Ulrich, *Dead Sea*, for the background of this topic.
39. Flint, *Dead Sea*, summarized on p. 239.
40. On this and the following section, see further ch. 12 by Wilson in this volume.
41. Brooke, 'Psalms', p. 6.

Flint's thesis continues by arguing that the Cave 11 Psalter was composed with relation to the solar calendar in use by the Qumran community (amongst others), representing a fifty-two-piece collection with a strong Davidic emphasis.[42]

The establishment of organizing principles tends to confirm the nature of the collection as a Psalter, especially when the Psalters are compared, as Gerald Wilson has done. Wilson looks at the shaping of both the MT and the Cave 11 scroll *as a whole*, and sees the Qumran scroll focusing on the need for divine deliverance for Jerusalem. The hope for this deliverance is found in David. The Davidic messiah's role is prominent, forming the final vision and hope of the Psalter. In contrast the MT Psalter concludes with the focus on the kingship of Yahweh, in the *yhwh malak* psalms (missing from 11QPsª) and the closing doxology on his creative power (Pss. 145 – 150). David's role is diminished.[43]

The LXX version of Book V, which differs from the MT largely in the addition of more superscriptions of authorship to David, plus the extra Ps. 151, seems to hold a mediating place between the two Psalters.

The significance of looking at these Psalters in this way is the light it sheds on the received canonical Psalter. The move away from messianic expectation parallels the downplaying of that element within Judaism following the disaster of the Jewish Revolt, in contrast to the heightened messianism of the pre-Revolt Cave 11 Psalter. When viewed in this way, the MT Psalter increasingly appears to be the latest edition – indeed, as the Psalter ultimately accepted by both Judaism and Christianity, it has had the final canonical word.[44]

Editing the Psalter

The questions relating to the nature of the Psalter(s) in the

---

42. Flint, *Dead Sea*, pp. 238–239.

43. Wilson, 'Qumran *Psalms Scroll*', pp. 463–464.

44. The manuscript evidence reveals an increasing alignment with the MT from the middle of the first century, and with the later scrolls (late first and second centuries) from Masada (MasPsª) and Nahal Hever (5/6Hev-Se4Ps) exhibiting pronounced MT affinity.

Dead Sea Scrolls have provoked an awareness and appreciation of editorial purpose in the placing of individual songs and smaller collections in relation to each other. The pioneer in this arena has been Gerald Wilson, whose ground-breaking dissertation, *The Editing of the Hebrew Psalter*, drew scholarly attention back to the much maligned superscriptions and book divisions. Psalm 1 provides the clue to how to read the Psalms – it is to be meditated on day and night, as Torah.[45] They may then be read chronologically, from David himself (Books I and II), to the loss of the kingdom (Book III), exile (Book IV) and expectation of the coming rule of God (Book V).

These insights into the shaping of the Psalter are most valuable, not only for understanding individual psalms on their own, but also for seeing psalms in relation to each other. Ultimately, the insight gained into the purposes of the editor(s) gives insight into the late first century CE, when this Psalter reached its final form. As such, the study of the MT Psalter places us in the very midst of the New Testament world!

The use of the Psalms in the Second Temple period

This insight leads us into the final aspect of the scrolls that we will note. That is, the place of the Psalms in interpretation. We have already noted the existence of seven Qumran scrolls that cite psalms in some manner: three *pesharim*, 4QFlorilegium, 4QTanhumim, 4Q Catena A, and 11QMelchizedek. The *pesharim* provide cases-in-point for understanding the place of the Psalms in Qumran. This form of continuous, charismatically 'inspired' commentary is otherwise known only for prophetic works, which can only mean that the Psalms are viewed in the same way.[46] All of

---

45. Wilson, *Editing*, p. 207.

46. Six copies of commentaries on Isaiah, two of Hosea and Zephaniah, and one each of Micah, Nahum and Habakkuk survive. The 'inspiration' gives the definitive interpretation of the prophecies for the last days, which their readers have already begun to experience.

these texts are mined for explanation of the events of the last days – the days of the faithful community – and of the eschatological characters who will bring deliverance to God's people.

This appropriation of the Psalms as prophetic of the messianic age is shared by the New Testament writers, as Pss. 37, 68 and 118 (subjects of the *pesharim*) are applied by both first-century communities to themselves and their history, but particularly to the passion of Jesus the Messiah. These are not only psalms of worship, they are the oracles of the Lord for the last days.

Conclusion

The Qumran scrolls grant us a view of the Psalms that the finished Psalters of the MT and LXX, being complete and fixed, cannot do. They show us the very process of creation at the midpoint of its development. This survey of the make-up of the manuscripts has attempted to offer some sense of the dynamic that the individual compositions display in their changing relations to each other prior to being cast in the permanency of immovable print. This was a living corpus during the very time the New Testament, and early Christianity itself, was developing. Perhaps some of that dynamic can be seen to continue even beyond the finalization of the canon.

14. THE EVANGELISTS AND THE PSALMS

Dale A. Brueggemann

Introduction

Jesus chided his disciples, not just for failure to believe his predictions of death and resurrection, but for failure to believe on the basis of what the Old Testament had said:[1] 'everything written about me in the law of Moses, the prophets, and the psalms must be fulfilled' (Luke 24:44). Arguably, he was not looking at select messianic predictions but referring to a message written 'in all the scriptures' (v. 27).[2] This encourages us to see the New Testament finding a messianic maximum in the Old Testament rather than a minimum.

---

1. Hays, 'Reading', p. 229; citing Evans, *Luke*, p. 910, to support the phrase 'on the basis of '.
2. Some think Jesus dealt with select messianic texts, e.g., Marshall, *Luke*, p. 897; others take a broader, generally typological, approach, e.g., Bock, *Luke*, p. 918; Hays, 'Reading', p. 229; Moberly, *Bible*, p. 51; Morris, *Luke*, p. 370.

Quotations of the psalms in the Gospels and Acts

As in all the New Testament, the Gospels and Acts quote widely
from the Psalter, especially from the royal and lament psalms, but
also from others.[3]

Psalm	Language	Gospels and Acts
2:1–2	'Why do the nations conspire, and the peoples plot in vain? The kings of the earth set themselves, and the rulers take counsel together, against the LORD and his anointed . . .'	Acts 4:25–26
2:7	'You are my son, today I have begotten you.'	Acts 13:33
6:3	'My soul is sorely troubled.' (LXX)	John 12:27
6:8	'Depart from me, all you workers of evil . . .'	Matt. 7:23; Luke 13:27
8:2	'Out of the mouth of babes and nursing children you have perfected praise.' (LXX)	Matt. 21:16
16:10	'For you do not give me up to Sheol, or let your faithful one see the Pit. You show me the path of life.'	Acts 2:28–31; 13:35
22:1	'My God, my God, why have you forsaken me?'	Matt. 27:46; Mark 15:34
22:7–8	'All who see me mock at me; they make mouths at me, they shake their heads; "Commit your cause to the LORD; let him deliver – let him rescue the one in whom he delights!"'	Matt. 27:39, 41–43
22:15	Thirst	John 19:28
22:18	'. . . for my clothing they cast lots.'	Matt. 27:35; Mark 15:24; Luke 23:34; John 19:23–24
31:5	'Into your hand I commit my spirit . . .'	Luke 23:46

---

3. NA[27] and UBS[4] index New Testament use of the Old Testament; also see
   Shires, *Finding*. For current discussion of the use of Psalms in the New
   Testament, see Moyise and Menken, *Psalms*.

Psalm	Language	Gospels and Acts
34:20	'He keeps all their bones; not one of them will be broken.'	John 19:36
35:19	'. . . those who hate me without cause . . .'	John 15:25
41:9	'. . . who ate of my bread, has lifted the heel against me.'	John 13:18
42:5, 11; 43:5	'soul . . . cast down/deeply grieved'	Matt. 26:38; Mark 14:34
62:12	'. . . you repay to all according to their work.'	Matt. 16:27
69:4	'. . . hate me without cause.'	John 15:25
69:9	'It is zeal for your house that has consumed me . . .'	John 2:17
69:21	'. . . for my thirst they gave me vinegar to drink.'	John 19:28–30
69:25	'May their camp be a desolation; let no one live in their tents.'	Acts 1:20
78:2	'I will open my mouth in a parable; I will utter dark sayings from of old.'	Matt. 13:35
78:24	'. . . he rained down on them manna to eat, and gave them the grain of heaven. Mortals ate of the bread of angels.'	John 6:31
82:6	'You are gods . . .'	John 10:34
89:20	'I have found my servant David . . .'	Acts 13:22 (cf. 1 Sam. 13:14)
91:11–12	'For he will command his angels concerning you . . . On their hands they will bear you up, so that you will not dash your foot against a stone.'	Matt. 4:6; Luke 4:10
104:12	'. . . the birds of the air have their habitation . . . among the branches.'	Matt. 13:32; Mark 4:32; Luke 13:19
110:1	'The LORD says to my lord, "Sit at my right hand . . ."'	Matt. 22:44; Mark 12:36; Luke 20:42–43; Acts 2:34–35; cf. Matt. 26:64; Mark 14:62; Luke 22:69
118:22–23	'The stone that the builders rejected has become the chief cornerstone. This is the LORD's doing; it is marvellous in our eyes.'	Matt. 21:42; Mark 12:10–11; Luke 20:17; Acts 4:11; cf. Eph. 2:20–22; 1 Pet. 2:4–8

Psalm	Language	Gospels and Acts
118:25–26	'Hosanna' and 'Blessed is the one who comes in the name of the LORD.'	Matt. 21:9; 23:39; Mark 11:9; Luke 19:38; John 12:13
132:11	'The LORD swore to David a sure oath from which he will not turn back: "One of the sons of your body I will set on your throne."'	Acts 2:30
146:6	'. . . who made heaven and earth, the sea, and all that is in them . . .'	Acts 4:24
148:1	'. . . praise him in the heights!'	Matt. 21:9; Mark 11:10

Uses of the psalms in the Gospels and Acts

To prove Jesus' arguments

'You are gods' (82:6)

Jesus claimed to be one with the Father in offering eternal life, so opponents wanted to stone him as a blasphemer (John 10:28–33). Jesus responded, 'Is it not written in your law,[4] "I said, you are gods"?' (v. 34, quoting Ps. 82:6), and described the *ʾĕlōhîm* as those 'to whom the word of God came' (v. 35), a commissioning phrase for prophets and kings.[5] Debate continues over how to interpret the *ʾĕlōhîm*. Some think they are human, either rulers and judges, or perhaps all of Israel, who received God's word at Sinai;[6] others think they are heavenly beings to whom God gave a word of commission, either angels[7] or beings otherwise included as members of the heavenly council, whether envisaged

---

4. 'Law' sometimes refers to all of Scripture, e.g., 1 Cor. 14:21 (quoting Isa. 28:11–12; cf. Deut. 28:49; Jer. 5:15); Rom. 3:19–20 (quoting Ps. 143:2); John 12:34 (drawing on non-Pentateuchal messianic promises).

5. E.g., 1 Kgs 6:11; 1 Chr. 22:8; Isa. 2:1; Jer. 1:2; Mic. 1:1; Zeph. 1:1.

6. Hanson, 'Citation'; 'Citation Reconsidered'.

7. Emerton, 'Interpretation'; 'Melchizedek'.

as real[8] or, using mythopoetic language,[9] as the 'gods' of the nations.[10]

Jesus argued from lesser to greater: if lesser judges could have the title *'ĕlōhîm*, why shouldn't the greater judge (John 10:34–38)? In so doing, he implied that, in the face of his interlocutors' un-*'ĕlōhîm*-like injustice, he was fulfilling the psalmist's prayer: 'Rise up, O *'ĕlōhîm*, judge the earth' (Ps. 82:8). Perhaps John had exactly this line in mind when he said, 'scripture cannot be annulled' (v. 35).[11]

'The LORD says to my lord, "Sit at my right hand until I make your enemies your footstool"' (110:1)

Ps. 110 puts an absolute perspective on the Davidic enthronement promise of Ps. 2.[12] The LORD (*yhwh*) enthrones his co-regent, whom David himself calls 'my lord' (*'ădōnî*).[13] Kidner says,

> While other psalms share with this one the exalted language which points beyond the reigning king to the Messiah, here alone the king himself does homage to this personage – thereby settling two important questions: whether the perfect king was someone to come, or simply the

8. Tsevat, 'God'.

9. Smick, 'Mythopoetic'.

10. Cf. Deut. 4:19; 32:8–9; Dan. 10; Sir. 17:17; *Jubilees* 15:31; *1 Enoch* 20:5.

11. Hanson, *Prophetic*, pp. 144–149, esp. 146.

12. Ps. 110 parallels the concerns of Ps. 2: both speak of the nations' subjugation (2:1–3, 8–12; 110:1a–2, 5–6), the shattering of Israel's enemies (2:9; 110:3, 6), the LORD's anger against opposing kings (2:5a; 110:5b), and final victory for a Davidic king who represents the LORD's universal kingship, either as 'son' (2:7) or as someone who sits at God's right hand (110:1; cf. *Midrash Ps.* 2:7). See Hay, *Glory*; Juel, *Messianic*, pp. 135–150.

13. The LXX does not keep the distinction between *YHWH* and *'ădōnî*; it translates both with *kyrios*, resulting in 'the lord said to my lord'. Perhaps the ascription of *Kyrios* to Jesus goes back to Ps. 110:1 (Dodd, *According*, p. 121; contra Hay, *Glory*, p. 121). Hay doubts that the original sense 'would readily beget the notion that the second "lord" is divine' (*Glory*, p. 106).

present ruler idealized; and whether the one to come would be merely man at his best, or more than this.[14]

The 'my lord' (*'ădōnî*) referred to David's royal descendant; however, anyone actually claiming to be called 'lord' (*kyrios*) with 'right hand' status in the heavenly throne room could fairly be claiming divinity. This inflamed Jesus' debates with Jewish leaders, as Watts indicates.

> To assert that one will sit at God's right hand and thereby arrogate God's prerogatives to oneself is offensive enough. But, after all the preceding tension, to do so at one's own trial by citing Daniel 7 which itself presupposes a courtroom confrontation, whereby a cloud-riding son of man is vindicated over beast-like and idolatrous nations is incendiary. Add to this Psalm 110's Melchizedekian promise with its implications of a change of polity (read demise of the present Temple leadership; cf. 11QMelch [13]) and Yahweh's crushing of the Messiah's enemies, and the lines could hardly be more clearly drawn. Mark's Jesus not only claims the highest possible status for himself but accuses his opponents not only of being Yahweh's enemies but of effectively playing the role of the fourth beast with the High Priest as the little horn.[15]

Jesus Christ is certainly, but not merely, David's messianic son; he is also David's exalted Lord – and thus Lord over his opponents.

To show that Jesus' life was predicted
The New Testament implies this for Ps. 110, but each of the following also merits an explicit note that something happened to fulfil language from the Psalter.

Jesus' parables (78:2)
Matthew concludes a series of parables with a quote from the Psalter: 'I will open my mouth to speak in parables; I will proclaim what has been hidden from the foundation of the world' (Matt.

---

14. Kidner, *Psalms 73 – 150*, p. 392.
15. Watts, 'Psalms', p. 41.

13:35). Jesus was the epitome of the Davidic sage, following the pattern of, but surpassing, an earlier son of David.[16]

Jesus' enemies hated him without cause

Hatred 'without cause' is an experience common to humanity; however, David was the paradigmatic righteous sufferer,[17] a royal figure who bore the brunt of hatred directed at God's kingdom. This was certainly the view of New Testament authors, and it may even have been pre-Christian messianic thought.[18] Neither Ps. 35:19 nor 69:4 was a prediction;[19] however, Jesus' experience followed the Davidic pattern 'to fulfil the word that is written in their law, "They hated me without a cause"' (John 15:25).

One who ate bread with Jesus betrayed him (41:9) [20]

The psalmist's experience of this was neither a prediction nor even uniquely Davidic; nonetheless, John appeals to it to depict Judas' betrayal as following a typological pattern: 'it is to fulfil the scripture, "The one who ate my bread has lifted his heel against me."' Perhaps John 13:18 is drawing not only on Ps. 41:9 but also on 2 Sam. 18:28, where men raised their hand against the king. There are also parallels between Judas and Ahithophel, whom Jewish tradition associates with Ps. 41: David and Jesus, their intended victims, both pray for deliverance on the Mount of Olives; Judas and Ahithophel both plan to act at night; both accounts contain the claim that the death of one man will bring peace to the people; and both hang themselves after the deed.[21]

---

16. 1 Kgs 4:32; Prov. 1:1; 10:1; 25:1.

17. 1 Sam. 25:31; 1 Kgs 2:31; Pss. 7:4; 35:7, 19; 69:4; 109:3; 119:161. See Block, 'Servant', pp. 49–55.

18. See Gese, 'Psalm 22'.

19. See also Pss. 38:19; 109:3.

20. The Synoptics also echo Ps. 41:9, but there the death of Jesus is the fulfilment, not the betrayal by one with whom he had eaten bread (Matt. 26:24; Mark 14:21; Luke 22:22).

21. Respectively 2 Sam. 15:31; 17:1, 3, 23; and Mark 14:26–42; John. 13:30; 11:50; Matt. 27:5. See Moyise, *Old Testament*, p. 68.

Jesus' thirst resulted in an offer of vinegar wine

Just before Jesus' death, 'when Jesus knew that all was now finished, he said (in order to fulfil the scripture), "I am thirsty"' (John 19:28). Some see this as fulfilling Ps. 69:21 or 22:15, although the cry 'I am thirsty' occurs in neither text; therefore, others see allusion instead to texts on spiritual thirst (e.g., Pss. 42:2; 63:1). Clearly it was literal thirst for which Jesus accepted some cheap vinegar wine; however, Daly-Denton says the tradition of Jesus' physical thirst and his acceptance of the bitter cup hints at that deeper thirst and also his even more bitter cup (cf. John 18:11).[22] John depicts this as fulfilling a Davidic pattern of suffering. It is also possible that John is continuing his own motif of spiritual hunger and thirst by reading several verses in dialogue (above texts plus John 4:34). Jesus would literally be thirsty, just as he was at the well with the Samaritan woman; however, just as he used his thirst there to speak of living water, here he uses it to speak of his determination to drink his cup of suffering.[23]

Tormentors cast lots for Jesus' clothes (22:18)

All four Gospels mention this incident, but John recounts it with a fulfilment formula. Aside from the fulfilment itself, it is not clear what significance the untorn garment would have held for the New Testament writers. Perhaps it signified the unbroken unity of the church established through Christ's death and coming resurrection.[24] Robe-tearings in early royal contexts provide useful background: a robe was torn when Samuel announced Saul's loss of kingship;[25] David tore Saul's cloak, which portended this; and Ahijah tore his robe into twelve pieces to depict the division of the kingdom.[26]

----

22. Daly-Denton, 'Psalms', p. 135; *David*, pp. 219–228.

23. Witkamp, 'Jesus' Thirst', p. 497.

24. Moyise, *Old Testament*, p. 69; citing Cyprian but rejecting that interpretation because the soldiers took this garment away from Jesus.

25. 1 Sam. 15:27–28. The Hebrew is ambiguous: 'he seized . . . his robe'. LXX, one Qumran text and most modern versions have Saul tearing Samuel's robe, but *Midrash Psalms* reverses this.

26. Respectively 1 Sam. 24:5, 11; 1 Kgs 11:29–31.

If it is possible that such a reading might have influenced the fourth
evangelist, then the tunic of Jesus that is not torn may refer to his royal
status, as inscribed with pointed intentionality by Pilate in the immediately
preceding scene . . . Thus, in an entirely unexpected way, God fulfils the
promise to David, 'I will establish the throne of his kingdom forever'.
Jesus [*sic*] robe is not torn. Nathan's oracle explains why. 'I will not take
my steadfast love from him as I took it from Saul' (2 Sam. 7:15).[27]

Jesus' experience fulfils something in the record of the psalmist's
suffering, though the psalm itself had no predictive sense.

Jesus' bones remained unbroken throughout his crucifixion

John uses a fulfilment formula to explain why Jesus' bones were
not broken, despite the practice of administering the coup de
grâce by breaking the victim's leg bones (John 19:31–33).[28] Some
link fulfilment with the prescription for the Passover lamb (Exod.
12:46; Num. 9:12); others point to the psalmist's sense of God's
preservation (Ps. 34:20). Verbal similarity cannot determine the
text(s) being quoted, and context allows both possibilities.
Eriksson notes John's use of the paschal lamb (John 18 – 19), and
that nothing is quoted from the Pentateuch throughout the
section, while much is quoted from the Psalms; therefore he opts
for Ps. 34:20 as the background.[29] Menken prefers to keep both
sets of texts in mind, treating them as 'analogous passages' in
John's mind: 'Jesus takes over the role of the righteous sufferer. At
the same time, these quotations indirectly announce the resurrection: in all of the psalms just mentioned [22; 41; 69], the salvation
of the righteous one is also a theme.'[30]

'You do not give me up to Sheol, or let your faithful one see the Pit' (16:10)

Kraus wonders, 'Is the singer speaking of a rescue from death,
or do we hear words that refer to a hope of resurrection?' He

---

27. Daly-Denton, 'Psalms', p. 133.
28. See Strange, 'Crucifixion'; Burke, 'Cross'; Green, 'Death'.
29. Eriksson, *Come*, p. 122.
30. Menken, 'Old Testament', p. 42.

concludes that the psalmist is talking about his own death.[31] By contrast, Kaiser and Moessner represent those who see Ps. 16 predicting resurrection,[32] and Kaiser even calls it a 'direct messianic prediction'.[33]

The psalmist was expressing confidence that, even in the face of death, God would show him 'the path of life', which was in God's 'presence' (v. 11). As Johnston explains, 'Sheol was not a fitting place for Yahweh's "holy one" (ḥāsîd) and the psalmist could expect some kind of deliverance from it', though it was left vague enough that a 'forward-looking, prophetic perspective' grew up around this promise.[34] Delitzsch's old comment still sums it up pretty well: 'David becomes the prophet of Christ; but he speaks of himself, and what he says also found its fulfilment in himself . . . Now that his hope has found in Christ its full historical and redemptive realization, it becomes through Christ a personal reality also for himself.'[35]

Peter argued confidently that 'David spoke of the resurrection of the Messiah' (Acts 2:31), and Paul adopted the same argument: David had 'died . . . and experienced corruption' (Acts 13:36), so it was left to Jesus to inherit the promise, 'You will not let your Holy One experience corruption' (v. 35).

Judas' office fell vacant, so another took his place
The psalmist wished, 'May their camp be a desolation; let no one live in their tents' (69:25). Peter found the first half of that wish fulfilled by the death of Judas Iscariot. Therefore he advised the apostles to replace Judas and thus fulfil another Davidic imprecation, 'may another seize his position' (109:8). Neither of these

---

31. Kraus, *Psalms*, vol. 1, p. 239; however, he says the psalmist's trust 'provided the early Christian witness for Christ with language and categorical conceptions in which also the ultimate could be expressed: the resurrection from death' (p. 241).

32. Kaiser, *Uses*, pp. 33–38; Moessner, '*Two* Lords'.

33. Kaiser, *Messiah*, p. 119.

34. Johnston, 'Psalm 16', pp. 221, 222; similarly *Shades*, pp. 202–203.

35. Delitzsch, *Psalms*, 1:288.

curses was a prediction;[36] rather they expressed the psalmists' wish for God's intervention in judgment. The apostolic situation saw the realization of that kind of hope.

Jesus displayed zeal for God's house

After Jesus drove the merchants from the temple, John comments, 'His disciples remembered that it was written, "Zeal for your house will consume me"' (John 2:17). Ps. 69:9 has 'has consumed me', but John's future tense applies the quotation to Jesus' death, which had not yet happened when he made this statement. Of course, Jesus applied this not just to the temple cleansing but to the destruction and rebuilding of the temple,[37] which his disciples did not understand until after the resurrection (John 2:19–22). This sets the temple cleansing, and thus Jesus' crucifixion and resurrection, against the background of Davidic experience. Jesus was fulfilling a Davidic pattern, and his resurrection was the hermeneutical key that unlocked it all.

Jesus' coronation as begotten son (2:7) and his seat at God's right hand (110:1)

Perhaps a coronation ritual for new Davidic kings, Ps. 2 reminds the king about the divine 'decree' which included the idealistic adoption formula, 'You are my son; today I have begotten you' (v. 7).[38] Jesus' resurrection-coronation fulfilled that promise,

---

36. One move that Christian interpreters use to lessen the bite of the Psalter's imprecations (e.g., Pss. 7; 35; 58; 59; 69; 83; 109; 137; 139) is to say they were not the psalmist's *wishes* for what God might do but his *prophecies* of what God would do. This is an unlikely translation in most places, impossible in others (e.g., Ps. 69:25–26), and clearly not the case where the psalmist notes his own personal satisfaction when his imprecations come to pass (Ps. 137:8–9). Indeed, people cannot take vengeance into their own hands but must leave it to God (Deut. 3:35; Rom. 12:19; Heb. 13:30), which the imprecations do.

37. First-century BCE Judaism expected the Messiah to 'purge Jerusalem from nations that trample her down to destruction' rather than from the unrighteous Jewish practices (*Pss. Sol.* 17:21–22).

38. See the way that later texts reflect on the oath to David (2 Sam. 7:8–16; 1 Chr. 17:3–15; Pss. 89:35–37; 132:11–12).

though the title had already figured in the divine attestation at Jesus' baptism and at his transfiguration. As had Jewish exegesis,[39] the Gospels adopted an eschatological tone in these echoes of Ps. 2:1–2. At Jesus' baptism there was both a voice and the Spirit coming from heavens that had opened up; and his transfiguration displayed theophanic cloud and glory on clothing and face, conversation with heavenly personages, and a heavenly voice.[40]

Upon Peter and John's release from custody after appearing before the council, the church gathered and prayed for courage to continue with a bold witness (Acts 4:24–30). Quoting Psalms before the council, and in prayer after their release, the church set this experience over against David's.[41] The psalmist's language assured them that they could face down 'kings of the earth' like Herod and 'rulers' like Pontius Pilate.

To show that Jesus is the 'Greater David'
This typology applied to the proofs based on Ps. 110:1 and was behind all of the fulfilment texts discussed in the previous section.

---

39. *Pss. Sol.* 17:21–25, 30–32 is almost a commentary on Ps. 2:1–4, emphasizing the destruction of hostile rulers (vv. 22–25) and subservience of the nations to the Messiah (vv. 29–31), whose rule extends Yahweh's kingdom. Watts notes: 'Later rabbinic literature appealed frequently to Ps. 2:1–4, often in the context of Yahweh's eschatological victory over Gog and Magog and Israel's defeat of idolaters (e.g., *b.Ber.* 7b; *Exod. R.* 1:1; *Midr. Ps.* 2:2, 4; the latter being an action of Yahweh as a warrior citing Is. 42:13). The psalm's subject is often understood to be the Messiah (*b.Sukk.* 52a; *Midr. Ps.* 2:3, 9, 10)' (Watts, 'Psalms', p. 27).

40. Baptism: Matt. 3:16–17; Mark 1:9–11; Luke 3:21–22; John 1:32, 34. Transfiguration: Matt. 17:1–9; Mark 9:2–10; Luke 9:28–36.

41. Acts 4:11, 24, 25–27, quoting Ps. 118:22; 146:6; 2:1–2. Peter relies on Davidic authorship of Ps. 2 though it has no title in either MT or LXX; and he considers David's words prophetic, since his words came 'by the Holy Spirit'. The label 'my servant' often applies to prophets (Num. 12:7–8; 1 Kgs 14:18; Rev. 10:7, etc.); however, 'my servant David' implies royal rather than prophetic appointment (2 Sam. 3:18; 7:5, 8, etc.). But note the contrasting views of Block ('Servant', pp. 26–32) and Hays ('If He').

In addition, a long list of examples demonstrate a David-Jesus typology, wherein the events of David's life foreshadow events in Jesus' life.

> The belief, universal in the Judaism contemporary with early Christianity, that King David was the 'author' of the psalms and that many of them tell of events in his career . . . is the unspoken presupposition that underlies the early Christian penchant for reading the psalms as prophetic of Jesus. The Jesus that emerges from the pages of the gospels is reminiscent not only of the David of the 'historical' narratives, but also of the imagined David of the psalmist. He is also suggestive of the expected 'new' David.[42]

Following Jesus' hermeneutic, Luke-Acts builds a comparative biography of David and Jesus.[43] Everywhere we look, we see David's language on Jesus' lips or otherwise linked to Jesus' experience, especially as it relates to his suffering and subsequent glory.

The passion narratives make wide use of Psalm 22. Briggs says of Ps. 22, 'These sufferings transcend those of any historical sufferer, with the single exception of Jesus Christ.'[44] Mays speaks the same way:

> One senses in simply reading the text a difference, a development of the type that raises it to its very limits and begins to transcend it. There is an intensity and comprehensiveness about the psalm which presses toward the ultimate possibilities that lie in the event sketched in the psalm: an afflicted person appealing in helplessness to God and then praising God for help.[45]

He admits 'the possibility that this feeling about the scope of the psalm is prompted by its association with the death of Jesus', but

---

42. Daly-Denton, 'Psalms', p. 120.

43. Doble, 'Psalms', p. 89.

44. Briggs, *Messianic*, p. 326.

45. Mays, 'Prayer', p. 324; citing Calvin (*Psalms 1–35*, p. 357) and Delitzsch (*Psalms*, 1:376), who say much the same thing.

concludes that 'it is there in the text itself'.[46] Even the details of Jesus' experience reflect those of the psalmist: Jesus' garments divided by lot, Jesus mocked, his thirst, his cry of dereliction.[47] McCann concludes, 'Either Jesus intentionally embodied the experience of the faithful suffering in Psalm 22, or the Gospel writers articulated their understanding of Jesus in the light of their knowledge of Psalm 22, or both.'[48] One way or the other, the Gospels insist that Ps. 22 finds its fulfilment in the suffering of Jesus.

Jesus willingly accepted the crowd's hosanna to the Son of David, 'who comes in the name of the LORD' (118:25f.). The phrase 'the one who comes/is to come' was perhaps an established expression for the expected Messiah or end-time prophet.[49] Several Johannine characters used it, expressing various levels of comprehension.[50]

Jesus claimed the Davidic promise that the rejected stone will become the cornerstone (118:22). This incendiary conclusion to the parable of the ruthless tenants unambiguously interprets it as a reference to the rejection and vindication of the Messiah. As far as the Jewish leaders were concerned, mixing potent entrance imagery from Zechariah and Ps. 118 was inflammatory, especially with Jesus' implied royal re-enactment.[51] On the other hand, the reversal motif of Ps. 118 would have encouraged the church to trust in the Lord rather than in rulers.[52]

Near the end of his public ministry Jesus sighed, 'Now my soul is troubled' (Ps. 6:3; John 12:27). In Gethsemane he explained his grief to Peter, James and John using words from Pss. 42 – 43, where

---

46. Mays, 'Prayer', p. 324.

47. Garments: Ps. 22:18 in Matt. 27:35; Mark. 15:24; Luke 23:34; John 19:24; mockery: Ps. 22:7f. in Matt. 27:39, 43; Mark 15:29; thirst: Ps. 22:15 in John 19:28; cry: Ps. 22:1 in Matt. 27:46; Mark 15:34.

48. McCann, *Theological*, p. 169.

49. Cf. Dan. 7:13; Mal. 3:1; Hab. 2:3. The triumphal entry uses not only Ps. 118 but also Zech. 9:9, which draws in Gen. 49:11 (Krause, 'One').

50. John 1:15; 4:25; 6:14; 7:25–31. See Daly-Denton, 'Psalms', p. 128.

51. Sanders, 'New Testament', p. 180.

52. Wagner, 'Psalm 118', pp. 173–174; citing Carroll, 'Uses', p. 518.

the psalmist asks three times, 'Why are you cast down?'[53] Jesus' final cry, 'Father, into your hands I commend my spirit' (Luke 23:46), also came from David's experience (Ps. 31:5). Jesus the righteous sufferer fulfilled the Davidic pattern of innocent suffering.

To prove Jesus' divinity

Whatever could be said in the Psalter of the LORD (Hebrew *yhwh*, Greek *kyrios*) could now be said of the Lord Jesus Christ. Jesus told his disciples, 'the Son of Man . . . will repay everyone for what has been done', a prerogative of the LORD, as the psalmist notes: 'O Lord . . . you repay to all according to their work.'[54] This concludes a passage on the cost of discipleship in view of the final judgment, which God has delegated to Jesus.[55]

Jesus approved of the crowd's shouted testimony, 'Hosanna to the Son of David' and 'Hosanna in the highest heaven'. He countered objections to the crowd's shouts with: 'have you never read, "Out of the mouths of infants and nursing babies you have prepared praise for yourself"'?'[56] *Hôšîʿâ nāʾ* had been a cry to the Lord meaning 'save now';[57] however, the shout developed from petition to acclamation.[58] Understood either way, Jesus was accepting petitions or praise that in the Psalms were lifted to the Lord, and rebuking those who begrudged him that right.

And, of course, the two texts used to prove Jesus' arguments were also used to prove his divinity (Pss. 82:6; 110:1; see above).

---

53. Pss. 42:5, 11; 43:5; LXX has 'grieved', so Matt. 26:38. The stanza/strophe arrangement shows that Pss. 42 – 43 were originally a single psalm.

54. Matt. 16:27; Ps. 62:12. The latter has *ʾădōnāy* rather than *yhwh*; nonetheless, it is clearly directed at Yahweh.

55. Matt. 16:24–28; cf. Acts 10:42; 17:31; cf. Matt. 13:41–43; 25:31–46. See Menken, 'Psalms', p. 70.

56. Ps. 8:2 in Matt. 21:16. LXX of Ps. 8:2 reads 'praise' (similarly NIV, NLT). The Hebrew is *ʿōz*, 'strength' (ASV, NASB, ESV, JPS, NJPS, NIV margin), or 'bulwark' (RSV, NRSV).

57. 2 Kgs 6:26; Pss. 12:1; 20:9; 28:9; 44:3; 60:5; 98:1; 108:6; 118:25.

58. Menken, 'Psalms', p. 70; Daly-Denton, 'Psalms', p. 127; Fitzmyer, 'Aramaic'; Lohse, *hōsanna*.

Conclusions

The Gospels and Acts find Jesus to be the fulfilment of the agony and ecstasy tied up in the Davidic dynasty's eternal promise. Many of the promises outstripped what a merely human descendant of David could ever experience, but these New Testament texts emphasize that they had to be fulfilled, and that Jesus did this. So they freely apply the prerogatives of the Lord in the Psalms to Jesus Christ the Lord, whether he was receiving petitions and praise or exercising divine judgment.

They use four overlapping methods to do all this. Sometimes the New Testament uses the Psalter to prove Jesus' arguments, sometimes to show that Jesus' life was predicted, and sometimes to show that Jesus is the 'Greater David'. Finally, any of those three methods might combine in an argument to prove Jesus' divinity.

This was not usually by prediction; rather, the typology established the basis of expectation. Sometimes this was by way of a typological connection deeply rooted in royal theology; however, the New Testament could also draw on incidentals from David's life and rely on the overarching David-Jesus typology to sustain the connection. What was vital was that the connection between David and Jesus be seen.

© Dale A. Brueggemann, 2005.

15. THE TARGUM OF PSALMS

Timothy M. Edwards

A chapter on Targum Psalms in this volume is most fitting and welcome, especially since it has been virtually ignored in Targum studies.[1] It is no exaggeration to say that scholarship on Targum Psalms[2] was in a state of stagnation between Bacher's seminal

---

1. 'Targum' literally means 'translation' and was used regularly for any translation; but the term came to refer specifically to the Aramaic translations of the Hebrew Bible, of which there are a number. These are referred to in the plural as 'Targumim'.

2. At present there are three published texts of Targum Psalms: de Lagarde, *Hagiographa*, taken from the first *Biblica Rabbinica*; Diez Merino, *Targum*, following MS Villa-Amil n. 5; and Cohen, *Miqrā'ôt*, a pointed text. There is also an unpublished critical edition of the Targum of Pss. 1 – 72 in transliteration: White, *Critical*. My study is based on all the above as well as MS 1106 (Wroclaw); Codex Solger 6.2 (Nürnberg); Codex Urbinati 1 (Vatican); MS Heb 110 (Paris). Clearly there is an urgent need for a fully accessible critical edition. [Stec, *Targum of Psalms*, is an English translation published while this paper was in press. Though not based on

article of 1872, 'Das Targum zur den Psalmen', and 1992,[3] as highlighted by the numerous encyclopaedia articles that simply summarize Bacher's main findings.[4] The inclusion of Targum Psalms is also welcome in light of the unfortunate modern scholarly prejudice which often writes off ancient exegesis as having little or nothing to contribute to the academic pursuit of the 'original meaning'.[5] This chapter, therefore, will serve both to introduce this neglected part of the Targum tradition, and to stimulate students and scholars alike in thinking about the way we read one of the most cherished parts of the Hebrew Bible.

Introduction to Targum Psalms

Before dealing with issues of date, language and style, it is necessary to place Targum Psalms within the broader context of the Targum tradition, and also of the advances in scholarship with regards to their function, particularly within a multilingual society.

Targum Psalms within the Targum tradition
The undue emphasis within scholarship on the *liturgical* function of the Targumim is perhaps the biggest reason for the neglect of Targum Psalms in academic study. The Psalms were never read and translated publicly in the synagogue,[6] and thus Targum

---

the complete manuscript collection, it is an important contribution to scholarship.]

3. This stagnation is now at an end, due particularly to the ongoing work of Moshe Bernstein: 'Translation'; 'Torah'; 'Righteous'.

4. Grossfeld, 'Targums'; Komlosh, 'Targum'; Schäfer, 'Targum'; Alexander, 'Targum'.

5. Cf. Braude, 'Midrash'.

6. The *baraita* (a Tannaitic source not found in the Mishnah – the Tannaim being sages from the first two centuries CE) in BT *Megillah* 21b implies that the *Hallel* is read and translated, thus implying that there was at least a Targum of Pss. 113 – 118 recited publicly. However, the reference to the *Hallel* is missing altogether in a number of the manuscripts. It is therefore

Psalms lacked a context on which research could be founded. Recent scholarship, however, has begun to delineate the pedagogical function of the Targumim within the rabbinic tradition that includes its use within the synagogue, school and house of study. Such a context is implied by the passage below from *Sifre Devarim*,[7] which places the Targumim as a bridge between the written Torah (Scripture) and the oral Torah (Mishnah and Talmud).[8]

> And [the Torah scroll] shall be with him, and he shall read from it all the days of his life, that he may learn to fear . . . the Lord his God [Deut. 17:19]. This teaches that sight leads to reading, reading leads to translation (*targûm*), translation leads to study (*talmûd*), study leads to action, action leads to fear of God.[9]

This educational role for the Targumim not only explains the numerous sources that posit such a context, but also explains why we have Targumim to those parts of the Hebrew Bible which were never read publicly in the synagogue. In fact it is quite possible that this educational role was the defining reason behind their development.[10]

The image of a bridge linking Scripture with tradition is ideal for the Targumim, as it is clear now that the Targumim assume knowledge of Hebrew. Although it has been supposed in much scholarship, the Targumim did not arise in response to a populace that no longer understood Hebrew. This means that they were not designed as replacements of the Hebrew text for non-Hebrew speakers, but as a companion to it, to be read in conjunction with

---

unwise to posit a specific liturgical context for Targum Psalms from this passage.

7. *Sifre Devarim* is a Tannaitic commentary on Deuteronomy. See Finkelstein, *Sifre*, for a critical edition of the text, and Hammer, *Sifre*, for an English translation.

8. See Fraade, 'Rabbinic', and 'Scripture', who delineates this pedagogical role very clearly.

9. *Sifre Devarim* 161. For this reading see Fraade, 'Torah', p. 55 n. 84.

10. See Smelik, *Targum*, pp. 31–39.

it.[11] Thus, when we approach Targum Psalms today we need to have these two factors in mind: first, it is an educational text and not a liturgical one; and secondly, it should always be read in conjunction with the Hebrew, and not in isolation from it.

This connection to the Hebrew text must always be borne in mind methodologically, even in the most expansive passages in Targum Psalms. For example, the translation of Ps. 68:9, although initially appearing to have little or no connection to the Hebrew, can be shown to be intimately connected to it:

MT: You provided (*nwp*)[12] abundant rain O God, You established your weary heritage.

Tg[13]: *When the house of Israel heard the voice of your might their souls flew away, immediately you caused the dew of resurrection to descend upon them*, You raised up O God choice rain upon your heritage and the congregation that was weary you established.

The association of this verse with the dew of resurrection is found in rabbinic literature,[14] and the Targum's interpretation is clearly linked to such passages. However, there are linguistic aspects that set the Targum apart from these interpretations, and seek to cement the interpretation to the Hebrew text. Each of the words underlined can be seen as 'translations' of the one Hebrew root, *nwp*. First, the root *nwp* is used in relation to snow in the earlier manuscripts of Sirach 43:17 from Qumran, yet is replaced in the later copies found at

---

11. This point is illustrated in the way the Targumim are always written either alongside the Hebrew text (as in MS 1106 and Cod. Solger 6.2) or with an introductory word or phrase from the Hebrew text (as in MS Heb. 110).

12. The meaning of the root *nwp* is unclear here, although the general sense is clear, hence the translation.

13. Additions to a one-to-one correspondence with the Hebrew are italicized.

14. Babylonian Talmud (BT) *Hagigah* 12b. Also see discussion by Sysling, *Tehiyyat*, pp. 158–161, on the 'midrash of the four keys' and the properties of rain and dew in the Bible and rabbinic literature.

Masada with the root *prḥ*, 'fly away', which is also found in the Targum here. Secondly, the root *nwp* in Ethiopic has the meaning of 'distil, drop like dew',[15] which possibly links the Targum's 'dew . . . to descend' with the Hebrew. Lastly, the root *nwp* is usually translated in the Targumim with *rwm*, and this is also found in this verse with the translation 'raised up'. It is possible therefore that the translator, in utilizing this interpretive tradition, also sought to communicate the underlying meanings and words of the Hebrew as much as possible, and thus uses three Aramaic roots to translate the one Hebrew root. If this is the case, it is a good example of the sophisticated nature of the translation and its intimate connection to the Hebrew, even in the more expansive renderings of particular verses. It highlights the need to consider the Targum alongside the Hebrew in order to fully comprehend its exegesis.

The language and date of Targum Psalms

Targum Psalms has been grouped linguistically under the heading of Late Jewish Literary Aramaic, along with the Targum of Job and Targum Pseudo-Jonathan to the Pentateuch.[16] This dialect is a purely literary creation, and contains a mixture of forms including both eastern and western Aramaic as well as various Hebraisms. This has possible consequences for its dating. The mixture of forms it contains suggests that Targum Psalms arose when Aramaic was no longer spoken, and thus could point to a post-Islamic conquest date. However, the fact that there are no references to Islam argues against this. This issue still needs further investigation, and is not the only one that affects the difficult task of dating this document.

The manuscript tradition for all the Targumim is medieval.[17]

---

15. BDB 631b. The Ethiopic may retain a meaning of the Hebrew that was known to the Rabbis.

16. See Cook, 'Psalms'; Kaufman, 'Targum'; 'Dating'. It appears that Cook and Kaufman reached the same conclusions independently.

17. York, 'Dating', deals with the issue of dating Targumic literature, with a thorough critique of Kahle's thesis and the case for an early, pre-Christian date for the Palestinian Targumim.

The texts have probably not remained the same through the long process of textual transmission,[18] so we must date individual traditions within each Targum as well as the corpus as a whole. For such dating to proceed on a stable footing, we must consider linguistic and exegetical issues alongside external evidence.[19] Such a stance assumes (justifiably) that the Targumim as we have them today resemble an archaeological tell, and thus need careful excavation to expose the various layers.[20]

With regards to Targum Psalms the situation is no different. There are indications of early traditions as well as of later additions, some possibly from the medieval period. Scholarly opinion, scant as it is, is divided between an early date of the fourth to fifth centuries,[21] and a later post-Talmudic date.[22] It would seem therefore that the safest way forward is the twofold dating highlighted above, providing a range within which to work. In a detailed study of fifteen Psalms, I conclude that the earliest datable individual tradition comes from the early second century,[23] while the document as we have it is clearly medieval.[24] Any firmer conclusion would lack sound basis and thus be foolhardy. However, by far the majority of exegetical traditions found in Targum Psalms are close

---

18. This is especially true for those Targumim that were never officially sanctioned, i.e. all except Targum Onkelos and Jonathan.

19. See Salvesen, 'Symmachus'.

20. So Gordon, *Studies*, p. 152; Levy, *Targum*, p. 131. Contrast Golomb, 'Methodological', who argues for assuming Targumic coherence on the basis of its midrashic character.

21. See Bacher, 'Targum', p. 471; Diez Merino, 'Haggadic'. This is based on: references to Rome and Constantinople in Ps. 108:11 and to Rome in Ps. 69:3, 15–16; Greek and Latin loan words; and an affinity with a non-MT *Vorlage* used by the LXX and Peshitta.

22. Churgin, *Tārgûm*, pp. 59–62; White, *Critical*, pp. 19–20. Both date it as post-Talmudic but prior to the Muslim conquest.

23. See Ps. 92:15 where the Targum appears to be depending on Aquila. Cf. Edwards, *Old*, pp. 30–34.

24. See Edwards, *Old*, p. 12 n. 52, for discussion on Targum Ps. 45:14 and the medieval Jewish scholar Moses ben Nahman (Nachmanides).

to Amoraic traditions,[25] which would suggest that a date before the fifth century for the 'original text' is very unlikely.

The style of Targum Psalms

J. Kugel has pointed out in his work on biblical poetry that rabbinic biblical interpretation, based upon what he describes as 'omnisignificance', does not take poetic structure into account.[26] Likewise Targum Psalms, despite its literary character, does not attempt to reproduce the poetics of the Hebrew original.[27] The 'poetic form' of the original is not important for the translator; the message is all-important, although not perhaps the original message of the biblical text. Thus, through translation of the original and supplements grafted into the text, the translator makes the Psalms communicate a specific message relevant to his readers and coincident with his particular worldview.[28] In this context it is important to highlight that the term 'original message' is a modern construct that would not be understood in the world of late antique Jewish (and Christian) exegesis. For the rabbis there is 'no before and after' in Torah, which itself is said to have 'seventy faces'. Thus the Targumim do communicate an original message: all interpretation is in a sense 'original', since the oral Torah itself was revealed on Sinai.[29]

---

25. The Amoraim are the sages of the post-mishnah period covering the mid-third to sixth centuries CE.

26. Kugel, *Idea*, pp. 96–109.

27. Targum Psalms is more interpretative and expansive on some psalms than others, and occasionally varies within a psalm. This sets it apart from the other Targumim that are consistently 'literal' or 'expansive'.

28. Samely, *Interpretation*, p. 183, helpfully places this Targumic exegesis in the context of a theology of revelation: the Targumim bring 'to the surface, not what the [Hebrew] words *say*, and not even what they (usually) *mean*, but what they (in the situation of revelation) *imply*' (emphasis original). Such a conclusion confirms Targumic exegesis as a part of the wider world of rabbinic exegesis, in which the Torah has 'seventy faces'.

29. See Mishnah Avot chs. 1 and 2 for the rabbinic chain of transmission that illustrates the belief that both the written *and* oral Torah (i.e. Scripture *and* tradition) were given by God to Moses and

Another feature of Targum Psalms, along with other Targumim, is multiple renderings on different verses, marked in different manuscripts by either *tārgûm 'aḥēr* or *lāšôn 'aḥēr* (both phrases meaning 'another translation').[30] These are not only found in the margins, but are also incorporated into the text,[31] and as such have been compared in function to the *dābār 'aḥēr* ('another interpretation') in rabbinic Midrashim.[32]

Having briefly introduced the general characteristics of Targum Psalms it is necessary to move on to the particular aspect of exegesis: how did Targum Psalms read the Psalms?

Exegesis in Targum Psalms

The fundamental fact that must be borne in mind at every turn in Targum scholarship is that the Targumim are inextricably bound up with the Hebrew text. We have described the Targum as a bridge that linked the written Torah with the oral Torah, and so without the Hebrew text they lose their *raison d'être*. Any research must therefore deal with the Targumim in association with the Hebrew text, and must analyse the translation carefully before attributing ideas or beliefs to the translators that are simply Aramaic representations of the ideas and beliefs of the Hebrew original. Any research must therefore be founded upon a thorough analysis of the translation of each psalm, highlighting any departures from a consistent translation technique, or additions to and departures from the Hebrew text. Once these differences have

---

then passed from generation to generation.

30. Targum Psalms contains fewer multiple renderings than the Targum of Job, and there are even differences within the manuscripts themselves, cf. Diez Merino, *Targum*, p. 132, where the number of *tārgûm 'aḥēr* in MS Villa-Amil n. 5 is compared to the Lagarde text.

31. For a concise summary of past scholarship on this feature see de Moor, 'Multiple', pp. 161–163.

32. *dābār 'aḥēr* is used to introduce a different interpretation for the same verse within rabbinic midrash.

been highlighted, they themselves need to be subjected to close examination in comparison to the Hebrew text, so as to understand what could have prompted them.[33] Thus, for example, it is necessary to assess fully the nature of additions before reaching conclusions as to their significance.

Secondly, one must also bear in mind that the Targum did not arise in a vacuum, but in creative partnership with other Jewish exegetical traditions. Comprehensive comparisons must therefore be made with other rabbinic and non-rabbinic Jewish traditions as well as with Christian interpretations,[34] so that Targumic exegesis is placed in as wide an historical context as possible.

This paper will conclude with a brief look at one particular psalm in Targum Psalms, and discuss its exegetical characteristics.

Targum of Psalm 81

Here is my translation of the Targum alongside the NRSV translation of the Hebrew:[35]

NRSV	Targum Psalms
To the leader: according to The Gittith. Of Asaph.	*For* praise on the stringed instrument that is coming from *Gath*[36] by Asaph:
1. Sing aloud to God our strength; shout for joy to the God of Jacob.	1. Praise before God our strength; shout out before the God of Jacob:

33. Such a position is especially important with Targum Psalms due to the poetic nature of the Hebrew text. It often includes difficult Hebrew words while also leaving much unsaid.

34. Relationship with Christian texts can be on three levels: (1) the same interpretation that has arisen because similar exegetical methods have been used on the same text by two distinct communities; (2) a shared interpretive tradition, usually Jewish and adopted by Christians, often unwittingly, or through Jewish-Christians; (3) polemical exegesis, i.e., the deliberate response by one group to exegesis made by 'the other'.

35. Verse numbers follow the English rather than the Hebrew.

36. The term *gat* could be both a personal name and a term connected to wine pressing.

NRSV	Targum Psalms
2. Raise a song, sound the tambourine, the sweet lyre with the harp.	2. Raise a voice in praise, arrange the timbrels, the stringed instrument whose sound is pleasant with the lyres:
3. Blow the trumpet at the new moon, at the full moon, on our festal day.[37]	3. Sound the Shofar in the month of *Tishrei*, when the moon is *concealed*, the days of our feasts:
4. For it is a statute for Israel, an ordinance of the God of Jacob.	4. For it is a statute decreed for Israel,[38] a law of justice to the God of Jacob:
5. He made it a decree in Joseph, when he went out over the land of Egypt. I hear a voice I had not known:	5. He placed it, a testimony on Joseph *who did not touch his master's wife, on the very day* he went out from jail and *ruled* over all the land of Egypt; a language [lit. lip] I didn't know, *I taught* and I heard.
6. 'I relieved your shoulder of the burden; your hands were freed from the basket.[39]	6. I removed his shoulders from enslavement, and his hands were taken up *from throwing clay for pots.*
7. In distress you called, and I rescued you; I answered you in the secret place of thunder; I tested you at the waters of Meribah. *Selah.*	7. In the time of the distress *of Egypt* you called and I saved you, I answered you in the secret place of *his Shekinah where fiery wheels cry out before him,* I examined you on the waters of quarrelling (for ever).
8. Hear, O my people, while I admonish you; O Israel, if you would but listen to me!	8. Hear my people and I will testify against you, Israel if you will receive my *Memra*:
9. There shall be no strange god among you; you shall not bow down to a foreign god.	9. There shall *not be worship of* foreign idols *among you*, and you shall not bow down to strange idols:

37. 'At the full moon' is better translated 'at the set time'; see my thesis, *Old*, p. 97 n. 33.

38. The passive construction is taken from MS Villa-Amil n. 5 and seems to be the better reading.

39. NRSV follows LXX without attribution. MT has 'your shoulder' and 'your hands'.

NRSV	Targum Psalms
10. I am the LORD your God, who brought you up out of the land of Egypt. Open your mouth wide and I will fill it.	10. I am the Lord your God that bought you up from the land of Egypt, open [lit. make wide] your mouth *with words of the law* and I will fill it *from everything good*:
11. But my people did not listen to my voice; Israel would not submit to me.	11. But my people did not accept my voice and Israel did not *desire my Memra*:
12. So I gave them over to their stubborn hearts, to follow their own counsels.	12. I drove him out in the thoughts of their heart, they went in the counsel of *their wickedness*:
13. O that my people would listen to me, that Israel would walk in my ways!	13. If only my people had listened to me, Israel would walk in my paths:
14. Then I would quickly subdue their enemies, and turn my hand against their foes.	14. In a short while I would humble their enemies and against their enemies I would return the blow of my might:
15. Those who hate the LORD would cringe before him, and their doom would last for ever.	15. Those who hate the Lord will *deny* Him [the Lord]; but He will be their strength for ever:[40]
16. I would feed you[41] with the finest of the wheat, and with honey from the rock I would satisfy you.'	16. I will cause you to eat from good things, fine bread, and I will satisfy you [with] honey from the rock:

The Hebrew clearly has an historical focus and in particular the paradigmatic exodus of Israel from Egypt and their subsequent wanderings in the wilderness. The Targum, although maintaining that context for the second half of the psalm, takes the reference to Joseph in v. 5 literally (i.e. the man Joseph and not the nation Israel).[42] This changes the focus of the first half of the psalm considerably, yet maintains a coherent interpretation for the whole

---

40. Or: 'Those who hate the Lord will deny him [Israel], but He [the Lord] will be their strength for ever.'

41. NRSV note: 'Cn Compare verse 16b: Heb *he would feed him*'.

42. As it does in the Targum of Ps. 80:2, and Targum Neofiti's reading of Ps. 80 in Gen. 49:22.

psalm by bringing the focus onto Israel for the second half. Our discussion will therefore pay particular attention to the application of vv. 3–6 to Joseph, before commenting briefly on v. 9 where another significant change occurs that highlights Targumic exegesis.

Verse 5 is pivotal in Targum Psalms' interpretation. The biblical text leaves us with two questions: (1) What is the 'decree' (lit. 'testimony') that is referred to? (2) Who goes out over Egypt? For the Targum, the 'testimony [placed] on Joseph' was the date on which he left jail, i.e. Rosh Hashanah (New Year), which was a reward for his faithfulness in face of the seduction of Potiphar's wife. This solution then leads smoothly on to the fact that it is Joseph who goes out from jail to rule over Egypt. Such an interpretation is achieved with a common Targumic method of giving the verb (went out) a new object (from jail) and the object (over Egypt) a new verb (to rule).

Such a reading of this psalm is not unique to the Targum. Rabbinic literature states that Joseph was released from jail on Rosh Hashanah,[43] and various early translations make similar changes to the prepositions to suggest that Joseph is the subject of this verse.[44] Aphrahat, the fourth-century Syrian Father, in his first Demonstration ('on Faith'),[45] also clearly links these verses with Joseph and in particular the reward for passing the test of his faith, a seeming reference to the incident with Potiphar's wife.[46] Such a selection of texts does not necessitate this being a shared interpretative tradition; it may simply show different groups and individuals using similar exegetical principles on the same text.[47]

However, such a reading could be problematic in that there are two aspects of the translation of v. 6 which seem to connect these verses with the sufferings of Israel in Egypt: 'enslavement'

---

43. See BT Rosh Hashanah 11a-b.
44. Cf. Aquila and Symmachus: 'at the time he went out *into* the land of Egypt'; Peshitta: 'when he came out *to* the land of Egypt'.
45. English translation in Wright, *Homilies*.
46. For a fuller discussion on all these traditions see my thesis, *Old*, pp. 69–71.
47. Another good example of this is Ps. 2:6, where the Targum, Symmachus and the New Testament interpret 'I have anointed my King'.

(Aramaic *šiʿbûdā*ʾ) translates 'burden' (Hebrew *sebēl*), and is a
unique translation in the Targumim, as is 'clay' (*ṭînāʾ*) for 'basket'
(*dûd*). The link between these translations and the exodus is clear
from two other passages. In the first, Targum Neofiti (TN), using
Exod. 1:12 as its source, places the following interpretation of a
dream in the mouth of Joseph in Gen. 40:18:

> MT: Joseph answered and said, 'This is its interpretation, the three
> baskets, they are three days.

> TN: Joseph answered and said, 'This is the interpretation *of the dream*;
> the three baskets are three *harsh <u>enslavements</u> of the future by which Israel will
> be enslaved in the land of Egypt, in <u>clay</u> (mortar), in bricks and working the face of
> the open fields.*'

Both words that are unusual translations in our verse are found
here, as additions to the Hebrew text, in a description of the
suffering of Israel in Egypt. It is possible therefore that the
Targumist used these words in his translation of Ps. 81 to connect
the sufferings described in v. 6 with those of Israel in Egypt. How
does this fit in with Targum Psalms having Joseph as the subject?
The answer could lie in the second relevant text. Here Targum
Pseudo-Jonathan (PsJn) of Gen. 37:17 reports an individual who
tells Joseph that his brothers have moved to Dothan:

> MT: And the man said, they have gone away for I heard them say, 'let us
> go to Dothan'.

> PsJn: And the man said they left from here, because I heard *from behind
> the curtain (of heaven) from this day the Egyptian slavery has started* . . .[48]

This text clearly links Joseph's sale to the Ishmaelites with the
beginning of the enslavement in Egypt. If the enslavement of
Joseph was seen as the beginning of Israel's bondage, then it is
fitting that he suffered in a similar way to those who suffered later

---

48. I am unaware of any parallel interpretation to this in rabbinic literature.

under Egyptian bondage.[49] In fact, Targum Psalms has creatively taken 'Joseph' to mean both the individual who was raised from slave to viceroy and the nation. Such an interpretive coup has been achieved by additions and vocabulary intended to point readers at the same time to the suffering of Joseph and the bondage of Israel in Egypt.

Such findings suggest that there is a shared interpretative tradition surrounding Joseph and the exodus seen in Targum Neofiti of Gen. 40, Targum Pseudo-Jonathan of Gen. 37 and Targum of Ps. 81, a tradition that has no parallels elsewhere, as far as I am aware.[50] This discussion highlights the importance of not treating Targum Psalms in isolation – it was never meant to be read in isolation either from the original Hebrew or from the broader rabbinic corpora of scriptural interpretation.

Rabbinic interpretations of v. 9 picked up on the unusual expression *bĕkā*, literally 'in you' (which parallels v. 5 and the testimony placed *in* Joseph) in relation to a 'foreign god', and linked it to the evil inclination that would eventually lead to idolatry.[51] Targum Psalms clearly interprets this phrase in a different way, as the context of the passage demands. It is the 'worship of foreign idols' which is not to be 'in' the community of Israel.

---

49. *Midrash Tehillim* relates Ps. 81:7 to Joseph. The passage refers v. 6a to Joseph and his release from jail, and then v. 6b to Joseph serving under the chief cook. It then cites the rabbis who relate this verse to the release of Israel from Egypt and that Joseph's descendants were not enslaved in contrast to the rest of the house of Israel. However, note BT *Rosh Hashanah* 11a, where 81:4 is said to refer to the date of Joseph's release from jail.

50. Zakowitch, *And You*, suggests that Gen. 47:12–26 is a secondary element in the narrative that put the blame for the Israelite enslavement on Joseph for mistreating the Egyptians when he ruled over the land. The LXX and Samaritan rendering of v. 21, which have 'enslave' as opposed to 'moved', support his claim. Such an interpretation suggests that the linking of Joseph to the bondage in Egypt may have a long history behind it. However, Targum Psalms is doing something different from this, as it places no blame on Joseph.

51. E.g. BT *Shabbat* 105b and parallels.

Such an interpretation is interesting in comparison to the Targumim of Deut. 32:12. There the MT describes how God alone led Israel, and that 'there was no foreign god with him'. Targum Neofiti translates: 'And there was no worship of foreign idols among them.'[52] Although the 'problem' in this text is different from that in Ps. 81:10, the similarity in the solution is striking, and indicates either the dependence of one text on another or more likely the adoption of a common tradition by different texts. The link between Ps. 81:10 and Deut. 32:12 is clear in the Hebrew, with the phrase 'foreign god' (*'ēl nēkār*) in both verses. Such a connection is sufficient for Targum Psalms to make the connection and utilize an earlier example of Targumic exegesis. Whether such utilization occurred or not is impossible to prove definitively, though there seems no doubt that some form of relationship exists between these texts.

It is striking to note the difference between the interpretation given to v. 5, where the Hebrew is read literally, and that in v. 9, where a potentially 'dangerous' literal reading is avoided. Clearly ancient biblical exegesis was not tied down by narrow exegetical categories that limit reading texts in one way, and one way only.

Conclusion

Targum Psalms, along with the other Targumim to the Hebrew Bible, has served for many as a repository of interpretative traditions which can be raided for evidence to support particular arguments, e.g. ancient *Vorlage* to the Hebrew Bible or Jewish interpretations in the New Testament. Such misuse is unfortunate but perhaps inevitable considering the lack of scholarly attention which the Targum has received in the past century. This essay, I trust, will encourage reading it as a document in its own right, containing evidence of how one of the most cherished parts of the Hebrew Bible was read in late antiquity.

---

52. So Targum Pseudo-Jonathan and Fragment Targum; Targum Onkelos has a slight variation.

In the introduction I also suggested that it should stimulate thinking about how we read the Psalter, since the Targum highlights the necessity of dependence on the original Hebrew, as well as the numerous possibilities that the original Hebrew presents for creative interpretations. Creativity is perhaps the most striking feature of ancient exegesis, as illustrated briefly above. This is refreshing in an age which focuses on uncovering an 'original meaning', a term that would sound particularly foreign to the exegete who was responsible for the Targum of Psalms.

APPENDIX 1: INDEX OF FORM-CRITICAL CATEGORIZATIONS

Compiled by Philip S. Johnston

Many scholars discuss form criticism of the Psalms, but few sources present the resultant categorization in accessible form. The following table presents the categorization of Gunkel and of several subsequent introductions, and will enable students to note both consensus and disagreement among these authors.

Abbreviations

Cn	Confidence Ps	CnC	Confidence Ps of the Community
		CnI	Confidence Ps of the Individual
Cov	Covenant Renewal Ps		
Cr	Creation Ps		
H	Hymn	HE	Hymn of Yahweh's Enthronement
		HZ	Hymn of Zion
His	Historical Ps		
L	Lament	LC	Lament of the Community
		LI	Lament of the Individual
Lit	Liturgy Ps		
Mix	Mixed Ps		
Pil	Pilgrimage Ps		
Pr	Prophetic Ps		
R	Royal Ps		
T	Torah Ps		
Th	Thanksgiving	ThC	Thanksgiving of the Community
		ThI	Thanksgiving of the Individual
W	Wisdom Ps		
#	acrostic		

Sources

Bellinger, W. H., *Psalms: Reading and Studying the Book of Praises* (Peabody: Hendrickson, 1990).

Day, J., *Psalms*, Old Testament Guides (Sheffield: JSOT Press, 1990).

Gillingham, S. E., *The Poems and Psalms of the Hebrew Bible* (Oxford: OUP, 1994).

Gunkel, H., *Introduction to Psalms: The Genres of the Religious Lyric of Israel*, tr. J. D. Nogalski (Macon: Mercer University Press, 1998).

Lucas, E. C., *Exploring the Old Testament, Vol. 3, The Psalms and Wisdom Literature* (London: SPCK, 2003).

Sabourin, L., *The Psalms: Their Origin and Meaning* (New York: Alba House, 2nd ed., 1974).

Seybold, K., *Introducing the Psalms*, tr. R. G. Dunphy (Edinburgh: T. & T. Clark, 1990).

Form-Critical Categorizatons

Psalm	Gunkel 1933	Sabourin 1974	Seybold 1990	Day 1990	Bellinger 1990	Gillingham 1994	Lucas 2003
1	W	W	W	W, T	W	W	W, T
2	R	R	R	R	R	R	R
3	LI	CnI	LI	LI	LI	LI	LI
4	CnI	CnI	CnI	LI	LI	CnI	CnI
5	LI	LI	LI	LI	LI	LI	LI
6	LI	LI	LI	LI	LI	LI	LI
7	LI	LI	LI	LI	LI	LI	LI
8	H	H	H	H	Cr	H	H
9-10 #	Mix	ThI	W	LI	LI	ThI	ThI
11	CnI	CnI	CnI	CnI	LI	CnI	CnI
12		LC		LC	LC	LI	LC
13	LI	LI	LI	LI	LI	LI	LI
14		Pr			LC	Pr	
15	Lit	Lit	Lit	Lit	Lit	Lit	
16	CnI	CnI	CnI	CnI	LI	CnI	CnI
17	LI	LI	LI	LI	LI	LI	LI
18	R, ThI	R	R	R, ThI	R	R	R
19	H	H	H, W	H-T	Cr, W	(H-W)	T

Psalm	Gunkel 1933	Sabourin 1974	Seybold 1990	Day 1990	Bellinger 1990	Gillingham 1994	Lucas 2003
20	R	R	R	R	R	R	R
21	R	R	R	R	R	R	R
22	LI	LI	LI	LI	LI	LI	LI
23	CnI	CnI	CnI	CnI	Cn	CnI	CnI
24	Lit	Lit	Lit	Lit	Lit	Lit	
25 #	LI	LI	LI, W	LI	LI	LI	LI
26	LI	LI	LI	LI	LI	LI	LI
27	CnI-LI	CnI	LI, CnI	CnI-LI	LI	CnI	LI
28	LI	LI	LI	LI	LI	LI	LI
29	H	H	H	H	H	H	H
30		ThI	ThI	ThI	ThI	ThI	
31	LI ThI	LI		LI	LI	LI	
32	ThI	ThI	ThI	ThI	W	ThI	ThI
33	H	H	H	H	H	H	H
34 #	ThI	ThI	ThI, W	ThI	ThI	ThI	ThI, W
35	LI	LI	LI	LI	LI	LI	LI
36		LI			LI	LI	
37 #	W	W	W	W	W	W	W
38	LI	LI	LI	LI	LI	LI	
39	LI	LI	LI	LI	LI	LI	LI
40	ThI-LI	ThI	ThI	ThI-LI	LI	ThI	
41	ThI	ThI	LI, ThI	ThI	ThI	ThI	LI
42-43	LI	LI	LI	LI	LI	LI	LI
44		LC	LC	LC	LC	LC	LC
45	R	R	R	R	R	R	R
46	HZ	HZ	HZ	HZ	HZ	HZ	HZ
47	HE	HE	HE	HE	HE	HE	HE
48	HZ	HZ	HZ	HZ	HZ	HZ	HZ
49	W	W	W	W	W	W	W
50		Pr		Cov	H, Pr	Pr	
51	LI	LI	LI	LI	LI	LI	LI
52		Pr		LI	LI	Pr	
53		Pr			LC	Pr	
54	LI	LI	LI	LI	LI	LI	LI
55	LI	LI	LI	LI	LI	LI	LI
56	LI	LI	LI	LI	LI	LI	LI
57	LI	LI	LI	LI	LI	LI	LI
58		LC		(LC)	LC	Pr	
59	LI	LI	LI	LI	LI	LI	
60		LC	LC	LC	LC	LC	LC

Psalm	Gunkel 1933	Sabourin 1974	Seybold 1990	Day 1990	Bellinger 1990	Gillingham 1994	Lucas 2003
61	LI	LI	LI	LI	LI	LI	LI
62	CnI	CnI	CnI	CnI	LI	CnI	CnI
63	LI	LI	LI		LI	LI	
64	LI	LI	LI	LI	LI	LI	LI
65	H	ThC		H	Cr	ThC	H
66	ThI-ThC	ThC	ThI	H-ThC-ThI	ThI	ThC	
67	H, ThC	ThC		(LC?)	ThC	ThC	ThC
68	H	ThC		H	H	ThC	
69	LI	LI	LI	LI	LI	LI	LI
70	LI	LI		LI	LI	LI	
71	LI	LI	LI	LI	LI	LI	LI
72	R	R	R	R	R	R	R
73	W	W	W	W	W	W	W
74		LC	LC	LC	LC	LC	LC
75	Pr	Pr			ThC	Pr	
76	HZ	HZ	HZ	HZ	HZ	HZ	HZ
77		LC		LI	LI	LC	
78		His		His	W	H, His	
79		LC	LC	LC	LC	LC	LC
80		LC	LC	LC	LC	LC	LC
81		Pr		Cov	H, Pr	Pr	
82		LC			H, Pr	LC	
83		LC	LC	LC	LC	LC	LC
84	HZ (Pil)	HZ	HZ	HZ (Pil)	HZ	CnI	HZ
85	Pr	LC	LC	LC	LC	LC	LC
86	LI	LI	LI	LI	LI	LI	LI
87	HZ	HZ	HZ	HZ	HZ	HZ	HZ
88	LI	LI	LI	LI	LI	LI	LI
89	R[47-52]	R	R, LC	R	R	R	R
90		LC	LC	(LC)	LC	LC	LC
91	W	W			Cn	CnI	CnI
92	ThI	ThI	ThI		ThC	ThI	ThI
93	HE	HE	HE		HE	HE	HE
94	LC-W-LI	LC		LC-LI	LI	LC	
95		Pr			HE	Pr	H
96	H	HE	HE	HE	HE	HE	HE

Psalm	Gunkel 1933	Sabourin 1974	Seybold 1990	Day 1990	Bellinger 1990	Gillingham 1994	Lucas 2003
97	HE	HE	HE	HE	HE	HE	HE
98	H	HE	HE	HE	HE	HE	HE
99	HE	HE	HE	HE	HE	HE	HE
100	H (ThI)	H	H	H	H	H	H
101	R	R	R	R	R	R	R
102	LI	LI	LI	LI	LI	LI	LI
103	H	H	H	H	H	H	H
104	H	H	H	H	Cr	H	H
105	H	His	H	H, His	H	H, His	
106		LC		His	LC	LC	
107	(ThI) Mix	ThI	(ThI)	Th	ThC	ThI	ThC
108		LC			LC	LC	
109	LI	LI	LI	LI	LI	LI	LI
110	R	R	R	R	R	R	R
111 #	H, Mix	H	H, W	H	H	H	W
112 #	W	W	W	W	W	W	W
113	H	H	H	H	H	H	H
114	H	H	H	H	H	H	H
115		CnC			H	CnC	CnC
116	ThI	ThI	ThI	ThI	ThI	ThI	ThI
117	H	H		H	H	H	H
118	ThI	ThC	ThI	ThI	ThI	ThC	ThI
119 #	Mix	W	W	T	W	W	T
120	LI	LI		LI	LI	LI	
121		CnI			Cn	CnI	CnI
122	HZ, Pil	HZ	HZ	HZ	HZ	HZ	HZ
123		LC		LC	LC	LC	
124	ThC	ThC		ThC	ThC	ThC	ThC
125		CnC			Cn	CnC	CnC
126		LC		LC	LC	LC	LC
127		W			W	W	
128	W	W			W	W	
129	ThC	CnC		CnC	ThC	CnC	CnC
130	LI	LI	LI	LI	LI	LI	LI
131	CnI	CnI		CnI	Cn	CnI	CnI
132	R	R	R	R	R	R	R
133	W	W			W	CnC	
134		Lit		H	H	Lit	H
135	H	H	H	H	H	H	H

Psalm	Gunkel 1933	Sabourin 1974	Seybold 1990	Day 1990	Bellinger 1990	Gillingham 1994	Lucas 2003
136	H	H		H	ThC	H	H
137		LC	LC	LC	LC	LC	LC
138	ThI	ThI	ThI	ThI	ThI	ThI	ThI
139		W		LI	H	W	
140	LI	LI	LI	LI	LI	LI	LI
141	LI	LI	LI	LI	LI	LI	LI
142	LI	LI		LI	LI	LI	LI
143	LI	LI	LI	LI	LI	LI	LI
144	R[1-11]	R		R	R	R	R
145 #	H	H	H, W	H	H	H	H
146	H	H	H	H	H	H	H
147	H	H	H	H	H	H	H
148	H	H	H	H	H, Cr	H	H
149	H	H	H	H	H	H	H
150	H	H	H	H	H	H	H

APPENDIX 2: INDEX OF SELECTIVE PSALMS COMMENTARIES

Compiled by Philip S. Johnston

There is much good if often brief commentary on selected psalms by well known scholars outside standard commentaries. However, this is often unknown and is therefore ignored. The following list gives some of the treatments published in recent decades.

Sources

Anderson = B. W. Anderson, *Out of the Depths* (Louisville: Westminster John Knox Press, 3rd ed., 2000).

Crenshaw = J. L. Crenshaw, *The Psalms: An Introduction* (Grand Rapids: Eerdmans, 2001).

Bellinger = W. H. Bellinger, *Psalms: Reading and Studying the Book of Praises* (Peabody: Hendrickson, 1990).

Broyles = C. C. Broyles, *The Conflict of Faith and Experience in the Psalms*, *JSOTSup* 52 (Sheffield: JSOT Press, 1989).

Brueggemann-P = W. Brueggemann, *The Psalms and the Life of Faith*, ed. P. D. Miller (Minneapolis: Fortress, 1995).

Brueggemann-M = W. Brueggemann, *The Message of the Psalms: A Theological Commentary* (Minneapolis: Augsburg, 1984).

Lucas = E. C. Lucas, *Exploring the Old Testament, Vol. 3, The Psalms and Wisdom Literature* (London: SPCK, 2003).

Magonet = J. Magonet, *A Rabbi Reads the Psalms* (London: SCM, 1994).

Mays = J. L. Mays, *The Lord Reigns* (Louisville: Westminster John Knox Press, 1994).

McCann = J. C. McCann, *A Theological Introduction to the Book of Psalms: The Psalms as Torah* (Nashville: Abingdon, 1993).

Miller = P. D. Miller, *Interpreting the Psalms* (Philadelphia: Fortress, 1986).

Westermann = C. Westermann, *The Living Psalms*, tr. J. R. Porter (Edinburgh: T. & T. Clark, 1989).

Ps.	Author and page
1	Anderson, 190; Bellinger, 132; Brueggemann-P, 190; Brueggemann-M, 38; Lucas, 34; McCann, 26; Miller, 81; Westermann, 297
2	Bellinger, 116; Lucas, 35; Mays, 108; McCann, 41; Miller, 87
3	McCann, 88
4	Westermann, 123
6	Bellinger, 60; Broyles, 179; Brueggemann-P, 54; Westermann, 74
8	Anderson, 134; Brueggemann-M, 36; McCann, 57; Westermann, 260
9–10	Broyles, 135; Brueggemann-P, 217
12	Bellinger, 68
13	Broyles, 183; Brueggemann-M, 58; Lucas, 37; Mays, 55; McCann, 90; Westermann, 68
14	Brueggemann-M, 44; Miller, 94
15	(Brueggemann-M, 42)
19	Anderson, 129; Lucas, 38; Magonet, 85; McCann, 28; Westermann, 252
22	Broyles, 187; Magonet, 99; McCann, 168; Miller, 108; Westermann, 79
23	Bellinger, 101; Brueggemann-M, 154; Lucas, 39; Magonet, 52; McCann, 127; Miller, 112; Westermann, 127
24	(Brueggemann-M, 42); Crenshaw, 155; McCann, 72; Westermann, 276
25	Brueggemann-P, 197; Magonet, 69
26	Bellinger, 63
27	Brueggemann-M, 152; Westermann, 146
29	Brueggemann-M, 142; Westermann, 229
30	Brueggemann-M, 126; Westermann, 166
31	Westermann, 173
32	Anderson, 80; Brueggemann-M, 95; McCann, 109
33	Anderson, 145; Brueggemann-M, 33; Lucas, 40; Westermann, 207
34	Brueggemann-M, 133
35	Broyles, 193; Brueggemann-M, 63
37	Bellinger, 133; Brueggemann-P, 235; Brueggemann-M, 42
39	Broyles, 196; Brueggemann-P, 109
40	Brueggemann-M, 128; Westermann, 178
42–43	Broyles, 201
44	Broyles, 139
46	Bellinger, 98; McCann, 136; Westermann, 283

Ps.	Author and page
108	Broyles, 149
109	Brueggemann-P, 268; Brueggemann-M, 81; McCann, 112
111	(Brueggemann-M, 45)
112	Brueggemann-M, 45
113	Brueggemann-M, 161; McCann, 79; Westermann, 201
114	Brueggemann-M, 140
115	Crenshaw, 128; Magonet, 131
116	Westermann, 189
117	Brueggemann-M, 159; McCann, 55
118	Mays, 136; McCann, 166; Westermann, 271
119	Brueggemann-M, 39; McCann, 30; Westermann, 294
121	Magonet, 119; Westermann, 289
122	McCann, 152; Westermann, 280
123	Westermann, 43
124	Brueggemann-M, 139; Lucas, 50; Magonet, 127; Westermann, 50
126	Westermann, 46
127	Miller, 131
130	Anderson, 87; Brueggemann-M, 104; McCann, 86; Miller, 138; Westermann, 116
131	Brueggemann-M, 48
132	Bellinger, 120
133	Brueggemann-M, 47
134	Magonet, 145
135	Brueggemann-M, 159
137	Brueggemann-M, 74; McCann, 117
138	Brueggemann-M, 131; Lucas, 50; Westermann, 197
139	Anderson, 91; Miller, 144; Westermann, 265
143	Brueggemann-M, 102
145	Brueggemann-P, 123; Brueggemann-M, 29; Magonet, 35; Westermann, 221
146	Brueggemann-P, 126; Brueggemann-M, 162; Magonet, 141
147	Brueggemann-M, 163
148	Brueggemann-M, 165; Westermann, 255
149	Brueggemann-P, 124; Brueggemann-M, 165
150	Brueggemann-P, 125, 192; Brueggemann-M, 167; Lucas, 51; McCann, 55

BIBLIOGRAPHY

Aejmelaeus, A., *The Traditional Prayer in the Psalms*, BZAW 167 (Berlin: de Gruyter, 1986).

Albertz, R., *A History of Israelite Religion in the Old Testament Period*, vol. 1 (London: SCM, 1994).

Albrektson, B., *History and the Gods: An Essay on the Idea of Historical Events as Divine Manifestations in the Ancient Near East and in Israel* (Lund: Gleerup, 1967).

Alexander, P. S., 'Targum, Targumim', *ABD*, vol. 6, pp. 320–331.

Allen, L. C., 'David as Exemplar of Spirituality: The Redaction Function of Psalm 19', *Bib* 67 (1986), pp. 544–546.

Allen, L. C., 'The Value of Rhetorical Criticism in Psalm 69', *JBL* 105 (1986), pp. 577–598.

Allen, L. C., *Psalms 101 – 150*, WBC 21 (Nashville: Thomas Nelson, 2nd ed. 2002).

Allen, R. B., *Praise! A Matter of Life and Breath* (Nashville: Thomas Nelson, 1980).

Alter, R., *The Art of Biblical Poetry* (New York: Basic, 1985).

Assmann, J., *Agyptische Hymnen und Gebete* (Zurich and Munich: Artemis Verlag, 1975).

Auffret, P., *The Literary Structure of Psalm 2*, JSOTSup 3 (Sheffield: JSOT Press, 1977).

Auffret, P., *Merveilles à nos yeux: étude structurelle de vingt psaumes dont celui de 1 Ch 16, 8–36*, BZAW 235 (Berlin: de Gruyter, 1995).

Auffret, P., 'L'étude structurelle des psaumes: réponses et compléments I', *ScEs* 48 (1996), pp. 45–60.

Auffret, P., 'L'étude structurelle des psaumes: réponses et compléments II', *ScEs* 49 (1997), pp. 39–61.

Auffret, P., 'L'étude structurelle des psaumes: réponses et compléments III',
    ScEs 49 (1997), pp. 149–174.

Auffret, P., *Là montent les tribus: étude structurelle de la collection des Psaumes des
    Montées, d'Ex 15, 1–18 et des rapports entre eux*, BZAW 289 (New York and
    Berlin: de Gruyter, 1999).

Austin, J. L., *How to do Things with Words: The William James Lectures delivered at
    Harvard University in 1955*, 2nd ed., ed. J. O. Urmson and M. Sbisà (Oxford:
    OUP, 1976).

Auwers, J.-M., *La Composition littéraire du Psautier: Un état de la question*, Cahiers
    de la Revue Biblique 46 (Paris: Gabalda, 2000).

Auwers, J-M., 'Les voies de l'exégèse canonique du Psautier', in J.-M. Auwers
    and H. J. de Jonge, eds., *The Biblical Canons*, BETL 163 (Leuven: Leuven
    University Press, 2003), pp. 5–26.

Babut, J.-M., *Idiomatic Expressions of the Hebrew Bible. Their Meaning and
    Translation through Componential Analysis*, BIBAL Diss. Ser. 5 (North
    Richland Hills, Texas: BIBAL Press, 1999).

Bacher, W., 'Das Targum zur den Psalmen', *MGWJ* 21 (1872), pp. 408–416,
    463–473.

Bail, U., 'Gerechtigkeit in der Mitte des Segens. Psalm 67', *BK* 58 (2003), pp.
    127–135.

Barr, J., *The Semantics of Biblical Language* (Oxford: OUP, 1961).

Barr, J., *Comparative Philology and the Text of the Old Testament* (Oxford: SCM
    Press, 1968).

Barth, C. F., *Die Errettung vom Tode in den individuellen Klage- und Dankliedern des
    Alten Testamentes* (Zollikon: Evangelischer, 1947); reprinted as *Die
    Errettung vom Tode*, ed. B. Janowski (Stuttgart: Kohlhammer, 1997), pp.
    11–139.

Barucq, A. and F. Daumas, *Hymnes et Prieres de l'Egypte Ancienne*, Litteratures
    Anciennes du Proche-Orient (Paris: Cerf, 1980).

Beauchamp, P., 'La prière à l'école des Psaumes', in *Testament biblique: Recueil
    d'articles parus dans Etudes* (Paris: Bayard, 2001), pp. 33–52.

Beckwith, R., 'The Early History of the Psalter', *TynBul* 46 (1995),
    pp. 1–27.

Begriche, J., 'Das priesterliche Heilsorakel', *ZAW* 52 (1934), pp. 81–92.

Bellinger, Jr, W. H., *Psalmody and Prophecy*, JSOTSup 27 (Sheffield: JSOT Press,
    1984).

Bellinger, Jr, W. H., *Psalms: Reading and Studying the Book of Praises* (Peabody:
    Hendrickson, 1990).

Bellinger, Jr, W. H., 'Psalm xxvi: a test of method,' *VT* 43 (1993), pp. 452–461.

Bellinger, Jr, W. H., *A Hermeneutic of Curiosity and Readings of Psalm 61*, Studies in Old Testament Interpretation 1 (Macon: Mercer University, 1995).

Berlin, A., *The Dynamics of Biblical Parallelism* (Bloomington: Indiana University Press, 1985).

Berlin, A., *Biblical Poetry Through Medieval Jewish Eyes* (Bloomington: Indiana University Press, 1991).

Bernstein, M., 'Translation Technique in the Targum to Psalms: Two Test Cases. Psalms 2 and 137', in E. H. Lovering, ed., *SBL Seminar Papers 1994* (Atlanta: Scholars Press, 1994), pp. 326–345.

Bernstein, M., 'Torah and Its Study in the Targum of Psalms', in J. Gurock and Y. Elman, eds., *Hazon Nahum: Studies in Honour of Dr Norman Lamm on the Occasion of his Seventieth Birthday* (Hoboken: Yeshiva University Press, 1997), pp. 39–67.

Bernstein, M., 'The Righteous and the Wicked in the Aramaic Version of Psalms', *JAB* 3 (2001), pp. 5–26.

Berry, D. K., *The Psalms and Their Readers: Interpretive Strategies for Psalm 18*, JSOTSup 153 (Sheffield: JSOT Press, 1993).

Beyerlin, W., *Die Rettung der Bedrängten in den Feindpsalmen der Einzelnen auf institutionelle Zusammenhänge untersucht* (Göttingen: Vandenhoeck & Ruprecht, 1970).

Block, D. I., 'My Servant David: Ancient Israel's Vision of the Messiah', in R. S. Hess, M. D. Carroll R., eds., *Israel's Messiah in the Bible and the Dead Sea Scrolls* (Grand Rapids: Baker, 2003), pp. 17–56.

Bock, D. L., *Luke*, BECNT 3 (Grand Rapids: Baker, 1996).

Boulton, M., 'Forsaking God: a Theological Argument for Christian Lamentation', *SJT* 55 (2002), pp. 58–78.

Bouzard, Jr, W. C., *We Have Heard With Our Ears, O God: Sources of the Communal Laments in the Psalms*, SBLDS 159 (Atlanta: Scholars Press, 1997).

Braude, W. G., *The Midrash on Psalms*, 2 vols. (New Haven: Yale University Press, 1954).

Braude, W. G., 'Midrash as Deep Peshat', in S. Brunswick, ed., *Studies in Judaica, Karaitica and Islamica* (Ramat Gan, Israel: Bar Ilan University Press, 1982), pp. 31–38.

Briggs, C. A., *Messianic Prophecy: The Prediction of the Fulfillment of Redemption Through the Messiah* (New York: Scribners, 1886; reprinted Peabody: Hendrickson, 1988).

Briggs, R. S., _Words in Action: Speech Act Theory and Biblical Interpretation. Toward a Hermeneutic of Self-Involvement_ (Edinburgh: T. & T. Clark, 2001).

Brooke, G. J., 'The Psalms in Early Jewish Literature', in S. Moyise and M. J. J. Menken, eds., _The Psalms in the New Testament_ (London and New York: T. & T. Clark, 2004), pp. 5–24.

Brown, P. and Levinson, S. C., _Politeness: Some universals in language usage_, Studies in Interactional Sociolinguistics 4 (Cambridge: CUP, 1978, 1987).

Brown, R. E., _The Death of the Messiah: From Gethsemane to the Grave_, 2 vols. (New York: Doubleday, 1994).

Brown, W. P., _Seeing the Psalms: A Theology of Metaphor_ (Louisville: Westminster John Knox Press, 2002).

Broyles, C. C., _The Conflict of Faith and Experience in the Psalms: A Form-Critical and Theological Study_, JSOTSup 52 (Sheffield: JSOT Press, 1989).

Broyles, C. C., _Psalms_, NIBC (Peabody: Hendrickson, 1999).

Brueggemann, W., 'From Hurt to Joy, From Death to Life', Interpretation 28 (1974), pp. 3–19; reprinted in _The Psalms and the Life of Faith_, ed. P. D. Miller (Minneapolis: Fortress, 1995), pp. 67–83.

Brueggemann, W., 'Psalms and the Life of Faith: A Suggested Typology of Function', _JSOT_ 17 (1980), pp. 3–32; reprinted in _The Psalms and the Life of Faith_, ed. P. D. Miller (Minneapolis: Fortress, 1995), pp. 3–32.

Brueggemann, W., _The Message of the Psalms: A Theological Commentary_ (Minneapolis: Augsburg, 1984).

Brueggemann, W., 'The Costly Loss of Lament', _JSOT_ 36 (1986), pp. 57–71; reprinted in _The Psalms and the Life of Faith_, ed. P. D. Miller (Minneapolis: Fortress, 1995), pp. 98–111.

Brueggemann, W., _Israel's Praise: Doxology against Idolatry and Ideology_ (Philadelphia: Fortress, 1988).

Brueggemann, W., 'The Psalms as Prayer', _Reformed Liturgy and Music_ 23 (1989), pp. 13–26; reprinted in _The Psalms and the Life of Faith_, ed. P. D. Miller (Minneapolis: Fortress, 1995), pp. 33–66.

Brueggemann, W., _Abiding Astonishment: Psalms, Modernity, and the Making of History_ (Louisville: Westminster John Knox Press, 1991).

Brueggemann, W., 'Bounded by Obedience and Praise: The Psalms as Canon', _JSOT_ 50 (1991), pp. 63–92; reprinted in _The Psalms and the Life of Faith_, ed. P. D. Miller (Minneapolis: Fortress, 1995), pp. 189–213.

Brueggemann, W., 'Praise and the Psalms: A Politics of Glad Abandonment', _The Hymn_ (Oct. 1992); reprinted in _The Psalms and the Life of Faith_, ed. P. D. Miller (Minneapolis: Fortress, 1995), pp. 112–132.

Brueggemann, W. and P. D. Miller, 'Psalm 73 as a Canonical Marker', *JSOT* 72 (1996), pp. 45–56.

Bühlmann, W. and K. Scherer, *Stilfiguren der Bibel: ein kleines Nachschlagewerk*, Biblische Beiträge 10 (Fribourg: Schweizerisches Katholisches Bibelwerk, 1973).

Bullock, C. H., *Encountering the Book of Psalms: A Literary and Theological Introduction* (Grand Rapids: Baker Academic, 2001).

Burke, D. G., 'Cross, Crucify', *ISBE*, vol. 1, pp. 825–830.

Buss, M. J., 'The Meaning of "Cult" and the Interpretation of the Old Testament', *Journal of Bible and Religion* 32 (1964), pp. 317–325.

Buttenwieser, M., 'Grammatical Excursus: The Precative Perfect', in M. Buttenwieser, *The Psalms*, The Library of Biblical Studies (New York: KTAV, 1969), pp. 18–25.

Caird, G. B., *The Language and Imagery of the Bible* (London: Duckworth, 1980).

Calvin, J., *Commentaries on the Book of Psalms*, vol. 1, *Psalms 1 – 35* (Grand Rapids: Baker, 1993).

Campbell, A. F., 'Form Criticism's Future', in M. A. Sweeney and E. Ben Zvi, eds., *The Changing Face of Form Criticism for the Twenty-First Century* (Grand Rapids: Eerdmans, 2003), pp. 15–31.

Carroll, J. T., 'The Uses of Scripture in Acts', in D. J. Lull, ed., *SBL Seminar Papers 1990* (Atlanta: Scholars Press, 1990), pp. 512–528.

Cartledge, T. W., 'Conditional Vows in the Psalms of Lament: A New Approach to an Old Problem', in K. G. Hogland et al., eds., *The Listening Heart: Essays in Wisdom and the Psalms in Honor of Roland E. Murphy, O. Carm.*, *JSOTSup* 58 (Sheffield: JSOT Press, 1987), pp. 77–94.

Casanowicz, I. M., *Paronomasia in the Old Testament* (Boston: Norwood Press, 1894).

Childs, B. S., *An Introduction to the Old Testament as Scripture* (Philadelphia: Fortress, and London: SCM, 1979).

Churgin, P., *Targûm Kĕtûbîm* (New York: Horeb, 1945).

Clements, R. E., *God and Temple* (Oxford: Blackwell, 1965).

Clements, R. E., 'Worship and Ethics: A Re-examination of Psalm 15', in M. P. Graham et al., eds., *Worship in the Hebrew Bible: Essays in Honor of John T. Willis*, *JSOTSup* 284 (Sheffield: Sheffield Academic Press, 1999), pp. 78–94.

Clines, D. J. A., 'Psalm Research Since 1955: I. The Psalms and the Cult', *TynBul* 18 (1967), pp. 103–126.

Clines, D. J. A., 'The Psalms and the King', *TSF Bulletin* 71 (1975), pp. 1–6, reprinted in *On the Way to the Postmodern: Old Testament Essays 1967–1998*, vol. 2, *JSOTSup* 292 (Sheffield: Sheffield Academic Press, 1998), pp. 687–700.

Clines, D. J. A., 'A World Established on Water (Psalm 24): Reader-Response, Deconstruction and Bespoke Interpretation', in J. C. Exum and D. J. A. Clines, eds., *The New Literary Criticism and the Hebrew Bible*, *JSOTSup* 143 (Sheffield: JSOT Press, 1993), pp. 79–90.

Cloete, W. T. W., *Versification and Syntax in Jeremiah 2 – 25: Syntactical Constraints in Hebrew Colometry*, SBLDS 117 (Atlanta: Scholars Press, 1989).

Cohen, M..E. ed., *Miqrā'ôt Gĕdôlôt Hāketer*, Psalms, vols. 1–2 (Israel: Bar Ilan University Press, 2003).

Cohen, M. E., *The Canonical Lamentations of Ancient Mesopotamia*, 2 vols. (Bethesda: CDL Press, 1988).

Cole, R. L., 'An Integrated Reading of Psalms 1 and 2', *JSOT* 98 (2002), pp. 75–88.

Cole, R. L., *The Shape and Message of Book III (Psalms 73 – 89)*, *JSOTSup* 307 (Sheffield: Sheffield Academic Press, 2000).

Collins, T., *Line-Forms in Hebrew Poetry*, Studia Pohl: Series Maior 7 (Rome: Pontifical Biblical Institute, 1978).

Cook, E. M., 'The Psalms Targum: Introduction to a New Translation with Sample Texts', in P. V. M. Flesher, ed., *Targum and Scripture. Studies in Aramaic Translations and Interpretation in Memory of Ernest G. Clarke* (Leiden: Brill, 2002), pp. 185–201.

Cooper, A., 'Ps. 24:7–10: Mythology and Exegesis', *JBL* 102 (1983), pp. 37–60.

Cooper, J. S., 'A Sumerian *Su-il-la* from Nimrud with a Prayer for Sin-sar-iskun', *Iraq* 32 (1970), pp. 51–67.

Craigie, P. C., *Psalms 1 – 50*, WBC 19 (Waco: Word, 1983).

Creach, J. F. D., *Yahweh as Refuge and the Editing of the Hebrew Psalter*, *JSOTSup* 217 (Sheffield: Sheffield Academic Press, 1996).

Creach, J. F. D., 'Like a Tree Planted by the Temple Stream', *CBQ* 61 (1999), pp. 34–46.

Crenshaw, J., *The Psalms: An Introduction* (Grand Rapids: Eerdmans, 2001).

Croatto, J. S., 'Psalm 23:1–6: A Latin American Perspective', in J. R. Levison and P. Pope-Levison, eds., *Return to Babel: Global Perspectives on the Bible* (Louisville: Westminster John Knox Press, 1999), pp. 57–62.

Croft, S. J. L., *The Identity of the Individual in the Psalms*, *JSOTSup* 44 (Sheffield: JSOT Press, 1987).

Cross, F. M., *Canaanite Myth and Hebrew Epic* (Cambridge, Mass.: Harvard University Press, 1973).

Crow, L. D., 'The *Rhetoric* of Psalm 44', *ZAW* 104 (1992), pp. 394–401.

Crow, L. D., *The Songs of Ascents (Psalms 120 – 134): Their Place in Israelite History and Religion*, SBLDS 148 (Atlanta: Scholars Press, 1996).

Crüsemann, F., *Studien zur Formgeschichte von Hymnus und Danklied in Israel*, WMANT 32 (Neukirchen-Vluyn: Neukirchener Verlag, 1969).

Culley, R. C., *Oral Formulaic Language in the Biblical Psalms*, NMES 4 (Toronto: University of Toronto Press, 1967).

Dahmen, U., *Psalmen- und Psalter-Rezeption im Frühjudentum. Rekonstruktion, Textbestand, Struktur und Pragmatik der Psalmenrolle 11QPs^a aus Qumran*, STDJ 49 (Leiden and Boston: Brill, 2003).

Dahood, M., *Psalms 1–50*, AB 16 (Garden City: Doubleday, 1965).

Dahood, M. and T. Penar, 'The *Grammar* of the Psalter', in M. Dahood, *Psalms 101–150*, AB 17a (New York: Doubleday, 1970), pp. 361–456.

Dalglish, E. R., *Psalm Fifty-One in the Light of Ancient Near Eastern Patternism* (Leiden: Brill, 1962).

Daly-Denton, M., *David in the Fourth Gospel: The Johannine Reception of the Psalms 101–150*, AGJU 47 (Leiden: Brill, 2000).

Daly-Denton, M., 'The *Psalms* in John's Gospel', in S. Moyise and M. J. J. Menken, eds., *The Psalms in the New Testament* (London: T. & T. Clark International, 2004), pp. 119–138.

Davidson, R., *The Vitality of Worship: A Commentary on the Book of Psalms* (Grand Rapids: Eerdmans, 1998).

Davies, G. H., 'The *Ark* in the Psalms', in F. F. Bruce, ed., *Promise and Fulfilment: Essays Presented to Professor S. H. Hooke* (Edinburgh: T. & T. Clark, 1963), pp. 51–61.

Day, J., *Psalms*, Old Testament Guides (Sheffield: JSOT Press, 1990).

deClaissé-Walford, N. L., *Reading from the Beginning: The Shaping of the Hebrew Psalter* (Macon: Mercer University Press, 1997).

Delekat, L., *Asylie und Schutzorakel an Zionheiligtum* (Leiden: Brill, 1967).

Delitzsch, F., *Biblical Commentary on the Psalms*, 3 vols. (Grand Rapids: Eerdmans, 1952).

Dobbs-Allsopp, F. W., *Weep O Daughter of Zion: A Study of the City-Lament Genre in the Hebrew Bible* (Rome: Pontifical Biblical Institute, 1993).

Doble, P., 'Psalms in Luke-Acts', in S. Moyise and M. J. J. Menken, eds., *The Psalms in the New Testament* (London: T. & T. Clark International, 2004), pp. 83–118.

Dodd, C. H., _According to the Scriptures: The Substructure of New Testament Theology_ (London: Nisbet, 1953).

Duncan, J. A., 'Book of Deuteronomy', _EDDS_, pp. 198–202.

Durham, J. I., 'The King as "Messiah" in the Psalms', _RevExp_ 81 (1984), pp. 425–435.

Eaton, J. H., _Psalms_, TBC (London: SPCK, 1967).

Eaton, J. H., _Kingship and the Psalms_, SBT 32 (London: SCM, 1976); 2nd ed., The Biblical Seminar 3 (Sheffield: JSOT Press, 1986).

Eaton, J. H., 'The Psalms and Israelite Worship', in G. W. Anderson, ed., _Tradition and Interpretation: Essays by Members of the Society for Old Testament Study_ (Oxford: Clarendon Press, 1979), pp. 238–273.

Eaton, J. H., _Psalms of the Way and the Kingdom: A Conference with the Commentators_, JSOTSup 199 (Sheffield: Sheffield Academic Press, 1995).

Edwards, T., _The Old, the New and the Rewritten: The Interpretation of the Biblical Psalms in the Targum of Psalms, in Relationship to other Exegetical Traditions, both Jewish and Christian_, DPhil Thesis (Oxford, 2003).

Emerton, J. A., 'The Interpretation of Psalm 82 in John 10', _JTS_ 11 (1960), pp. 329–332.

Emerton, J. A., 'Melchizedek and the Gods: Fresh Evidence for the Jewish Background of John x.34–36', _JTS_ 17 (1966), pp. 399–401.

Eriksson, L. O., _'Come, Children, Listen to Me!' Psalm 34 in the Hebrew Bible and in Early Christian Writings_, ConBOT 32 (Stockholm: Almqvist & Wiksell, 1991).

Eshel, E., et al., '4Q448, 4QApocryphal Psalm and Prayer', in E. Eshel et. al., eds., _Qumran Cave 4, VI, Poetical and Liturgical Texts, Part 1_, DJD XI (Oxford: Clarendon Press, 1998), pp. 403–425.

Eshel, H. and E. Eshel, '4Q448, Psalm 154 (Syriac), Sirach 48:20, and 4QpIsaᵃ', _JBL_ 119 (2000), pp. 645–659.

Estes, D. J., _Hear, My Son: Teaching and Learning in Proverbs 1 – 9_, NSBT 4 (Leicester: Apollos, 1997).

Evans, C. F., _Saint Luke_, TPINTC (London: SCM, 1990).

Falkenstein, A. and W. von Soden, _Sumerische und akkadische Hymnen und Gebete_ (Stuttgart: Artemis, 1953).

Fass, D., E. Hinkelman, and J. Martin, eds., _Proceeding of the IJCAI Workshop on Computational Approaches to Non-Literal Language: Metaphor, Metonymy, Idiom, Speech Acts and Implicature_ (Boulder: University of Colorado, 1991).

Ferris, Jr, P. W., _The Genre of Communal Lament in the Bible and the Ancient Near East_, SBLDS 127 (Atlanta: Scholars Press, 1992).

Finkelstein, L. and H. Horowitz, *Sifre on Deuteronomy* (New York and Jerusalem: Jewish Theological Seminary of America, 1993).

Firth, D. G., 'Responses to Violence in Some Lament Psalms of the Individual', *SK* 17 (1996), pp. 317–328.

Firth, D. G., 'Context and Violence in Individual Prayers for Protection', *SK* 18 (1997), pp. 86–96.

Firth, D. G., 'Testimony as Instruction: Psalms that Share the Experience of Violence with the Community', *SABJT* 7 (1998), pp. 12–22.

Firth, D. G., 'Psalms of Testimony', *OTE* 12 (1999), pp. 440–454.

Firth, D. G., 'Stages of Prayer through the Psalms', *SABJT* 10 (2001), pp. 1–10.

Firth, D. G., *Responses to Violence in Complaint Psalms of the Individual*, PBTM (Carlisle: Paternoster, 2005)

Fitzmyer, J. A., 'Aramaic Evidence Affecting the Interpretation of *Hosanna* in the New Testament', in G. F. Hawthorne and O. Betz, eds., *Tradition and Interpretation in the New Testament: Essays in Honor of E. Earle Ellis* (Tübingen: Mohr/Siebeck, 1987), pp. 110–118.

Flint, P. W., *The Dead Sea Psalms Scrolls and the Book of Psalms*, STDJ 17 (Leiden: Brill, 1997).

Flint, P. W., 'Psalms Scrolls from the Judaean Desert', in J. H. Charlesworth, ed., *The Dead Sea Scrolls: Hebrew, Aramaic and Greek Texts with English Translations*, vol. 4A (Tübingen: Mohr/Siebeck and Louisville: Westminster John Knox Press, 1997).

Foster, B., *Before the Muses*, 2 vols. (Bethesda: CDL Press, 1993).

Foster, J. L., 'The Hymn to Aten: Akhenaten Worships the Sole God', *CANE* vol. 3, pp. 1751–1761.

Foster, J. L., *Hymns, Prayers, and Songs: An Anthology of Ancient Egyptian Lyric Poetry* (Atlanta: Scholars Press, 1996).

Fowler, M. D., 'The Meaning of lipnê YHWH in the Old Testament', *ZAW* 99 (1987), pp. 384–390.

Fraade, S., 'Rabbinic Views on the Practice of Targum, and Multilingualism in the Jewish Galilee of the Third to Sixth Centuries', in L. I. Levine, ed., *The Galilee in Late Antiquity* (New York, Jewish Theological Seminary of America, 1992), pp. 253–286.

Fraade, S., 'Scripture, Targum and Talmud as Instruction: A Complex Textual Story from the *Sifra*', in J. Magness and S. Gitin, eds., *Hesed ve-Emet: Studies in Honor of Ernest S. Frerichs* (Atlanta: Scholars Press, 1998), pp. 109–122.

Fraade, S., 'The Torah of the King (Deut. 17:14–20) in the Temple Scroll and Early Rabbinic Law', in J. Davila, ed., *The Dead Sea Scrolls as Background to Postbiblical Judaism and Early Christianity* (Leiden: Brill, 2003), pp. 25–60.

Freehof, S., 'Sound the Shofar – "Ba Kesse" Psalm 81:4', *JQR* 64 (1973–4), pp. 225–228.

Fuller, R., *Body Idioms: English idiomatic expressions relating to parts of the human body explained with their French equivalents*, Cahiers du centre interdisciplinaire de recherches en histoire, lettres et langues 19 (Angers: Université Catholique de l'Ouest, 1996).

Gelander, S., 'Convention and originality: identification of the situation in the Psalms', *VT* 42 (1992), pp. 302–316.

Geller, S. A., *Parallelism in Early Biblical Poetry*, HSM 20 (Missoula: Scholars Press, 1979).

Gerbrandt, G. E., *Kingship According to the Deuteronomistic History*, SBLDS 87 (Atlanta: Scholars Press, 1986).

Gerstenberger, E. S., 'Psalms', in J. H. Hayes, ed., *Old Testament Form Criticism* (San Antonio: Trinity University Press, 1974), pp. 179–223.

Gerstenberger, E. S., *Der bittende Mensch* (Neukirchen-Vluyn: Neukirchener Verlag, 1980).

Gerstenberger, E. S., *Psalms, Part I: With an Introduction to Cultic Poetry*, FOTL 14 (Grand Rapids: Eerdmans, 1988).

Gerstenberger, E. S., *Psalms, Part II, and Lamentations*, FOTL 15 (Grand Rapids: Eerdmans, 2001).

Gerstenberger, E. S., *Theologies in the Old Testament* (Minneapolis: Fortress, 2002).

Gese, H., 'Psalm 22 und das Neue Testament: Der älteste Bericht vom Tode Jesu und die Entstehung des Herrenmahles', *ZTK* 65 (1968), pp. 1–22.

Gillingham, S. E., *The Poems and Psalms of the Hebrew Bible* (Oxford: OUP, 1994).

Gillmayr-Bucher, S., 'Body Images in the Psalms', *JSOT* 28 (2004), pp. 301–326.

Girard, M., *Les psaumes redécouverts: De la structure au sens*, 3 vols. (Quebec: Bellarmin, 1994–6).

Glucksberg, S., *Understanding Figurative Language: from metaphors to idioms*, Oxford Psychology Series 36 (Oxford: OUP, 2001).

Golomb, D., 'Methodological Considerations in Pentateuchal Targumic Research', *JSP* 18 (1988), pp. 3–25.

Gordon, R. P., _Studies in the Targum to the Twelve Prophets_, VTSup 51 (Leiden: Brill, 1994).

Gottwald, N. K., _The Hebrew Bible: A Socio-Literary Introduction_ (Minneapolis: Fortress, 1985).

Gous, I. G. P., 'Reason to Believe: Cognitive Strategy in the Acrostic Psalm 34', _OTE_ 12 (1999), pp. 455–467.

Gowan, D. E., _Reclaiming the Old Testament for the Christian Pulpit_ (Edinburgh: T. & T. Clark, 1980).

Grant, J. A., _The King as Exemplar: The Function of Deuteronomy's Kingship Law in the Shaping of the Book of Psalms_, Academia Biblica 17 (Atlanta: SBL and Leiden: Brill, 2004).

Gregg, R.C., ed., _Athanasius: The Life of Antony and the Letter to Marcellinus_ (London: SPCK and New York: Paulist Press, 1980).

Green, J. B., 'Death of Jesus', _DJG_, pp. 146–163.

Grogan, G. W., _Prayer, Praise and Prophecy: A Theology of Psalms_ (Fearn: Christian Focus, 2001).

Grossfeld, B., 'Targums to the Hagiographa', _Encyclopaedia Judaica_, vol. 4 (1972), pp. 848–849.

Gunkel, H., _Die Psalmen,_ Göttinger Handkommentar zum Alten Testament II.2 (Göttingen: Vandenhoeck & Ruprecht, 1926).

Gunkel, H., _The Psalms: A Form-Critical Introduction_, tr. T. M. Horner (Philadelphia: Fortress, 1967); published originally as 'Psalterbuch', in H. Gunkel and L. Zscharnack, eds., _Die Religion in Geschichte und Gegenwart_ (Tübingen: J. C. B. Mohr [Paul Siebeck], 2nd ed., 1930), 4: cols 1628–1630.

Gunkel, H., _Introduction to Psalms: The Genres of the Religious Lyric of Israel_, tr. J. D. Nogalski (Macon: Mercer University Press, 1998); published originally as _Einleitung in die Psalmen: die Gattungen der religiösen Lyrik Israels_ (Göttingen: Vandenhoeck & Ruprecht, 1933).

Guterbock, H. G., 'The Composition of Hittite Prayers to the Sun', _JAOS_ 78 (1958), pp. 237–245.

Gwaltney, W. C., 'The Biblical Book of Lamentations in the Context of Near Eastern Literature', in W. W. Hallo et al., eds., _Scripture in Context_, vol. 2 (Winona Lake: Eisenbrauns, 1982), pp. 191–211.

Haller, M., 'Ein Jahrzehnt Psalmforschung', _TRu_ 1 (1929), pp. 377–402.

Halliday, M. A. K., 'Language Structure and Language Function', in J. Lyons, ed., _New Horizons in Linguistics_ (Harmondsworth: Penguin, 1970), pp. 140–165.

Hallo, W. W., 'Individual Prayer in Sumerian: The Continuity of a Tradition', *JAOS* 88 (1968), pp. 71–89.

Hallo, W. W., 'Letters, Prayers, and Letter-Prayers', *Proceedings of the Seventh World Congress of Jewish Studies, 1977*, vol. 2 (Jerusalem: Magness Press, 1981), pp. 17–27.

Hallo, W. W., 'Compare and Contrast: The Contextual Approach to Biblical Literature', in W. W. Hallo et al., eds., *Scripture in Context*, vol. 3 (Lewiston: Mellen, 1990), pp. 1–30.

Hallo, W. W., 'Lamentations and Prayers in Sumer and Akkad', *CANE* vol. 3, pp. 1871–1881.

Hallo, W. W. and J.-J. A. van Dijk, *The Exaltation of Inanna* (New Haven: Yale University Press, 1968).

Hammer, R., *Sifre A Tannaitic Commentary on the book of Deuteronomy* (New Haven and London: Yale University Press, 1986).

Hanson, A. T., 'John's Citation of Psalm 82', *NTS* 11 (1965), pp. 158–162.

Hanson, A. T., 'John's Citation of Psalm 82 Reconsidered', *NTS* 13 (1967), pp. 363–367.

Hanson, A. T., *The Prophetic Gospel: A Study of John and the Old Testament* (Edinburgh: T. & T. Clark, 1991).

Haran, M., *Temple and Temple Service in Ancient Israel* (Oxford: Clarendon, 1978).

Haran, M., '11QPs^a and the Canonical Book of Psalms', in M. Brettler and M. Fishbane, eds., *Minhah le-Nahum*, Nahum M. Sarna Festschrift, *JSOTSup* 153 (Sheffield: JSOT Press, 1993), pp. 193–201.

Hay, D. M., *Glory at the Right Hand: Psalm 110 in Early Christianity*, SBLMS (Nashville: Abingdon, 1973).

Hays, J. D., 'If He Looks Like a Prophet and Talks Like a Prophet, Then He Must be . . . : A Response to D. I. Block', in R. S. Hess and M. D. Carroll R., eds., *Israel's Messiah in the Bible and the Dead Sea Scrolls* (Grand Rapids: Baker, 2003), pp. 57–70.

Hays, R. B., 'Reading Scripture in the Light of the Resurrection', in E. F. Davis and R. B. Hays, eds., *The Art of Reading Scripture* (Grand Rapids and Cambridge: Eerdmans, 2003), pp. 216–238.

Hillers, D. R., 'Delocutive Verbs in Biblical Hebrew', *JBL* 86 (1967), pp. 320–324.

Hillers, D. R., 'Ritual Procession of the Ark and Ps. 132', *CBQ* 30 (1968), pp. 48–55.

Hillers, D. R., 'Some Performative Utterances in the Bible', in D. P. Wright et al., eds., *Pomegranates and Golden Bells: Studies in Near Eastern Ritual, Law, and*

Literature in Honor of Jacob Milgrom (Winona Lake: Eisenbrauns, 1995), pp. 757–766.

Holladay, W. L., *Jeremiah 1 and 2*, Hermeneia (Philadelphia: Fortress, 1986, 1989).

Holladay, W. L., *The Psalms through Three Thousand Years: Prayerbook of a Cloud of Witnesses* (Minneapolis: Fortress, 1993).

Holladay, W. L., '*Hebrew Verse Structure* Revisited (I): Which Words "Count"?', *JBL* 118 (1999), pp. 19–32.

Holladay, W. L., '*Hebrew Verse Structure* Revisited (II): Conjoint Cola, and Further Suggestions', *JBL* 118 (1999), pp. 401–416.

Hosch, H. E., 'Psalms 1 and 2: A Discourse Analysis', *Notes on Translation* 15 (2001), pp. 4–12.

Houston, W., 'The King's Preferential Option for the Poor: Rhetoric, Ideology and Ethics in Psalm 72', *BibInt* 7 (1999), pp. 341–367.

Howard, Jr, D. M., 'The Case for Kingship in the Old Testament Narrative Books and the Psalms', *TJ* 9 (1988), pp. 19–35.

Howard, Jr, D. M., 'The Case for Kingship in Deuteronomy and the Former Prophets', *WTJ* 52 (1990), pp. 101–115.

Howard, Jr, D. M., *The Structure of Psalms 93 – 100*, BJSUCSD 5 (Winona Lake: Eisenbrauns, 1997).

Howard, Jr, D. M., Review of N. Whybray, *Reading the Psalms as a Book*, *RBL*, http://www.bookreviews.org/pdf/2475_1563.pdf (posted 15 April 1998).

Howard, Jr, D. M., 'Psalm 94 Among the Kingship of YHWH Psalms', *CBQ* 61 (1999), pp. 667–685.

Howard, Jr, D. M., 'Recent Trends in Psalms Study', in D. W. Baker and B. T. Arnold, eds., *The Face of Old Testament Studies: A Survey of Contemporary Approaches* (Grand Rapids: Baker, 1999), pp. 329–368.

Hunt, J. H., *The Hymnic Introduction of Selected Suilla Prayers Directed to Ea, Marduk and Nabu*, PhD dissertation (Brandeis University, 1994).

Irsigler, H., 'Psalm-Rede als Handlungs-, Wirk- und Aussageprozeß: Sprech-aktanalyse und Psalmeninterpretation am Beispiel von Psalm 13', in K. Seybold and E. Zenger, eds., *Neue Wege der Psalmenforschung: Für Walter Beyerlin* (Freiburg: Herder, 1994), pp. 63–104.

Jacobsen, T., *The Harps that Once ... Sumerian Poetry in Translation* (New Haven and London: Yale University Press, 1987).

Jacobson, D. L., 'The Royal Psalms and Jesus Messiah: Preparing to Preach on a Royal Psalm', *WW* 5 (1985), pp. 192–198.

Jacobson, R. A., '*Many are Saying': The Function of Direct Discourse in the Hebrew Psalter*, JSOTSup 397 (London: T. & T. Clark International, 2004).

Jenni, E., 'Verba gesticulationis im Hebräischen', in W. Groß, H. Irsigler and
T. Seidl, eds., *Text, Methode und Grammatik: Wolfgang Richter zum 65.
Geburtstag* (St Ottilien: EOS, 1991).

Jesurathnam, K., 'Towards a Dalit Liberative Hermeneutics: Re-reading the
Psalms of Lament', *Bangalore Theological Forum* 34 (2002), pp. 1–34.

Jobling, D., 'Deconstruction and the Political Analysis of Biblical Texts: A
Jamesonian Reading of Psalm 72', *Semeia* 59 (1992), pp. 95–127.

Johnson, A. R., *Sacral Kingship in Ancient Israel* (Cardiff: University of Wales
Press, 1955).

Johnson, A. R., *The Cultic Prophet and Israel's Psalmody* (Cardiff: University of
Wales Press, 1979).

Johnston, P. S., 'Psalm 16, Sheol, and the Holy One', in P. E. Satterthwaite et
al., eds., *The Lord's Anointed: Interpretation of Old Testament Messianic Texts*
(Carlisle: Paternoster, 1995), pp. 213–222.

Johnston, P. S., Review of F. Lindström, *Suffering and Sin*, *BibInt* 4.2 (1996), pp.
239–242.

Johnston, P. S., *Shades of Sheol: Death and Afterlife in the Old Testament* (Leicester:
Apollos and Downers Grove: InterVarsity, 2002).

Johnston, P. S., 'Ordeals in the Psalms?', in J. Day, ed., *Temple and Worship
in Biblical Israel*, JSOTSup 422 (London: T. & T. Clark International,
2005).

Juel, D., *Messianic Exegesis: Christological Exegesis of the Old Testament in Early
Christianity* (Philadelphia: Fortress, 1987).

Kaiser, Jr, W. C., *The Uses of the Old Testament in the New* (Chicago: Moody,
1985).

Kaiser, Jr, W. C., *The Messiah in the Old Testament*, SOTBT (Grand Rapids:
Zondervan, 1995).

Kaufman, S., 'Targum Pseudo-Jonathan and Late Jewish Literary Aramaic',
in M. Ben Asher et al., eds., *Studies in Bible and Exegesis*, vol. 3 (Givat Ram:
Bar Ilan University Press, 1993), pp. 363–382 (Hebrew).

Kaufman, S., 'Dating the languages of the Palestinian Targums and their use
in the Study of First Century Texts', in D. Beattie and M. McNamara,
eds., *The Aramaic Bible: Targums in their Historical Context* (Sheffield:
Sheffield University Press, 1994), pp. 118–141.

Keel, O., *The Symbolism of the Biblical World: Ancient Near Eastern Iconography and
the Book of Psalms* (London: SPCK and New York: Seabury, 1978).

Kidner, D., *Psalms 73 – 150*, TOTC (Leicester: IVP and Downers Grove:
InterVarsity, 1975).

Kim, E. K., 'Holy War ideology and the rapid shift of mood in Psalm 3', in S. L. Cook and S. C. Winter, eds., *On the Way to Nineveh: Studies in Honor of George M. Landes* (Atlanta: Scholars, 1999), pp. 77–93.

Kinoti, H. W., 'Psalm 23:1–6: An African Perspective', in J. R. Levison and P. Pope-Levison, eds., *Return to Babel: Global Perspectives on the Bible* (Louisville: Westminster John Knox Press, 1999), pp. 63–68.

Kirkpatrick, A. F., *The Book of Psalms with Introduction and Notes* (Cambridge: CUP, 1902).

Klein, J., *Three Shulgi Hymns: Sumerian Royal Hymns Glorifying King Shulgi of Ur* (Bar-Ilan University Press, 1981).

Köhler, L., *Hebrew Man* (London: SCM, 1956).

Komlosh, Y., 'Targum Psalms', *Encyclopaedia Biblica*, vol. 8, p. 756 (Hebrew).

König, E., *Stilistik, Rhetorik, Poetik in Bezug auf die biblische Literatur* (Leipzig: Dieterich, 1900).

Korpel, M. C. A. and J. C. de Moor, 'Fundamentals of Ugaritic and Hebrew Poetry', *UF* 18 (1986), pp. 173–212; reprinted in W. van der Meer and J. C. de Moor, eds., *The Structural Analysis of Biblical and Canaanite Poetry*, *JSOTSup* 74 (Sheffield: JSOT Press, 1988), pp. 1–61.

Kraus, H.-J., *Psalms, A Commentary*, tr. H. C. Oswald, 2 vols. (Minneapolis: Augsburg, 1988–89).

Kraus, H.-J., *Theology of the Psalms* (Minneapolis: Fortress, 1992).

Krause, D., 'The One Who Comes Unbinding the Blessing of Judah: Mark 11.1–10 as a Midrash on Genesis 49.11, Zechariah 9.9, and Psalm 118.25–26', in C. A. Evans and J. A. Sanders, eds., *Early Christian Interpretation of the Scriptures of Israel: Investigations and Proposals*, SSEJC 5 (Sheffield: Sheffield Academic Press, 1997), pp. 141–153.

Kugel, J. L., *The Idea of Biblical Poetry: Parallelism and Its History* (New Haven: Yale University Press, 1981).

Kuntz, J. K., 'King Triumphant: A Rhetorical Study of Psalms 20 and 21', *HAR* 10 (1986), pp. 157–176.

Kuntz, J. K., 'Grounds for Praise: The Nature and Function of the Motive Clause in the Hymns of the Hebrew Psalter', in M. P. Graham et al., eds., *Worship in the Hebrew Bible: Essays in Honour of John T. Willis*, *JSOTSup* 284 (Sheffield: Sheffield Academic Press, 1999), pp. 148–183.

Kuntz, J. K., 'Wisdom Psalms and the Shaping of the Hebrew Psalter', in R. A. Argall et al., eds., *For a Later Generation: The Transformation of Tradition in Israel, Early Judaism, and Early Christianity* (Harrisburg: Trinity Press International, 2000), pp. 144–160.

Kutscher, R., _Oh Angry Sea (a-ab-ba hu-luh-ha): The History of a Sumerian Congregational Lament_ (New Haven: Yale University Press, 1975).

Kwakkel, G., _'According to My Righteousness': Upright Behaviour as Grounds for Deliverance in Psalms 7, 17, 18, 26, and 44_, OTS 46 (Leiden: Brill, 2002).

Lagarde, P. de, _Hagiographa_ Chaldaice (Osnabrück: O. Zeller, 1967).

Lakoff, G., _Women, Fire and Dangerous Things: What Categories Reveal about the Mind_ (Chicago: University of Chicago Press, 1990).

Lakoff, G. and M. Johnson, _Metaphors we live by_ (Chicago: University of Chicago Press, 1996).

Lambert, W. G., _Babylonian Wisdom Literature_ (Oxford: Clarendon Press, 1960).

Lambert, W. G., '_Dingir.sa.dib.ba_ Incantations', _JNES_ 33 (1974), pp. 267–322.

Lande, I., _Formelhafte Wendungen der Umgangssprache im Alten Testament_ (Leiden: Brill, 1949).

Lauha, R., _Psychophysischer Sprachgebrauch im Alten Testament: Eine struktursemantische Analyse von ruaḥ, nepeš, Lēb. I. Emotionen_, Annales Academiae Scientiarum Fennicae: Dissertationes Humanarum Litterarum 35 (Helsinki: Suomalainen Tiedeakatemia, 1983).

Lebrun, R., _Hymnes et priers Hittites_ (Louvain-la-Neuve: Centre d'Histoire, 1980).

Levin, S., 'Let my _Right Hand_ Wither', _Judaism_ 45 (1996), pp. 282–286.

Levine, H. J., _Sing Unto God a New Song: A Contemporary Reading of the Psalms_, Indiana Studies in Biblical Literature (Indianapolis: Indiana University Press, 1995).

Levinson, S. C., _Pragmatics_, Cambridge Textbooks in Linguistics (Cambridge: CUP, 1983).

Levinson, S. C., '_Three_ levels of meaning', in F. R. Palmer, ed., _Grammar and Meaning: Essays in Honour of Sir John Lyons_, F. S. Lyons (Cambridge: CUP, 1995), pp. 90–115.

Levy, B. B., _Targum Neophyti 1 a Textual Study_ (Lanham, University Press of America, 1986).

Lewis, C. S., _Reflections on the Psalms_ (London: Literat, 1958).

Limburg, J., '_Down-to-Earth_ Theology: Psalm 104 and the Environment', _CurTM_ 21 (1994), pp. 340–346.

Lindström, F., _Suffering and Sin: Interpretations of Illness in the Individual Complaint Psalms_, ConBOT 37 (Stockholm: Almqvist & Wiksell, 1994).

Lohse, E., _hōsanna_, TDNT, 9:682–684.

Lombaard, C. J. S., '_By_ Implication. Didactical Strategy in Psalm 1', _OTE_ 12 (1999), pp. 506–514.

Long, B. O., 'Recent Field Studies in Oral Literature and the Question of *Sitz im Leben*', *Semeia* 5 (1976), pp. 35–49.

Lübbe, J. C., 'Idioms in the Old Testament', *JfS* 11 (2002), pp. 45–63.

Lunn, N., 'Paronomastic Constructions in Biblical Hebrew', *Notes on Translation* 10 (1996), pp. 31–52.

Luther, M., *The Large Catechism of Martin Luther*, tr. R. Fischer (Philadelphia: Fortress, 1959).

Lyons, J., *Semantics*, 2 vols. (Cambridge: CUP, 1977).

Macky, P. W., 'The Multiple Purposes of Biblical Speech Acts', *Princeton Seminary Bulletin* 8 (1987), pp. 50–61.

Mandolfo, C., *God in the Dock: Dialogical Tension in the Psalms of Lament*, JSOTSup 357 (Sheffield: Sheffield Academic Press, 2002).

Marcus, J., *The Way of the Lord: Christological Exegesis of the Old Testament in the Gospel of Mark* (Louisville: Westminster John Knox Press, and Edinburgh: T. & T. Clark, 1992).

Marshall, I. H., *The Gospel of Luke: A Commentary on the Greek Text*, NIGTC (Grand Rapids: Eerdmans, 1978).

Maul, S. M., '*Herzberuhigungsklagen*': Die sumerisch-akkadischen Ersahunga-Gebete (Wiesbaden: Otto Harrassowitz), 1988.

Mays, J. L., 'Prayer and Christology: Psalm 22 as Perspective on the Passion', *ThTo* 3 (1985), pp. 322–331.

Mays, J. L., 'The Place of the Torah-Psalms in the Psalter', *JBL* 106 (1987), pp. 3–12.

Mays, J. L., 'The Question of Context in Psalm Interpretation', in J. C. McCann, ed., *The Shape and Shaping of the Psalter*, JSOTSup 159 (Sheffield: JSOT Press, 1993), pp. 14–20.

Mays, J. L., *The Lord Reigns: A Theological Handbook to the Psalms* (Louisville: Westminster John Knox Press, 1994).

Mays, J. L., *Psalms* (Louisville: Westminster John Knox Press, 1994).

McCann, J. C., 'Psalms', in L. E. Keck, ed., *The New Interpreter's Bible* 4, (Nashville: Abingdon, 1996), pp. 641–1280.

McCann, J. C., 'The Psalms as Instruction', *Interpretation* 46 (1992), pp. 117–128.

McCann, J. C., *A Theological Introduction to the Book of Psalms: The Psalms as Torah* (Nashville: Abingdon, 1993).

McCarter, P. K., 'The River Ordeal in Israelite Literature', *HTR* 66 (1973), pp. 403–412.

McCarthy, D. P., 'A Not-So-Bad Derridean Approach to Psalm 23', *Proceedings, Eastern Great Lakes and Midwest Biblical Society* 8 (1988), pp. 177–192.

322 INTERPRETING THE PSALMS

McConville, J. G., 'King and Messiah in Deuteronomy and the Deuteronomistic History', in J. Day, ed., *King and Messiah in Israel and the Ancient Near East: Proceedings of the Oxford Old Testament Seminar*, JSOTSup 270 (Sheffield: Sheffield Academic Press, 1998), pp. 271–295.

McConville, J. G., *Deuteronomy*, Apollos Old Testament Commentary, 5 (Leicester: Apollos and Downers Grove: Inter-Varsity Press, 2002).

McFall, L., 'The Evidence for a Logical Arrangement of the Psalter', *WTJ* 62 (2000), pp. 223–256.

McKenzie, S. L. and S. R. Haynes, *To Each Its Own Meaning: An Introduction to Biblical Criticisms and Their Application*, rev. ed. (Louisville: Westminster John Knox Press, 1999).

Meador, B. de Shong, *Inanna: Lady of Largest Heart. Poems of the Sumerian High Priestess Enheduanna* (Austin: University of Texas Press, 2000).

Meer, W. van der, and J. C. de Moor, eds., *The Structural Analysis of Biblical and Canaanite Poetry, JSOTSup* 74 (Sheffield: JSOT Press, 1988).

Menken, M. J. J., 'Old Testament Quotations in the Gospel of John', in J. M. Court, ed., *New Testament Writers and the Old Testament* (London: SPCK, 2002), pp. 29–45.

Menken, M. J. J., 'The Psalms in Matthew's Gospel', in S. Moyise and M. J. J. Menken, eds., *The Psalms in the New Testament* (London: T. & T. Clark International, 2004), pp. 61–82.

Merino, L. Diez, 'Haggadic Elements in the Targum of Psalms', in *Proceedings of the Eighth World Congress of Jewish Studies, Division A: The Period of the Bible* (Jerusalem, World Union of Jewish Studies, 1982), pp. 136–137.

Merino, L. Diez, *Targum de Salmos: Edition Principe del Ms. Villa-Amil n.5 de Alfonso de Zamora* (Madrid: Consejo Superier de Investigaciones Científicas, 1982).

Mettinger, T. N. D., *In Search of God* (Minneapolis: Fortress, 1988).

Michel, D., *Tempora und Satzstellung in den Psalmen*, Abhandlungen zur Evangelischen Theologie, Band 1 (Bonn: H. Bouvier Verlag, 1960).

Milik, J., 'Fragment d'une Source du Psautier (4QPs89) et fragments des Jubilés, du Document de Damas, d'un phylactère dans la Grotte 4 de Qumran', *RB* 73 (1966), pp. 94–106.

Miller, P. D., 'Current Issues in Psalms Studies', *WW* 5 (1985), pp. 132–143.

Miller, P. D., *Interpreting the Psalms* (Philadelphia: Fortress, 1986).

Miller, P. D., Review of E. K. Kim, *The Rapid Change of Mood in the Lament Psalms, Interpretation* 41 (1987), pp. 88–89.

Miller, P. D., *Deuteronomy*, Interpretation (Louisville: John Knox Press, 1990).

Miller, P. D., 'The Beginning of the Psalter', in J. C. McCann, ed., *The Shape and Shaping of the Psalter, JSOTSup* 159 (Sheffield: JSOT Press, 1993), pp. 83–92.

Miller, P. D., 'Dietrich Bonhoeffer and the Psalms', *PSB* 15 (1994), pp. 274–281; reprinted in *Israelite Religion and Biblical Theology, JSOTSup* 267 (Sheffield: Sheffield Academic Press, 2000), pp. 345–354.

Miller, P. D., *They Cried to the Lord: The Form and Theology of Biblical Prayer* (Minneapolis: Fortress, 1994).

Miller, P. D., 'Kingship, Torah Obedience and Prayer', in K. Seybold and E. Zenger, eds., *Neue Wege der Psalmenforschung* (Freiburg: Herder, 1995), pp. 127–142.

Miller, P. D., 'The End of the Psalter: A Response to Erich Zenger', *JSOT* 80 (1998), pp. 103–110; reprinted in *Israelite Religion and Biblical Theology, JSOTSup* 267 (Sheffield: Sheffield Academic Press, 2000), pp. 310–317.

Mitchell, D. C., *The Message of the Psalter: An Eschatological Programme in the Book of Psalms, JSOTSup* 252 (Sheffield: Sheffield Academic Press, 1997).

Moberly, R. W. L., *The Bible, Theology, and Faith: A Study of Abraham and Jesus* (Cambridge: CUP, 2000).

Moessner, D. P., '*Two* Lords "at the Right Hand?" The Psalms and an Intertextual Reading of Peter's Pentecost Speech (Acts 2:14–36)', in R. P. Thompson and T. E. Phillips, eds., *Literary Studies in Luke-Acts* (Macon: Mercer University Press, 1998), pp. 215–232.

Moon, C. H., 'Psalm 23:1–6: An Asian Perspective', in J. R. Levison and P. Pope-Levison, eds., *Return to Babel: Global Perspectives on the Bible* (Louisville: Westminster John Knox Press, 1999), pp. 69–72.

Moor, J. de, 'Multiple Renderings in the Targum of Isaiah', *JAB* 3 (2001), pp. 161–180.

Moore, G., ed., *Hymns Old and New: New Anglican Edition* (Bury St Edmunds: Kevin Mayhew, 1996).

Morris, C. W., 'Foundations of the Theory of Signs', in O. Neurath et al., eds., *Encyclopedia of Unified Science* (Chicago: University of Chicago, 1938), pp. 77–137.

Morris, L., *Luke*, TNTC, rev. ed. (Leicester: IVP, 1988).

Mowinckel, S., *The Psalms in Israel's Worship*, tr. D. R. Ap-Thomas, 2 vols. (Oxford: Blackwell and Nashville: Abingdon, 1962).

Moyise, S., *The Old Testament in the New* (London and New York: Continuum, 2001).

Moyise, S. and M. J. J. Menken, eds., *The Psalms in the New Testament* (London: T. & T. Clark International, 2004).

Muraoka, T., *Emphatic Words And Structures In Biblical Hebrew* (Jerusalem: The Magnes Press and Leiden: Brill, 1985).

Nasuti, H. P., *Defining the Sacred Songs: Genre, Tradition and the Post-Critical Interpretation of the* Psalms, *JSOTSup* 218 (Sheffield: Sheffield Academic Press, 1999).

Negoiţă, A. and Ringgren, H., 'hāghāh', *TDOT*, vol. 3, pp. 321–324.

Nowell, I., 'Psalm 88: A Lesson in Lament', in L. Boadt and M. S. Smith, eds., *Imagery and Imagination in Biblical Literature: Essays in Honor of Aloysius Fitzgerald, F. S. C.*, CBQMS 32 (Washington: Catholic Biblical Association of America, 2001), pp. 105–118.

Ntreh, A., 'The Survival of the Earth: An African Reading of Psalm 104', in N. Habel, ed., *The Earth Story in the Psalms and the Prophets*, The Earth Bible 4 (Sheffield: Sheffield Academic Press, 2001), pp. 98–108.

O'Connor, M., *Hebrew Verse Structure* (Winona Lake: Eisenbrauns, 1980, 1997).

Ormseth, D. H., 'The Psalms and the Rule of God', *WW* 5 (1985), pp. 119–121.

Otto, E., *Theologische Ethik des Alten Testaments* (Stuttgart: Kohlhammer, 1994).

Parry, D. W., 'The "Word" or the "Enemies" of the Lord? Revisiting the Euphemism in 2 Sam. 12:14', in S. M. Paul et al., eds., *Emanuel: Studies in Hebrew Bible, Septuagint and Dead Sea Scrolls in Honor of Emanuel Tov*, *VTSup* 94 (Leiden and Boston: Brill, 2003), pp. 367–378.

Paul, S. M., 'Euphemistically "speaking" and a covetous eye', *HAR* 14 (1994), pp. 193–204.

Payne, A., 'Confessions of a Teenage Praise Junkie', *The Briefing* 173 (20 Feb. 1996), pp. 1–5.

Pedersen, J., *Israel: Its Life and Culture*, 2 vols. (Atlanta: Scholars Press, 1921, 1991, and London: OUP, 1926).

Pinto, B. de, 'The Torah and the Psalms', *JBL* 86 (1967), pp. 154–174.

Pleins, D., *The Psalms: Songs of Tragedy, Hope, and Justice* (Maryknoll: Orbis, 1993).

Ploeg, J. P. M. van der, 'Le sens et un problème textuel du Ps LXXXIX', in A. Caquot and M. Delcor, eds., *Mélanges bibliques et orientaux en l'honneur de M. Henri Cazelles* (Neukirchen-Vluyn: Neukirchener Verlag, 1981), pp. 471–481.

Poorthuis, M., ed., *Mijn God, Mijn God, Waarom Hebt Gij Mij Verlaten? Een interdisciplinaire bundel over psalm 22* (Baarn: Ten Have, 1997).

Prinsloo, G. T. M., 'Analysing Old Testament Poetry: An Experiment in Methodology with Reference to Psalm 126', *OTE* 5 (1992), pp. 225–251.

Prinsloo, G. T. M., 'Tremble Before the Lord: Myth and History in Psalm 114', *OTE* 11 (1998), pp. 306–325.

Prinsloo, G. T. M., 'Psalm 130: Poetic Patterns and Social Significance', *OTE* 15 (2002), pp. 453–469.

Prinsloo, W. S., *Die Psalms Leef: 'n eksegetiese studie van psalm 3, 15, 23, 112, 126, 131, 136, 149* (Pretoria: NGKB, 1991).

Prinsloo, W. S., 'Psalm 116: Disconnected Text or Symmetrical Whole?' *Biblica* 74 (1993), pp. 71–82.

Prinsloo, W. S., 'Psalm 149: Praise Yahweh with Tambourine and Two-Edged Sword', *ZAW* 109 (1997), pp. 395–407.

Rad, G. von, 'The Tent and the Ark', in *The Problem of the Hexateuch and Other Essays* (Edinburgh: Oliver & Boyd, 1965), pp. 103–124.

Ravasi, G., *Il libro dei Salmi: commento e attualizzazione* (Bologna: Edizione Dehoniane, 1985).

Redford, D. B., 'Ancient Egyptian Literature: An Overview', *CANE* vol. 4, pp. 2223–2241.

Reid, S. B., *Listening In: A Multicultural Reading of the Psalms* (Nashville: Abingdon, 1997).

Reindl, J., 'Weisheitliche Bearbeitung von Psalmen: Ein Beitrag zum Verständnis der Sammlung des Psalter', in J. A. Emerton, ed., *Congress Volume Vienna 1980*, *VTSup* 32 (Leiden: Brill, 1981).

Rendsburg, G. A., 'Word Play in biblical Hebrew: an Eclectic Collection', in S. B. Noegel, ed., *Puns and Pundits: Word Play in the Hebrew Bible and Ancient Near Eastern Literature* (Bethesda: CDL Press, 2000), pp. 137–162.

Rendsburg, G. S. and S. L. Rendsburg, 'Physiological and Philological Notes to Psalm 137', *JQR* 83 (1993), pp. 385–339.

Ridderbos, N. H., 'Psalmen und Kult', in P. H. A. Neumann, ed., *Zur Neueren Psalmenforschung,* Wege der Forschung CXCII (Darmstadt: Wissenschaftliche Buchgesellschaft, 1976).

Ringgren, H., '*hll*', *TDOT*, vol. 3, pp. 404–410.

Roberts, J. J. M., 'The Religio-Political Setting of Psalm 47', *BASOR* 221 (1976), pp. 129–132.

Rodd, C. S., *Glimpses of a Strange Land: Studies in Old Testament Ethics* (Edinburgh: T. & T. Clark, 2001).

Roos, J. de, 'Hittite Prayers', *CANE* vol. 3, pp. 1997–2005.

Salvesen, A., 'Symmachus and the Dating of Targumic Traditions', *JAB* 2 (2000), pp. 233–245.

Samely, A., *The Interpretation of Speech in the Pentateuch Targums* (Tübingen: Mohr/Siebeck, 1992).

Sanders, J. A., *The Psalms Scroll of Qumrân Cave 11 (11QPsᵃ)*, DJD 4 (Oxford: Clarendon Press, 1965).

Sanders, J. A., 'Variorum in the Psalms Scroll (11QPsᵃ)', *HTR* 59 (1966), pp. 83–94.

Sanders, J. A., *The Dead Sea Psalms Scroll* (Ithaca: Cornell University Press, 1967).

Sanders, J. A., 'A New Testament Hermeneutic Fabric: Psalm 118 in the Entrance Narrative', in C. A. Evans and W. F. Stinespring, eds., *Early Jewish and Christian Exegesis: Studies in Memory of W. Hugh Brownlee* (Atlanta: Scholars Press, 1987), pp. 177–190.

Sappan, R., *The Typical Features of the Syntax of Biblical Poetry in its Classical Period* (Jerusalem: Kiryat-Sepher, 1981).

Sarna, N. M., *On the Book of Psalms: Exploring the Prayer of Ancient Israel* (New York: Schocken Books, 1993).

Saur, M., *Die Königspsalmen: Studien zur Enstehung und Theologie*, BZAW 340 (New York and Berlin: de Gruyter, 2004).

Schäfer, P., 'Das Targum zu den Hagiographen', *Theologische Realenzyklopädie*, vol. 6 (Berlin: de Gruyter, 1980), p. 223.

Schmidt, H., *Das Gebet der Angeklagten im Alten Testament*, BZAW 49 (Giessen: A. Töpelmann, 1929).

Schorch, S., *Euphemismen in der Hebräischen Bibel*, Orientalia Biblica et Christiana 12 (Wiesbaden: Harrassowitz, 2000).

Schroer, S. and T. Staubli, *Die Körpersymbolik der Bibel* (Darmstadt: Wissenschaftliche Buchgesellschaft, 1998); tr. as *Body Symbolism in the Bible* (Collegeville: Liturgical Press, 2001).

Schröten, J., *Entstehung, Komposition und Wirkungsgeschichte des 118. Psalms*, BBB 95 (Weinheim: Beltz Athenäum, 1995).

Schuller, E., 'Non-Canonical Psalms', in E. Eshel et al., eds., *Qumran Cave 4, VI, Poetical and Liturgical Texts, Part 1*, DJD 11 (Oxford: Clarendon Press, 1998), pp. 75–172.

Scott, R. B. Y., *The Psalms as Christian Praise* (London: Lutterworth Press, 1958).

Sedgwick, C. J., 'The Message of the Psalmists 12. Praise the Lord! Pss. 148 – 150', *Expository Times* 103 (1992), pp. 209–210.

Senior, D. P., *The Passion of Jesus in the Gospel of John* (Collegeville: Liturgical Press, 1991).

Seow, C. L., 'Ark of the Covenant', in *ABD*, vol. 1, pp. 386–393.

Seybold, K., *Die Psalmen*, Handbuch zum Alten Testament 1/15 (Tübingen: Mohr, 1996).

Shepherd, J. E., *The Book of Psalms as the Book of Christ: A Christo-Canonical Approach to the Book of Psalms*, PhD dissertation (Westminster Theological Seminary, 1995).

Sheppard, G. T., *Wisdom as a Hermeneutical Construct: A Study in the Sapientializing of the Old Testament*, BZAW 151 (Berlin: de Gruyter, 1980).

Sheppard, G. T., 'Theology of the Book of Psalms', *Interpretation* 46 (1992), pp. 143–155.

Shires, H. M., *Finding the Old Testament in the New* (Philadelphia: Westminster, 1974).

Simon, U., *Four Approaches to the Book of Psalms: From Saadiyah Gaon to Abraham Ibn Ezra*, tr. L. J. Schramm (Albany: State University of New York, 1991).

Sjöberg, Å. and E. Bergmann, *The Collection of Sumerian Temple Hymns*, Texts from Cuneiform Sources 3 (Locust Valley: J. J. Augustin, 1960).

Skehan, P. W., 'Qumran and Old Testament Textual Criticism', in M. Delcor, ed., *Qumrân. Sa piété, sa théologie et son milieu* (Paris: Editions Duculot and Leuven: Leuven University Press, 1978), pp. 163–182.

Skehan, P. W., 'Gleanings from Psalm Text from Qûmran', in A. Caquot and M. Delcor, eds., *Mélanges bibliques et orientaux en l'honneur de M. Henri Cazelles* (Neukirchen-Vluyn: Neukirchener Verlag, 1981), pp. 439–452.

Skehan, P. W., E. Ulrich and P. W. Flint, 'Psalms', in *Qumran Cave 4, XI, Psalms to Chronicles*, DJD XVI (Oxford: Clarendon Press, 2000).

Smelik, W., *The Targum of Judges* (Leiden: Brill, 1995).

Smick, E. B., 'Mythopoetic Language in the Psalms', *WTJ* 44 (1982), pp. 88–98.

Smith, M. S., 'The Heart and Innards in Israelite Emotional Expressions: Notes from Anthropology and Psychobiology', *JBL* 117 (1998), pp. 427–436.

Sonnet, J.-P., *The Book Within the Book: Writing in Deuteronomy*, 14 (Leiden: Brill, 1997).

Stamm, J. J., 'Ein Vierteljahrhundert Psalmenforschung', *TRu* 23 (1955), pp. 1–68.

Starbuck, S. R. A., *Court Oracles in the Psalms: The So-Called Royal Psalms in their Ancient Near Eastern Context*, SBLDS 172 (Atlanta: Scholars Press, 1999).

Stec, D. M., *Targum of Psalms*, Aramaic Bible 16 (Collegeville: Liturgical Press, 2004).

Stolz, F., *Psalmen im nachkultischen Raum*, Theologische Studien 129 (Zurich: Theologischer Verlag, 1983).

Strange, J. F., 'Crucifixion', *IDBSup*, pp. 199–200.

Swanson, D., 'How Scriptural is Re-Written Bible?', *RevQ* 21 (2004), pp. 407–427.

Sysling, H., *Tehiyyat Ha Metim* (Tübingen: Mohr, 1996).

Szörenyi, A., *Psalmen und Kult im Alten Testament* (Budapest: Sankt Stefans, 1961).

Talmon, S., '*Pisqeh be'emsa' pasuq* and 11QPsᵃ ', *Textus* 5 (1966), pp. 11–21; tr. from '*Mizmôrîm Hîsônîm ballasôn ha'ibrît miqqûmrân*', *Tarbiz* 35 (1966), pp. 214–234 (Hebrew).

Tanner, B. L., 'Hearing the Cries Unspoken: An Intertextual Feminist Reading of Psalm 109', in A. Brenner and C. R. Fontaine, eds., *Wisdom and Psalms*, FCB 2 (Sheffield: Sheffield Academic Press, 1998), pp. 283–301.

Tate, M. E., *Psalms 51 – 100*, WBC 20 (Dallas: Word Books, 1990).

Terrien, S., *The Psalms: Strophic Structure and Theological Commentary* (Grand Rapids: Eerdmans, 2003).

Thiselton, A. C., *New Horizons in Hermeneutics* (London: HarperCollins, 1992).

Tigay, J. H., 'Some more delocutives in Hebrew', in R. Chazan et al., eds., *Ki Baruch Hu: Ancient Near Eastern, Biblical, and Judaic Studies in Honor of Baruch A. Levine* (Winona Lake: Eisenbrauns, 1999), pp. 409–412.

Toorn, K. van der, 'Ordeal', *ABD*, vol. 5, pp. 40–42.

Toorn, K. van der, *Sin and Sanction in Israel and Mesopotamia: A Comparative Study* (Assen: Van Gorcum, 1985).

Toorn, K. van der, 'Theology, Priests, and Worship in Canaan and Ancient Israel', *CANE*, vol. 3, pp. 2043–2058.

Tournay, R. J., *Seeing and Hearing God in the Psalms: The Prophetic Liturgy of the Second Temple in Jerusalem*, JSOTSup 118 (Sheffield: JSOT Press, 1991).

Tov, E., 'Excerpted and Abbreviated Biblical Texts from Qumran', *RevQ* 16 (1995), pp. 581–600.

Tsevat, M., *A Study of the Language of the Biblical Psalms*, JBL Monograph Series IX (Philadelphia: Society of Biblical Literature, 1955).

Tsevat, M., 'God and the Gods in Assembly: An Interpretation of Psalm 82', *HUCA* 40–41 (1969–70), pp. 123–137.

Ulrich, E., 'Book of Isaiah', *EDDS*, pp. 384–388.

Ulrich, E., *The Dead Sea Scrolls and the Origins of the Bible* (Grand Rapids: Eerdmans and Leiden: Brill, 1999).

Urbrock, W. J., 'The Earth Song in Psalms 90 – 92', in N. Habel, ed., *The Earth Story in the Psalms and the Prophets*, The Earth Bible 4 (Sheffield: Sheffield Academic Press, 2001), pp. 65–83.

VanderKam, J. C., *The Dead Sea Scrolls Today* (London: SPCK and Grand Rapids: Eerdmans, 1994)

VanGemeren, W. A., 'Psalms', in F. E. Gaebelein, ed., *The Expositor's Bible Commentary* 5 (Grand Rapids: Zondervan, 1991).

Van Pelt, M. V. and W. C. Kaiser, Jr, '*hgh* I', *NIDOTTE*, vol. 1, pp. 1006–1008.

Vanhoozer, K., *Is There a Meaning in This Text? The Bible, The Reader, and the Morality of Literary Knowledge* (Grand Rapids: Zondervan and Leicester: Apollos, 1998).

Vaux, R. de, *Ancient Israel* (London: Darton, Longman and Todd, 1961).

Vermes, G., *The Complete Dead Sea Scrolls in English* (London: Penguin, 1998).

Velde, H. te, 'Theology, Priests, and Worship in Ancient Egypt', *CANE*, vol. 3, pp. 1731–1749.

Vincent, M. A., 'The Shape of the Psalter: An Eschatological Dimension?', in P. J. Harland and C. T. R. Hayward, eds., *New Heaven and New Earth: Prophecy and the Millenium, Essays in Honour of Anthony Gelston*, VTSup 77 (Leiden: Brill, 1999), pp. 61–82.

Waard, J. de, 'Do you use "clean language"? Old Testament Euphemisms and their Translation', *TBT* 22 (1971), pp. 107–115.

Wagner, A., *Sprechakte und Sprechaktanalyse im Alten Testament: Untersuchungen im biblischen Hebräisch an der Nahtstelle zwischen Handlungsebene und Grammatik*, BZAW 253 (Berlin: de Gruyter, 1997).

Wagner, A., 'Die Bedeutung der Sprechakttheorie für Bibelübersetzungen, aufgezeigt an Gen 1,29, Ps 2,7 und Dtn 26,17–19', in J. Krašovec, ed., *The Interpretation of the Bible: The International Symposium in Slovenia, JSOTSup* 289 (Sheffield: Sheffield Academic Press, 1998), pp. 1575–1588.

Wagner, A., 'Die Stellung der Sprechakttheorie in Hebraistik und Exegese', in A. Lemaire, ed., *Congress Volume Basel 2001*, VTSup 92 (Leiden: Brill, 2002), pp. 55–84.

Wagner, J. R., 'Psalm 118 in Luke-Acts: Tracing a Narrative Thread', in C. A. Evans and J. A. Sanders, eds., *Early Christian Interpretation of the Scriptures of Israel: Investigations and Proposals*, SSEJC 5 (Sheffield: Sheffield Academic Press, 1997), pp. 154–178.

Wallace, H. N., 'What Chronicles Has to Say about Psalms', in M. P. Graham and S. L. McKenzie, eds., *The Chronicler as Author: Studies in Text and Texture*, JSOTSup 263 (Sheffield: Sheffield Academic Press, 1999), pp. 267–291.

Waltke, B. K., 'A Canonical Process Approach to the Psalms', in J. S. and P. D. Feinberg, eds., *Tradition and Testament: Essays in Honor of Charles Lee Feinberg* (Chicago: Moody Press, 1981), pp. 3–18.

Waltke, B. K., 'Theology of the Psalms', *NIDOTTE*, vol. 4, pp. 1100–1115.

Walton, J. H., *Ancient Israelite Literature in its Cultural Context* (Grand Rapids: Zondervan, 1989).

Walton, J. H., 'Hymns, Prayers, and Incantations', in *Ancient Israelite Literature in Its Cultural Context* (Grand Rapids: Zondervan, 1989), pp. 135–166.

Warren, A. L., 'A Trisagion Inserted in the 4QSam^a Version of the Song of Hannah, 1 Sam. 2:1–10', *JJS* 45 (1994), pp. 278–285.

Warren, A. L., *Modality, Reference and Speech Acts in the Psalms*, PhD dissertation (Cambridge University, 1998).

Warren, A. L., 'Some Linguistic Strategies for Politeness in Biblical Hebrew and West African Languages', *TBT* forthcoming (Paper presented at UBS TTW03, Iguaçu, Brazil, June 2003).

Watson, W. G. E., *Classical Hebrew Poetry*, JSOTSup 26 (Sheffield: JSOT Press, 1984, 2nd ed. 1986).

Watts, J., *Psalm and Story: Inset Hymns in Hebrew Narrative*, JSOTSup 139 (Sheffield: JSOT Press, 1992).

Watts, R. E., 'The Psalms in Mark's Gospel', in S. Moyise and M. J. J. Menken, eds., *The Psalms in the New Testament* (London: T. & T. Clark International, 2004), pp. 25–45.

Weiser, A., *The Psalms: A Commentary*, tr. H. Hartwell, OTL (Philadelphia: Westminster Press, 4th ed. 1962).

Wendland, E. R., 'Genre Criticism and the Psalms: What Discourse Typology Can Tell Us about the Text (with Special Reference to Psalm 31)', in R. D. Bergen, ed., *Biblical Hebrew and Discourse Linguistics* (Winona Lake: Eisenbrauns, 1994), pp. 374–414.

Westermann, C., 'Zur Sammlung des Psalters', *Theologia Viatorum* 8 (1961–2), pp. 278–284.

Westermann, C., *Praise and Lament in the Psalms*, tr. K. R. Crim and R. N. Soulen (Atlanta: John Knox and Edinburgh: T. & T. Clark, 1981).

Westermann, C., *The Living Psalms* (Edinburgh: T. & T. Clark and Grand Rapids: Eerdmans, 1989).

White, E., *A Critical Edition of the Targum of Psalms: A Computer Generated Text of Books I and II*, PhD dissertation (McGill University, 1988).

White, H.C., ed., *Speech Act Theory and Biblical Criticism*, Semeia 41 (Decatur: Scholars Press, 1988).

Whybray, N., _Reading the Psalms as a Book_, JSOTSup 222 (Sheffield: Sheffield Academic Press, 1996).

Williams, R. J., _Hebrew Syntax: An Outline_ (Toronto: University of Toronto Press, 2nd ed. 1967).

Williamson, H. G. M., 'Reading the Lament Psalms Backwards', in B. A. Strawn and N. R. Bowen, eds., _A God So Near: Essays on Old Testament Theology in Honor of Patrick D. Miller_ (Winona Lake: Eisenbrauns, 2003), pp. 3–16.

Willis, J. T., 'Psalm 1 – An Entity', _ZAW_ 9 (1979), pp. 381–401.

Wilson, G. H., _The Editing of the Hebrew Psalter_, SBLDS 76 (Chico: Scholars Press, 1985; reissued 2004).

Wilson, G. H., 'The Use of Royal Psalms at the "Seams" of the Hebrew Psalter', _JSOT_ 35 (1986), pp. 85–94.

Wilson, G. H., 'The Shape of the Book of Psalms', _Interpretation_ 46 (1992), pp. 129–142.

Wilson, G. H., 'Shaping the Psalter: A Consideration of Editorial Linkage in the Book of Psalms', in J. C. McCann, ed., _The Shape and Shaping of the Psalter_, JSOTSup 159 (Sheffield: JSOT Press, 1993), pp. 72–82.

Wilson, G. H., 'The Qumran _Psalms Scroll_ (11QPs^a) and the Canonical Psalter: Comparison of Editorial Shaping', _CBQ_ 59 (1997), pp. 448–464.

Wilson, G. H., Review of P. W. Flint, _The Dead Sea Psalms Scrolls and the Book of Psalms_, _JQR_ 90 (2000), pp. 515–521.

Wilson, G. H., 'Songs for the City: Interpreting Biblical Psalms in an Urban Context', in S. B. Reid, ed., _Psalms and Practice: Worship, Virtue and Authority_ (Collegeville: Liturgical Press, 2000), pp. 231–243.

Wilson, G. H., 'Psalms and Psalter: Paradigm for Biblical Theology', in S. J. Hafemann, ed., _Biblical Theology: Retrospect and Prospect_ (Leicester: Apollos and Downers Grove: InterVarsity Press, 2002), pp. 100–110.

Wilson, G. H., _NIV Application Commentary: Psalms_, vol. 1 (Grand Rapids: Zondervan, 2002).

Wilson, G. H., _NIV Application Commentary, Psalms_, vol. 2 (Grand Rapids: Zondervan, forthcoming).

Wilson, G. H., 'King, Messiah, and the Reign of God: Revisiting the Royal Psalms and the Shape of the Psalter', in P. W. Flint and P. D. Miller, eds., _The Book of Psalms: Composition and Reception_, VTSup 99 (Leiden: Brill, 2004).

Wilson, G. H., 'The Qumran, Masoretic, and Greek Psalters: Shape and Canon', in E. Herron, ed., _Festschrift in Honor of Emmanuel Tov_ (Grand Rapids: Eerdmans, forthcoming).

Wilson, I., 'Merely a Container? The Ark in Deuteronomy', in J. Day, ed., *Temple and Worship in Biblical Israel*, JSOTSup 422 (London: T. & T. Clark International, 2005).

Witkamp, L. T., 'Jesus' Thirst in John 19:28–30: Literal or Figurative?', *JBL* 115 (1996), pp. 489–510.

Wolff, H. W., *Anthropology of the Old Testament* (London: SCM, 1974).

Wright, C. J. H., *Old Testament Ethics for the People of God* (Leicester: IVP, 2004).

Wright, W., *The Homilies of Aphraates* (London: Williams and Norgate, 1869).

York, A. D., 'The Dating of Targumic Literature', *JSJ* 5 (1974), pp. 49–62.

Zakowitch, Y., '*And You Shall Tell Your Son . . .' The Concept of the Exodus in the Bible* (Jerusalem, Magnes, 1991).

Zenger, E., *A God of Vengeance? Understanding the Psalms of Divine Wrath* (Louisville: Westminster John Knox Press, 1996).

Zenger, E., 'Dass alles Fleisch den Namen seiner Heiligung segne (Ps. 145.21). Die Komposition Psalms 145 – 150 als Antoss zu einer christlich-jüdischen Psalmenhermeneutik', *BZ* 41 (1997), pp. 1–27.

Zenger, E., 'The Composition and Theology of the Fifth Book of the Psalms, Psalms 107 – 145', *JSOT* 80 (1998), pp. 77–102.

Zenger, E., 'The Psalter as a Book: Observations About its Origin, Composition, and Function', in P. D. Miller and D. M. Howard, Jr, eds., *The Psalms in Recent Research*, SBTS (Winona Lake: Eisenbrauns, forthcoming); tr. from 'Der Psalter als Buch: Beobachtungen zu seiner Entstehung, Komposition und Funktion', in E. Zenger, ed., *Der Psalter in Judentum und Christentum*, Herders Biblische Studien 18 (Freiburg: Herder, 1998), pp. 1–57.

Zenger, E., 'Der Psalter als Heiligtum', in B. Ego et al., eds., *Gemeinde ohne Tempel: Zur Substituierung und Transformation des Jerusalemer Tempels und seines Kults im Alten Testament, antiken Judentum und frühen Christentum*, WUNT 118 (Tübingen: Mohr/Siebeck, 1999), pp. 115–130.

Zyl, A. H. van, '1 Sam 1:2 – 2:11 – A Life-world Lament of Affliction', *JNSL* 12 (1984), pp. 151–161.

Zuber, B., *Das Tempussystem des biblischen Hebräisch. Eine Untersuchung am Text*, BZAW 164 (Berlin: de Gruyter, 1986).